The North-East Diaries Vol 3

The North-East Diaries Vol 3

Times They Are A-Changin'

J.R. Bates

Names may have been changed to conceal the identity
of certain characters in the book.

ISBNs:
Paperback: 978-1-80541-577-0
eBook: 978-1-80541-578-7

http://www.jrbates-author.co.uk

Contents

Prologue
If I Could Turn Back Time
(More Batesy & Pals)

———————————————————■———————————————————

I'm sitting in my recliner with a single-malt in hand and feeling somewhat despondent and nervous. It's the evening of my 70th birthday, August 4th, 2021, and most people in the UK are feeling exactly the same as myself as the Covid situation trundles on without an end in sight. Today has produced lots of online Facebook contact with best wishes a' plenty but very little in the way of actual human interaction. I've had three people wish me happy birthday from outside our front-garden fence but I can't remember who they were because they all wore masks and stood the regulation distance apart. Unfortunately my wife Lorraine doesn't drink anymore since her stroke and both of our Westies have refused to join me... so I imbibe alone in a reflective mood.

I have much to be thankful for I muse. I've managed the three-score years and ten which is pretty much what the bible promised me although there have been times when that target seemed quite unreachable. I have a decent number of birthday cards on the mantelpiece. They have all been removed from their envelopes only after the said envelopes have been wiped with antiseptic wipes just in case the postie person is a Covid carrier. One of the cards informs me that I'm 'never too old to party' and that makes me feel morose... but also glad that I'm still here to read it. Many folk throughout the country must be having those same thoughts and giving thanks... and many of course will be grieving for those who have succumbed to this nasty virus.

Of course Covid is just the latest in a long line of nasties to rear its odious head. When you reach your seventieth year all kinds of vile diseases are lurking behind the curtains and waiting to jump on you when you're not looking. Have a quick shufti around the walls in your doctor's surgery waiting room... the posters will frighten the life out of you. Those thoughts give me no comfort whatsoever.

I drain my tumbler and I have a moment of panic as I suddenly think... 'have I remembered to check myself for testicular cancer recently?'... Yes... No?... think James think!... then after a second or two I remember that I have... because there was a bit of a rumpus yesterday when I began my checking in the Tesco fresh fruit and vegetables aisle. I'm sure there wouldn't have been such a furore if we'd been in the Co-op... they'd probably have helped me.

I pour myself another whisky. Lorraine's eyes swivel... eyeing the glass to make sure that I haven't poured a really big one, which will mean a night in the spare-room because of my inebriated snoring and fighting in my sleep. The thing is... I've yet to lose a sleep fight after a few glasses of malt. Mind you I did end up once with a broken toe when I lashed out during a particularly boisterous fight with my dream adversary and managed to kick the bedroom wall... and I still can't remember how that came about.

All that aside I feel quite grateful to our current government who have handled the Covid situation with such aplomb. We're on first name terms with our ruling elite nowadays and one has to remark that Boris, Matt and Rishi have led the country from the front. It is so humbling to realise that those brilliantly talented commanders and intellectuals are following the same rules as we common folk. Mask wearing, hand washing, distance keeping and avoiding social gatherings whilst using their analytical minds to keep our country safe. Aye that'll be right!

Over the past few years I have however become... as with most other folk, slightly concerned with the way the United States is heading. Firstly under the stewardship of an orange-skinned president. Heavens' above folks... the world's most powerful country being led by a crude Satsuma. Because of this the politics of lies and nastiness seemed to have reared their ugly heads. Then of course, as you're all aware, the Satsuma was grudgingly replaced by a doddery bloke whom you'd imagine being more at home in fluffy slippers and a nice cardigan... and certainly not the fella you'd want with his finger on the nuclear button. So here's hoping that the land of the free finds a way to recover from its current malaise and avoids becoming yet another dictatorship.

As the warm glow of the Glenfiddich reaches my cockles my mind begins to wander and I'm suddenly faced with a conundrum. Very little is precisely known about the journey that the Covid virus is taking. So for argument's sake what if it can actually be active in your body without you suspecting?

What if it can be selective about the parts of your body that it attacks? I've just had my booster jab and once again I'd offered up my left arm for the injection. So... think about it... what if the virus knows this and thinks to itself 'hmmm that left arm is well protected... let's have a bash at his right arm'. Maybe my right arm will succumb to Covid but my left arm will be completely healthy. Not that my right arm will begin coughing and lose its sense of taste... that would be silly, but you see my train of thought. So to my way of thinking it follows that maybe I should ask my local surgery for additional boosters in my legs... that makes sense... but what about all the other bits in-between? Would a leg injection protect my bum? How high up would the injection fluid reach? And what about my head?

Spare room it was for me... and well before midnight. Shabby birthday.

I lay awake for ages, warm and glowing and well-served but still with a modicum of sensible to work with and I began thinking about the second half of my life. Where had those thirty-five years gone? Because it just seemed like yesterday that I was still ensconced in Hull and about to make the huge leap back to Blyth and my roots. Then who should worm their way into my head but the three folk who'd had such a huge bearing on my life... Charlie Chuck, Tug and Frances and as my eyes closed the years ticked back over to the time of redemption and moving on.

CHAPTER 1

China in Your Hand

———————————————■———————————————

Hull – early 1987 and my new business has taken off and is flying. Night Shadow Lingerie now has permanent stalls on four local markets – Hull, Skirlington, Bridlington and Withernsea. I haven't a clue what I'm doing or why it is successful but because of Charlie's money I'm now the boss or the owner or CEO... call it what you will but I was enjoying the ride. I've recently opened my first bricks and mortar shop in Chanterlands Avenue in Hull and that first opening day has been so busy and lucrative that I'm absolutely shattered come closing time. Not only that but one of the lady customers has invited me out on a date. She asked me quite brazenly whilst purchasing her 'teddy' and she was such a good-looker that I'd instantly agreed. So after closing up, the locking of the shop and the banking of the cash in the night safe I made a mad dash home for a shower and spruce up before our arranged night out. It was to be at a Chinese restaurant then on to a club. I was quite partial to a Chinese meal and occasionally enjoyed a sweet and sour takeaway so that part of the evening should go smoothly... aye that'll be right!

Has any Geordie born person ever managed to master chopsticks? I mean the eating implements, not the piano thingy, because it never crossed my mind when I turned up for our date that I'd end up trying to waggle food into my mouth between two skinny bamboo knitting needles. Had I known what was about to unfold I could at least have practiced for a few days. Unfortunately that wasn't to be and I was thrust in at the deep-end for an evening of discomfort and humiliation as well as the learning of a salutary lesson... when eating at a sit-down Chinese restaurant, wear a bib and carry a fork.

To be fair the evening started off on the front foot. Belinda, my date for the evening turns up looking like a million dollars and totally fanciable She links my arm as we walk from our meeting place to her chosen restaurant. She's wearing one of those 'little black' numbers with a plunging neckline and I'm fighting valiantly to stop my eyes from popping out.

We were shown to our table quickly when we arrived and were then served so promptly that it came as something of a shock... because in a Brit restaurant we'd have had to wait until the staff could be bothered to finish their ciggies and get up off their backsides. The initial glass of beer went down well too, because I wasn't even aware that the Chinese brewed beer. I was informed by our waiter that the glass of Tsingtao beer I was drinking used bitter melon instead of hops... and it was that process which gave the beer such a distinctive taste... and boy was it potent.

Hindsight is a great thing but on that particular occasion foresight would have been much more appropriate. I'd

2

been incredibly nervous about a date arranged in haste with someone I'd barely shared more than two sentences with. So, back in my flat... I'd decided to have a quick single malt livener to quieten the nerves while I decided which fashion ensemble to knock her dead with. Then one malt became two... Glenlivet on this occasion and the second glass was fuller than the first. Then yet another swift gargle just before I left the house as the taxi tooted outside and I was set for the evening. A wee snifter never hurt anybody... did it?

The thing is folks... a good single malt always takes its time to work its magic and it creeps up on you slowly... very slowly on this occasion. I was sitting in the restaurant attempting to do the Billy Connolly thing and make myself windswept and interesting with my stimulating conversation. It was then that I felt the first stirrings of a single-malt ambush. The half glass of Tsingtao had hastened the march of the Glenlivet and it worried me because I could feel it working its way up my body. I was desperate to hold it back because my feet and legs were already feeling squiffy. The sensation was somewhere up around my hips by the time our food arrived. I took a big deep breath as I focused on pulling myself together and making the most of my attractive partner and the easy ambience of the restaurant.

Our food arrived. Belinda had taken control of the ordering... immediately suspecting that I was out of my depth when I'd ran my confused gaze over the menu. Jiaozi, Wonton, Zongzi, Tangyuan, Changsha stinky tofu... ehhh? Howay man, where on earth was the chicken and chips followed by rice pudding with a few sultanas scattered on top?

3

A bespectacled and nervous looking young lad who couldn't have been any more than sixteen proceeded to transfer an array of small pots onto our table from his trolley... while the head waiter looked on, napkin over his arm. To be fair the food smelled okay but I didn't have a clue as to what I was about to eat. By this time the Glenlivet is up inside my rib-cage and still climbing. I stare apprehensively at the crowd of pots then glance at the head waiter with a confused expression on my face.

He understood the soundless question... and smiled, "Dim-sum."

I catch Belinda's eye and whisper "That's not very nice... the poor lad doesn't look that thick."

She giggles and flaps a hand in my direction, "You're so funny... ha-ha-ha. That's why I liked you. You've had this before though... haven't you?"

"Course I have."

"I really love the chicken feet... what's your favourite?"

I'm not sure if she's cracking a joke. Chicken feet... get real man. Who on earth ever ate chicken feet? I remember watching my dad having a go at pig's trotters on one occasion and feeling all cockly as he attacked them with gusto. But chicken feet, that can't be right can it? There's no meat on chicken feet just wrinkly skin and sharp toenails. Aye... she's definitely winding me up.

"I'm quite partial to spicy newt in sticky sauce," I reply.

The response was unexpected, "That's not on the menu here but I know they do that particular dish in one of the York restaurants."

Now she's got me off balance. Was that response a proper response or some reverse ridicule? I'm not sure so I let go of the thought train and drain my glass of Tsingtao. I hold up a finger then make a circle motion towards the waiter. A soundless re-order of the beer which appears on our table within a minute or two with my empty glass whisked away. The Glenlivet has now reached the top of my chest and my arms begin to feel like they belong to someone else. Nevertheless it's now time to tuck in but I can't spot my knife and fork... and there's not even a spoon.

I play for time to work out the intricacy of the situation and hold my finger up again to attract the waiter's attention, "Hey-there bonny lad, can I have two malt whiskies, large ones?"

"No whisky sir," head waiter says with a disapproving frown on his face, "Baijiu we have... it is China spirit drink something like whisky."

"Okay fella, two large barjews... and some cutlery wouldn't go amiss either."

Belinda gives a frown and a little hand gesture towards the waiter. "Sorry Tang, ignore that we have the sticks."

She glares at me. The malt is working its way up my neck and everything clicks into place just as my brain is overrun. She's taking two chopsticks out of their paper sleeves just as the two glasses of Baijiu spirit drink are plonked unceremoniously in front of me.

"I don't drink spirits... you should have asked," Belinda chides me, "Tea is usually taken with dim-sum with rice wine to follow." She's not a happy bunny. She's sitting opposite me but avoiding eye contact and I'm aware I'm out of my comfort zone and not in her good books.

I pick up the two sticks sitting in front of my plate and remove them from their paper sleeve. I take a deep breath and think to myself 'howay man Jim you can do this... cometh the hour cometh the divvy.' I pick up my napkin and begin to tuck it into the top of my shirt. Belinda throws me a look of disgust and makes a production of flapping her napkin open and placing it on her lap. I grimace and remove my napkin and follow her lead by doing the flapping thing and placing mine on my lap too. In the centre of our napkins are embroidered dragons breathing fire and to be fair they look the business.

She sips at funny coloured tea from a fragile bone-china cup then begins clicking her chopsticks as she transfers various concoctions from their containers into her bowl. She's so adept... and for a few seconds I'm transfixed and watching how she does it. It's like watching an artist at work. Bottom stick stays stiff, top one does the waggling... easy-peasy lemon-squeezy. My turn.

I drain the first glass of Baijiu. Then the Baijiu and Glenlivet meet in my head for the first time and between them they have a good old chinwag and decide to teach me a lesson.

I pick up the chopsticks and place them in my hand in exactly the same position as Belinda has hers. I dive in for my first attack on the array of bowls and heated containers and bugger me if I don't come up with a chicken's foot. I've done it. I've picked up some food with chopsticks... it's easy man. What on earth was I so worried about? Then I feel my head thickening and my eyes going woggly. I'm beginning to see double and I'm staring at the chicken's foot that I've managed to successfully transfer to my bowl... or is it two chickens' feet? No, definitely just the one foot I decide as I squint with one eye closed.

I don't know what to do with it... because I certainly can't eat it. What if one of the toenails gets stuck in my throat. Choking to death in a Chinese restaurant isn't at the top end of my bucket list. Then the pie-eyed stupid kicks in and I begin to snort... imagining some poor hen hobbling around on crutches. I manage to stifle the snorts and pretend that I'm coughing and cover my mouth with a handkerchief. It seems to work and Belinda carries on with the food tucking-in. I pull myself together and decide to have a crack at one of those big meaty dumpling fellas in the big container, because the alcohol has given me the munchies. I'm ravenous by now and they look really tasty.

Huge mistake... huge, huge mistake.

I manage to focus intently for the few seconds it takes to position my target dumpling between the sticks. Squeeze dumpling gently with the pressure on the top stick then lift slowly... all good. Keep exerting pressure and now carefully transfer to the feeding bowl. I'm just a hairsbreadth away and I almost make it... almost but not quite. As I manoeuvre the dumpling through the descent to bowl bit of the operation my sticks decide to go walkabout and cross over. Dumpling does a swallow dive... then hits the edge of the table before landing unceremoniously in my lap. The restaurant seems deathly quiet and there's no comment from Belinda but I'm not brave enough to look up in case any of the other diners are watching. I sit there for what seems like an age... staring at the dumpling nestling on the napkin in my lap. Some of the sauce has splashed my shirt and I give it a perfunctory rub with my hanky without looking up. Then the munchies retreat and the squeaks make an appearance. I can't stop myself. I'm staring at my lap and I begin to giggle.

"For Christ's sake Jim... what's so bloody funny with that?" My date for the evening was not impressed with her date for the evening. She'd left her sense of humour in her handbag. "You're drunk... for heaven's sake get a grip... it's... well it's embarrassing." If looks could kill... my life would have been over.

Question... have you ever had a bit too much to drink and seen something which creases you up so much that you can't stop laughing? Yes? Of course you have... we all have, and this was my moment and I couldn't stop the chortles... I was in full-on squeak mode. Giggling and gasping I point to the pork dumpling in my lap.

"It looks like one of my bollocks popped out my pants."

"Ughhh..."

"And the dragon is having a right old nibble... hee-hee-hee."

"Eeyeew..." she screws up her face, "you're disgusting and childish... and I thought you would be fun... God how wrong was I?" Fortunately she was keeping her voice low so as not to attract too much attention. She tugged the front of her dress higher. I watch with my double vision as she does so. She glares at me... all four boobs now modestly hidden.

To be honest I was past caring. Tonight had been a big mistake and we all make them. But I'd be paying for the meal so I wasn't going to be beaten. Then I had a brainwave. It suddenly dawned on me that I could use my chopstick like a lance... and with that thought in mind I speared my lap dumpling... and it worked. I delicately transferred the speared victim towards my mouth and began to chomp on the tasty lump like a toffee apple. It was a brilliant brainwave from a brilliant mind so I proceeded to work my way through all the other spearable food on the table... and you know what?... I didn't give a fig if the other diners were watching. I finished off the other drinks too... and all beneath the gaze of utter contempt from Belinda.

That evening wasn't one of my finest in truth but it certainly turned out to be memorable. I did manage to escort my date to a taxi rank but I wouldn't see Belinda again after that evening. But at least I'd managed two dates on the same night... our first and our last.

Life returned to normal and trundled on after that embarrassing escapade. Actually it more than trundled... it sprinted and ushered in a period of success that I still can't understand to this day. That success was mainly because of a lady called Frances... Fran for short, whom I'd employed on a temporary fortnight's contract in December to sort out the accounts bookwork. As it turned out she would be with me for the following eighteen months and to all intents and purposes she would run the business. She was one smart cookie. A lady in her late fifties who was a bona-fide signed-up man-hater to the nth degree... but for some reason she liked me and for whatever reason we gelled almost instantly. Fran was a totally focussed and self-confident lady who spoke her mind and didn't suffer fools gladly. However... she'd made it abundantly clear after our first week together that she considered me to be one of those fools, and within a few short weeks she would become the woman who transformed said Mr Silly into Captain Sensible...ish.

CHAPTER 2

Itsy-Bitsy Teeny-Weeny

———————◼———————

It was a Wednesday, half-day closing for the shop, before my mid-week wander over to the Avenues pub for an afternoon wind-down. Fran and I were standing behind the counter with her in teacher mode. Customers had been few and far between. She'd been logically walking me through the day-book entries and explaining double entry book-keeping. I tried to feign interest but honestly I was none the wiser. In return I'd been pontificating on my latest idea for the expansion of the business. To my way of thinking I'd come up with a super money-making idea but Fran wasn't convinced in the slightest.

"No Jim no, that's not the way to go. Come on young man that's not a bright move." Fran was not impressed with my latest proposition and was all for kicking it into touch.

"How not?"

"Another two stalls at markets so far apart does not make financial sense."

"Why not? the stalls we have are making money... so more stalls equals more money, surely?"

"Not so Jim, not so... it just means an increased workload. You're adding to your cost base. More petrol expenses for a start and you'll need to increase your stock holding quite substantially. The only way you can do that at the moment is to go into overdraft and the bank charges will take the biggest chunk out of any profit. Think about it... it's winter... folk aren't going out so much and money's tight after the Christmas. The Withernsea stall has been losing money for a few weeks now, and I have my suspicions as to why that is. The losses at Withernsea cancel out the Skirlington profit, so in effect you only have two stalls and the shop making money. Those profits are just sufficient to cover shop rental, utility bills and staff wages. So we're basically treading water which means to take on extra debt at this time is not a smart move. But of course you're the boss and the final decision is yours."

She had a habit of doing that. Telling me what she thought was the right course of action then daring me to cross her.

"So what do you think I should do?"

"You'll do whatever you like... as is your right but I'll tell you what I'd do if the business was mine."

"Okay... fire away. You've obviously given it some thought."

"No Jim, I've given it a lot of thought... and really that's your job."

"Okay... okay Fran just spit it out. You're going to give me your take on things whether I like it or not."

She smiled at that comment. She began to roll herself a cigarette. I'd never been able to understand why this pushing sixty old biddy... who by the way was handsomely paid and lived in a fully owned semi-detached house in a nice area of Hessle rolled her own cigarettes. I'd never asked because she could be very caustic with her responses and a closed book when it came to her personal life. It was nothing to do with me anyway.

"If it were my decision I would abandon all the stalls apart from the one here in Hull. You're putting too much effort into those outlying pitches for very little return. Your petrol expenses would immediately shrink and your outgoings for market rent and third-party wages will disappear. Instead of weekly you'll only need one trip a fortnight down to Lorella's in Leicester to buy in new stock. That's freeing up a day for you... which means you can work here earning money instead of burning money and you won't be paying someone else to run the shop, as well as saving a load of petrol and vehicle wear and tear."

"Yeh but the profit would shrink too."

"Maybe... maybe not, but even so the shrinkage would be minimal and your stock won't be taking a battering out in the open day after day and in all weathers, so that will minimize the stock degrade. I've calculated that shrinkage at the moment is running at around three percent due to theft and possibly mis-selling. Believe me Jim when I say that three percent is a big number for a small business. If you decide to go with the new model I'm proposing then we can cut most of that loss out completely. At the present time you're running around working lots of hours for very little return. If your idea of smart business is just to plough on working those hours just to keep your head above water and make a living then carry on as you are... but I honestly think you can target resources a lot more efficiently than that."

Frances was making a good case but I wasn't convinced, "I hear what you're saying Fran... honestly, but going down to one stall and the shop... isn't that just admitting defeat."

"No Jim it's not defeat it's a tactical withdrawal and a rational decision for the wellbeing of the business... and it makes sense to consolidate your resources and take a different route for making profit."

Something else was bothering me, "But that means I'll have to let Lucy, Joan and Kim go. I can't carry on paying them if their stalls are mothballed."

"That's true but they're not your children Jim. You're making a business decision and decisions have consequences. Pay them double rate for their last week on their stalls and thank them for their hard work. They'll understand... and if they don't then tough. You're in business to make money and in my opinion this particular model has run its race."

"Aye... maybe... if that's what I decide."

"Of course... I'm only offering advice." Fran grinned as she stubbed out her cigarette. Then the shop bell dinged as a good-looking middle-aged woman entered the shop. Fran left me to do the salesman's chat-and-sell part of the business that she hated so much as she slunk away into the stock room.

It would take a few weeks of soul-searching and nudging from Fran before I came to the decision to pull the plug on the stalls and tell the three ladies who ran them for me that I no longer required their services. I agonized over that decision but a look at our bank balance finally convinced me to follow Fran's advice. We were currently churning lots of money... but churn wasn't turning into profit and we were only just managing to keep the business in the black without any uptick on the sales graph.

On the night I made my decision I'd lain awake going over and over the conflicting scenarios and wrestling with the consequences of taking Fran's advice. Suddenly, and quite out of the blue, a discussion with one of my old Grammar school teachers sprung into my head. It had been my old geography teacher Mr Wilson... or Fat Alec as he was affectionately known to the pupils. He'd sat me down in an empty room a few weeks after an unfortunate altercation we'd had and began to speak to me in a way that none of the other teachers had ever attempted.

He spoke that day about how we pupils were going to leave school soon, and head into the world, separately, for ever. He said I wouldn't be able to grasp it yet but my horizons were about to expand in ways I wouldn't believe. For the teenage me it was a revelation to hear an adult address me like that... not as a kid to whom he needed to impart information, but as a human being with whom he wanted to share some wisdom.

What stayed with me was the image he used: he told me to use my ears and listen intently when I came upon someone using the voice of experience. He said my life would be akin to walking through a dark tunnel and there would be times in that darkness when a light would appear and if I used my natural instinct then I would be drawn to that light like a moth to a flame. That light more often than not would turn out to be a voice and that voice would be the voice of common sense and insight. If I managed to listen and learn when that voice entered my world then I would thrive, but if I ignored it then the darkness would return and my journey would continue in the pitch black.

My teacher's advice... remembered that night, became a sort of symbolic compass point warning me against the dangers of my own self-importance and egotism. His words reminded me to remain open to that which might further illuminate a darkness I hadn't even realised I couldn't see. The remembered advice of my teacher formed a subtle threshold. It had been a speech that passed by quietly in a deserted classroom... but that evening it pushed open a door in my mind.

"Okay bonny lass it's all done and dusted," I said to Fran as she came into the shop that Saturday morning after her week off work with some sort of bug. "The stalls are now non-existent other than the Hull market one. The ladies have been paid off and they accepted the decision without any unpleasantness. All of their stock is now here and counted off."

Fran didn't comment. She smiled as she brushed past me to have a look in the stock-room and to take her coat off.

I heard the groan, "For goodness sake Jim... it's chocker."

"I know but it was your idea."

"Aye that's as maybe, but it was your decision."

"Knew you'd say that. But now we've got to shift that lot somehow. Got any more bright ideas?"

She gave me a jaundiced look. "How much stock was missing?"

I referred to my notebook. For once I'd been most thorough. "One Basque, two teddies, two crop-tops, a bra and brief set, three packs of Tanga briefs and two of those men's posing pouch things with the elephant trunk. There's also a small pile of stock just outside the toilet door that looks the worse for wear and is probably unsaleable."

"Okay... I was sort of expecting something like that. I can do a write-down and it won't impact us too much. I'll take the grubby stock home with me and give it a wash and spruce up... perhaps we can make up a basket and sell them as seconds."

"Yeh that sounds fine in theory Fran... but where do we go from here? There's far too much stock to turn over from just the shop and the Hull stall and next month is a biggy. The tax and insurance is due on the Transit... and it needs a service... God knows how much that will come to. It definitely needs a couple of new tyres and the two-month bill for Lorella is due to be paid and we can't cross them."

Fran held up a hand to stem my flow, "Calm yourself down Jim. I've a few ideas... if you're prepared to think outside the box."

I was really hoping she had some good ideas. As for thinking outside the box... it was a statement that unnerved me... nevertheless, "Okay... I'm all ears, fire away."

She was about to begin when the shop door opened and a young lass of about twenty years old came in accompanied by an older woman in her forties. They had the same facial features so I reckoned it was mother and daughter. Time for me to go to work as I noticed Fran slipping out of the door. She was no doubt off to the local baker's shop to buy our lunch.

"How may I help you ladies?" I asked as I sported my best smile. Strangely enough I'd concluded that the vast majority of ladies who came into the shop preferred to be assisted by a male rather than a female. One of the customers had told me this was because women felt they were being judged when served by a female but felt more like they were being admired when served by a decent looking man. It didn't bother me one way or the other and I could only remember two occasions when a lady had entered the shop then turned and immediately left when they saw a male sales person. Both times the ladies had been of the vintage variety.

"This is my daughter Linda and she's getting married next month," said the mother figure. "We're hoping to spot something extra special for the honeymoon... you know?... something romantic." She gave me a great big crooked grin through yellow teeth. Her daughter smiled, with a bit of a blush working its way up her cheeks. Her smile however was welcoming and given self-consciously through pearly white teeth.

No offence intended but smile aside, the lass wasn't the bonniest female I'd ever encountered and she was standing there with hunched shoulders. No matter, it was my job to make her feel special.

"Do you have anything particular in mind because we have many different lingerie items to tempt our regular clientele. Are you thinking luxurious, exclusive, seductive, saucy? It's your honeymoon... well your daughter's and her husband's." The young lass hadn't attempted to make eye contact so I was addressing the mother.

Mouthy mother smiled and continued while Linda stared at the floor with a lopsided grin. "We were thinking saucy weren't we Linda. Something to get Richard's teeny pecker up hopefully." She gave a loud laugh whilst Linda seemed to shrink after her mother's comment. I felt sorry for the lass. She was plain... well actually not even plain... but she was a human being with feelings and her mother wasn't helping her at all. And presumably she'd inherited those looks from her mother.

"Saucy... yes we do saucy... but do you have anything specific in mind... you know like a see-through negligee, a Basque, stockings and suspender belt, a bustiere or a playsuit maybe?"

Then the mother started being silly as well as embarrassing, "Well you're the expert. What would give a man the hots if he was lucky enough to be on honeymoon with one of us two?" she chuckled.

I couldn't afford to be rude because we needed the money but inside my head I'm thinking, 'if it was with yourself pet a bottle of Glenfiddich and a photo of Bridget Bardot would do the trick'. I couldn't say that out loud of course. Time to find out how much they were prepared to spend.

"Well for me the see-through negligee would do the trick with a half cup... maybe quarter cup bra in red and black with the matching suspender belt and stockings. A romantic feast indeed for a hungry man."

"Knickers?" I thought at first the mother was being dismissive but realised quickly that it was a question.

"None... would be saucier with a see-through," I replied.

"Ooohh we are a naughty boy aren't we?... let the fox see the rabbit ehhh?"

19

I pulled out the best smile I could muster. I didn't like this woman one little bit but I couldn't show it. She was embarrassing her daughter and making a fool of herself in the process.

"Take her through and give her a fitting then. Go on Linda go on... show the nice man what's on offer," then she laughed an ignorant laugh at her own comment as she pushed her daughter towards the changing room at the back of the shop. This was going to be a difficult exercise because the stock room was now overflowing and our sole changing room was also crammed full of stock boxes. Thankfully the shop bell dinged and Fran returned at that precise moment, carrying a cardboard tray with sandwiches, donuts and a couple of apple turnovers in full view.

"Aahh Fran... can you look after Mrs...?

"Smeaton... Lizzie Smeaton," said Fran. "We know each other well... don't we Lizzie?"

The woman seemed to have lost her tongue. She didn't seem best pleased to be confronted by Fran.

"Go on Jim, do your fitting or whatever it is you do. I'll keep a close eye on Lizzie here."

Keep a close eye on Lizzie... what did that mean? The atmosphere had changed somewhat and the loudmouth mother now seemed very cowed and submissive. I made a mental note to find out the full story later on but first I had a young woman to see to.

She was standing in the stockroom surrounded by boxes when I walked in and shut the heavy curtain between the shop and the storage area. She looked very nervous and she spoke in little more than a whisper.

"I don't want to do a fitting. The changing room is full and I don't want to take my clothes off in front of you. Can't you just give me the things you said and let me get out."

I was really pleased she'd said that. With the changing room out of commission I had no wish to watch this young woman in a state of undress.

"Can you talk loudly though... as if I was trying the things on and make some nice comments so my mam will hear?"

I gave her a wide smile and a wink, "Just hang your blouse up there Linda," was my first loud comment, then a minute or two later, "Take the skirt and slip off too and just hang them over the chair back there... yep, that's it, looking good, super."

We spent the next five minutes with myself making the occasional loud comment and both of us grinning as I searched the boxes for her wedding night ensemble. She seemed so relieved.

I had to whisper when I asked, "What is your bust measurement?"

"I'm a 34c."

"Thought so... that's the exact size I've just pulled out," I said... dangling a black and red half-cup in front of her, "Okay then that's all the required lingerie for your big day. Let's get it all bagged up and when we step out into the shop pretend you're still buttoning your top to make it seem real."

She smiled and said, "Thank you for... well... you know for being a gentleman. I've not met too many of those in my life. Oh and whatever the bill comes to put a fiver on top. My mam's a nightmare but she has a pocketful of cash and I don't know where she's got it all from."

I gave her a big smile and a peck on the cheek. "Okay... will do. Go and have yourself a brilliant wedding day."

With that final thought we both stepped out into the shop with Linda buttoning up the top buttons on her blouse. Her mother made no comment whatsoever as I put the honeymoon lingerie into a 'Night Shadow' printed carrier and she didn't turn a hair when I presented her with the inflated total. She pulled out a wad of notes and paid in cash... even refusing her change. But she didn't hang about for any small talk and was really eager to escape the shop.

When they'd left Fran and I stood quietly reflecting for a while before I broke the silence.

"I didn't really do a fitting... with the clothes off and that."

"I know."

"How?"

"I just do because you're so readable... and a big softie."

"She was alright... the daughter Linda."

"Shame she has to have that waste of skin for a mother."

"So what's that story with you and her?... and what are these ideas you have for the business?"

Suddenly there was a small crowd of females around the front window. They were pointing, giggling and checking their purses and it was obvious we were about to be inundated.

She left my question on hold, "What are you doing tonight Jim?"

"Dunno... I haven't anything planned. What for?"

"You've got my address. Bring your pj's and toothbrush and a decent bottle of malt whisky. We need longer than a few minutes to discuss all the things that need discussing."

"Ehhh?"

"You'll be using the spare room… and don't look so worried because you're far too green for me," she laughed… a nice friendly laugh. "We need an uninterrupted couple of hours to get everything out in the open and for me to tell you what my business plan is. It's totally different to the physical shop template we're following at the moment. Are you up for it or not?"

"Aye I'm up for it… sounds sensible."

"Eight o'clock then."

"Sounds good to me."

Just then the bell dinged as the door burst open and four bonny lasses giggled their way into the shop. Time for Jim to work his sales magic.

We had a brilliant slew of sales that afternoon because unbeknown to me Fran had paid one of her contacts to leaflet as many pubs and shops in the area as could be managed before mid-day. It worked a treat. Ten percent discount on any purchase for one day only and a ten percent discount on all future purchases for those customers who registered their name and address. After lunchtime in particular was manic and we made a lot of money… and we secured a lot of addresses. Thank heavens for that because we needed it.

The business paid for my evening bottle of malt and a bottle of Gordon's gin for Fran. If we were to have a session then let's make it a memorable one. I left the Transit at home and took a taxi that evening. No point chancing a lost licence.

CHAPTER 3

Our House

———————————■———————————

Fran's home was exactly as I'd expected. Nipping clean and functional without a hint of pretentiousness. Everything in her house was conservative and understated... and somehow lifeless. It gave me the same feeling as I had about my place. It wasn't a home... it was a place to live in. A place to wake up in and go to bed in... a place to have an occasional meal and to sit alone watching telly but certainly not a hideaway to be enjoyed.

I made all the right noises of course when complimenting Fran on the décor and the furnishings but somehow it rang hollow and she knew it.

"Give it a rest Jim you're not selling now. It's four walls... an upstairs and downstairs and a garden front and back. It does its job and keeps me warm in winter and off the streets when it's dark and it's somewhere to park the car... no more and no less."

"Aye... well, all I was trying to say was that I've seen worse. Not recently of course but there must be even tattier places than this hovel."

She laughed at that and gestured with her hand for me to sit myself down on the settee. "I hope you've arrived with alcohol."

I gave a grin and reached inside my holdall... emerging with the bottle of whisky first and then the Gordon's gin which had been tucked beneath my pyjamas to stop the bottles from chinking against each other. Pyjamas I'd had a heck of a job finding because it was many years since I'd last worn any.

"I don't need any mixers for the whisky but I forgot to bring any for your Gordon's."

By this time she was opening the dark wood door of a unit I thought was a record cabinet. It wasn't... it was full of bottles... mostly full bottles of every spirit you could imagine. She turned around with a bottle of Schweppes tonic in hand.

"Howay Fran what are you playing at... you've got more spirits in there than an Aleister Crowley seance. Why on earth did you ask me to bring alcohol with me?"

She gave a little laugh, "Because I want to discuss the business with you Jim... to have a chat and a decision-making evening. I'm supplying the bed and breakfast and you're supplying the drinks... seems fair to me. I wasn't about to pay full whack for your night out."

"You're not Scottish by any chance?"

She smiled, "No... just sensible and don't worry... when you get up in the morning I won't charge much for your breakfast."

"Ha-ha-ha very funny... there's definitely some Scot in there somewhere."

"Northumbrian actually Jim from up your neck of the woods... Alnwick. But that was a long time ago... a lifetime in fact." That came as a surprise but she stopped abruptly and I knew better than to pursue the matter.

She reached up into a glass fronted display cabinet and took out two spirit tumblers before coming to sit beside me on the settee. She placed the tumblers over slate coasters on the glass topped coffee table in front of us and proceeded to open the bottle of Bunnahabhain Scotch and poured me a half glassful. Then she opened the gin bottle and poured herself a half glass too before topping it up with tonic.

"Cheers," she held her glass out towards me.

"Cheers," I replied and we chinked and sipped.

We talked about many and diverse subjects for the first hour... bits and bobs... this and that, and none of it about Night Shadow, but it was pleasant to have a two-way chat with Fran. She had views and opinions about most things. The Second world war which she'd lived through as a young lass took up a big part of that hour and in the main it was fascinating stuff. For my part I told her about my life up to that point with the usual suspects featuring heavily... the important folk, Charlie, Tug, Titch, Sheila and my kids... my parents, my sister and my nephew Billy. Then my Grammar school years. It all came out so easily and she listened intently when it was my turn to unload.

As the drink kicked in Fran began to talk more personally about her younger years and I learned that she'd been born in 1929... the offspring of a skilled whitesmith father and her mother a farmhand's daughter. Her father very clever and her mother uneducated which didn't make for a blissful marriage. She didn't elaborate on that bit of information. Leaving Alnwick in early 1940 the family moved to Seaton Carew with the father working in Hartlepool at a zinc works of some description and her mother working as a milkmaid at a local farm. Fran could vividly remember the German bombers coming over regularly in an attempt to bomb the steelworks and shipyards in the area. The family were living in a place called 'The Green' and she remembered one evening in particular when a bomb dropped close by and blew out all the windows showering them in glass fragments. Shortly afterwards she was evacuated to a little village called Carlton Husthwaite near Thirsk where she told me she spent four happy years with a lovely family quite unlike hers. But she also told me that she was orphaned in August 1941. Her mother and father both died after an air-raid on West Hartlepool where they'd been attending a blacked out 40th birthday party for one of her father's work colleagues. Over twenty people died that night when a German parachute mine landed in the street where the party was being held.

Fran halted her memories for a moment... staring into the past and not savouring the moment... then simply said, "Houghton Street... and I can't get that name out of my mind. Houghton Street is where they died... but at least they were together for one final time." Then she clammed up.

We sat silently for quite a while just thinking and sipping. I was wanting to ask her if she'd gone to the funeral and did she get to see her parents before burial but it didn't seem right somehow. Apart from that my malt was taking some getting down the hatch because it was so peaty. I'd thought to impress Fran with my choice of whisky and had gone for one which I'd never tried before and it was really expensive. At that moment I was wishing I'd stuck to my usual tipple.

Fran seemed to realise this and said, "Whisky not going down too well Jim?"

"Nah, not really, it's not too clever. It's catching the back of my throat and it just tastes rough to me."

"So why did you buy it?"

"Dunno really... thought I'd give it a bash."

"Trying to impress me ehhh? do you want a swap?"

"What?"

I'll swap you a bottle of Grouse for your bottle of..." she turned the bottle to read the label, "Buhhnahab... Buurnabihairn... bloody hell Jim I can't even pronounce it and you can't drink it. What do you say? My full bottle of Grouse for your already opened bottle of Bunnies brains?"

She had quite a sense of humour after a drink and I thought to myself that anything would be better than the rough stuff I was currently sipping, "Aye okay, you're on."

Fran grinned then stood up and poured the malt I'd left in my glass back into the culprit bottle then replaced the stopper and whisked my expensive bottle away. A minute later she was unscrewing the cap from a bottle of Grouse and pouring me a fresh glass of whisky. "It's just a cheapy and a blend but it's pointless drinking something that isn't doing the trick." She pushed the glass into my hand and I took a sip.

I grinned, "That's better."

We sat for a while savouring the moment and the strange friendship we were striking up. Then she began.

"So Jim... my idea for the business."

I gave a grin, "Just the one idea?"

"No... okay I mean ideas then... plural, more than one. I've a few things to run past you but I'll pull them out of the hat one at a time."

"Okay Fran... go for it."

Fran topped up the glasses. The Grouse was palatable and going down a treat but I didn't want another Chinese restaurant episode so I pulled in my horns and slowed down the intake.

She began, "What does the market stall in Hull come under?... is it Night Shadow?" she asked.

"Yes of course."

"Okay so that needs changing as soon as possible to whatever... Nellie's Knickers... Freda's Frillies or something which detaches it from the shop and the main business."

"Ehhh... what for?"

"I'll tell you in a minute. Also... don't pay the pitch fees with card or cheque in future. Make sure it's cash only."

"Right... for what reason?"

"Hmmm... you're probably going to have a different opinion of me after this chat but we need to begin using the stall as a cash cow that the taxman doesn't see. It's pointless taking money out of your pocket and putting it into his."

I wasn't shocked but I was surprised, "But why?"

"Because in eighteen months' time... two years tops there'll be so much competition out there that your profit margins will shrink. Your shop will be less productive and less attractive to potential buyers."

"Buyers?"

"Yes... buyers. Because you'll need to sell up at the top of the cycle and not when the business is in decline."

"Sell up... what for?"

"To make a whacking profit and move onto something else."

"I hadn't considered..."

"Well then it's time to start considering Jim. All small businesses have a finite life cycle. Competition appears, prices tumble, profits are squeezed and it becomes a grind just to keep afloat for no sensible reason other than dumb pride. In two years there'll be half a dozen lingerie shops in Hull and a dozen market stalls following behind. You've been the pathfinder so to speak and other folk will copy your business model. So you have to think ahead and set a target date for your sell-out, as well as inflating the profits of Night Shadow. Take your wedge when a daft buyer comes along... poorly advised. Then disappear into the sunset with a bulging wallet,"

Now I was quite shocked. Fran was turning into a female Al Capone. "You're joshing... right?"

"I never josh. I've never married Jim and I've never failed in my business endeavours. No-one paid off this house other than myself. No-one ever bought me a new car every three years other than myself. No-one ever filled my bank account and my share portfolio other than myself... and I didn't do it by being naive and playing footsie with the tax people.

"You've never paid tax?"

"Of course I have but the barest minimum that I could get away with. Cash has always done the trick for me... not cheques or overdrafts... and cash will do the same for you if you see the light and play the game."

"But the tax folk aren't stupid?"

"I didn't say they were but most of them have a frisson of arrogance about them. The trick is to get them to focus on your flagship business while you're making the real money behind the scenes."

"Frances... you are something of a surprise."

"Thank you... I'm assuming that's a compliment."

"Yeh... maybe, so how do we go about this operation? It sounds a bit complicated to me... no offence intended."

"None taken. Top that glass up then listen and learn."

I did as I was told and topped both glasses up before settling back to listen to Frances in full flow.

"First we do exactly as I said with the Hull stall. As far as anyone will be concerned the stall has nothing to do with Night Shadow. The profit from the stall is fed in through the shop accounts to inflate the trading profit. Then we buy in similar stock to that which we buy from Lorella but we buy in from a Bradford manufacturer who is quite prepared to trade with us on a cash only no receipt basis."

"But..."

"Don't interrupt... I've already set up a tentative deal if you agree to my plan. Cash to buy in the stock and cash when it's sold and the taxman is none the wiser. Because at the moment you're a static outlet waiting for the money to come to your shop... and this will dwindle when the locals get over the novelty and other outlets appear. So what I suggest is that we take your new Bradford stock to the money."

"Ehhh... how's that supposed to work?"

She gave a triumphant grin, "Pub landlords."

"What?"

"You carry on as normal with the shop and the renamed stall. Lorella stock only and going through the books as per usual with the incomings and outgoings all attributed to Night Shadow."

"I understand that bit but what's that thing about landlords?"

"The Bradford cash stock is taken out to events... maybe weekly but probably fortnightly. We set up events all around Yorkshire, Lancashire, Nottingham, Lincoln, Durham and maybe further afield... it all depends on the impact."

"What events?... I'm not getting it."

"That's where the pub landlords come in. Show me someone who likes to appear affluent with a pocketful of cash and I'll show you a pub landlord. Show me someone who likes to spend that cash and flash their extravagance and I'll show you a landlord's wife or doxy."

"Doxy?... I don't..."

"The bit on the side... the barmaid... the other woman." She paused and frowned, "Forget that comment and let's concentrate on the main players. What I propose is that we set up events... a landlords' night out with wives in tow for a lingerie fashion show. We approach good-sized pubs which have a function room and then we ask them to invite the local landlords... say within a ten-mile radius for a lingerie shindig with perhaps three young and attractive lasses modelling on a walk-through. It's a win-win all around. The host landlord has a crowd in for one of his dead nights... so to speak... midweek. So he pulls in a crowd of big spenders to boot. The guest landlords get to show off and flash the cash and their wives get to spend a chunk of it on some of the lingerie on show. We get to make a tasty profit without the tax folk involved and the modelling lasses have a night out and a decent payday." Repeat that twice a month and squirrel the cash away somewhere unobtrusive."

"So where do the lasses come from?"

"Least of your worries Jim. I'll advertise and you'll have more takers than you can shake a stick at. Ages from eighteen to twenty-three we'll aim for. Lasses that age like to prance and show off and be ogled. Twenty quid in their pockets... a night full of ooh's and aahh's and admiring comments plus their drinks and food paid for... they'll lap it up."

"So who pays that?"

"We pay the cash because we'll have inflated our prices to cover the lasses' money... and we'll talk the host landlord into the free drinks and food for the girls. We'll invest some cash into buying a few bottles... whisky and gin and we'll give the guest landlords and wives a large snifter when they arrive. There's nothing like alcohol for driving the sensible out of someone's head and prizing the cash out of their pockets."

"Bloody hell Fran... you've got this all worked out. I have to say I'm somewhat gobsmacked... but what do you get out of it?"

She didn't answer for a while... sipping at her drink and then opening up a baccy tin and taking out the makings. She spoke as she constructed her smoke.

"Half of the profits from the shady side of the project?"

"Half?"

"Aye... half," she said as she finished off the making, licked the Rizzla and lit her rolly with a chunky glass table lighter.

"But that's..."

"Fifty percent."

"But how does that work? It's my stock and my business. How come you're wanting half of the cash?"

"Who's your Bradford supplier?"

"I don't know it's your contact."

"Precisely... and how do you pay him?"

"With cash... like you said."

"And that comes from where? Because we'll need to lay out north of five-hundred pounds... maybe double that."

"Five-hundred... a grand?" that figure seemed far too much."

"Yes because that will give us enough stock for the first two events. We don't want to be burning money driving back and forward to Bradford once or twice a week. And where would you get the cash from because as far as I can work out all your spare money for the foreseeable future is to pay Lorella and service the Transit. You've already told me that it has a whistling differential and needs some expensive work doing... so you don't have any wriggle room on the finance front."

"So?"

"So I'll invest enough cash to launch the event side of the business, but an investment deserves a just reward and I think half is a fair enough split... don't you?"

"What about the shop and stall?"

"They carry on as per usual. They're your business interests one hundred percent. The other bit however is either a joint venture or nothing."

I sat for a long while sipping at my whisky and lighting up a cigarette. I was going over it in my head because

Fran's comment about alcohol driving out the sensible and prizing out the cash could have applied to me... but somehow I doubted it. Then I remembered my old teacher Mr Wilson and his comment about a voice being a light in the darkness... so for better or worse I said...

"Okay... you've got a deal."

She stuck out her hand and we shook.

Then she said, "That handshake is more binding than any contract you're ever likely to sign. Contracts can be wriggled out of... but a handshake is a token of unbreakable trust between two people."

I nodded then grinned and replied, "Cut the claptrap Frances and pour the drinks, I still think you've some Scot in you somewhere. Fifty percent seems a fair outcome."

"You're a daft lad Jim... if you'd pretended to walk away I would have settled for forty with me handling the cash-flow."

I could only grin ruefully at that piece of information as I relaxed into the rest of the evening. We would end up talking the hours away and sorting the world out as the drinks took effect and we gabbled on into the small hours. The session would end up with me sleeping on the couch... and I can't remember how that came about because I woke up next day, close to midday with a blanket draped over me and my pyjamas still unused.

CHAPTER 4

On The Road Again

———————————— ■ ————————————

The next two months were frenetic and none of the folk involved seemed to have a spare minute. Gina who ran the Hull stall was given a pay increase and a set of instructions should she ever be asked questions about the stall owners. Those owners were now to all intents and purposes an outfit named Fashion-House with an address which didn't exist.

My Transit was now retired and sold off. Night Shadow had become the proud owner of a Bedford campervan. The Transit hadn't fetched a huge amount so this purchase had taken me to the limits of my spending power without dipping into overdraft. I'd come up a chunk short of the required amount and had to strike a deal with the seller to pay off the remaining third of the purchase price over the following three months. The procurement of that beauty however allowed us to transport sufficient stock and display equipment to the forthcoming events as well as the ability to transport our female models and our new tough-guy minder without having to use multiple vehicles.

Frances spent countless hours organising the financial side and the cash procurement of stock almost identical to that which we currently held. Each and every item was quality checked and price negotiated while at the same time she put out feelers both local and far afield for potential events. Our first event however would be held at my local pub the Priory Inn in their function room. It was a run through for us... a sort of pre-season friendly. With Frances handling the leafletting and advertising, it more or less guaranteed a bumper pay night for Alan the landlord.

Six models had been recruited by Fran and she told me it was easy. I don't know how she did it and I didn't delve too deeply other than to ask, "Why six, when we only have enough room to squeeze three into the camper?"

"Girls fall ill Jim... girls make other arrangements sometimes... dates with boyfriends... nights out... wrong time of the month. Girls pack jobs in the same as anyone else, but with six models we are never going to have to arrive with a girl or two missing and have a disappointing event. And every one of them is close to a size 12 and with similar body shape so we don't need to invest in a multiple demo stock selection."

Frances also arranged for a minder to protect the girls and sort out any inebriated punters who felt it was acceptable to have careless hands when around our scantily clad models. His name was Joss... short for Joskin which was a Hull term for a country bumkin or simpleton. He wasn't the brightest lad you would ever meet but he was built like a tank and was like a faithful puppy where Frances was concerned. I didn't know the full story but it was rumoured she'd saved Joss from a life on the streets and he would follow Frances to the ends of the earth if asked. When we were first introduced

I looked the bloke up and down and decided quite quickly to make him a pal. I certainly didn't want him as an enemy... so I asked him out for a pint shortly before our first event at the Priory. He readily agreed.

I'd chosen home advantage for our first meet-up. It was a Thursday evening, five days before our first lingerie run-out the following Tuesday. Joss would have preferred our evening to be at his favourite pub the Polar Bear on Spring Bank but I'd insisted on The Priory... my local with friendly faces around in case the evening didn't go well.

I was already sitting down with a pint of lager when Joss wandered in and after looking around and spotting me he gave me a smile as he ambled over to the bar. I signalled to the barmaid that this was the guy whose pint was in the pump and paid for. She gave me a grin in return and pulled his pint. She said something to him and then gave a flat hand gesture before pointing towards me when he reached into his pocket... letting him know that no money was required. He looked surprised... then lifting his pint he came over to my table and sat down.

"Thanks for the drink," he gave me a smile.

"Nae bother man... cheers," I said as we lifted our glasses and supped at the same time.

"Bit nippy out tonight," was his first foray into conversation.

I smiled and nodded, "Aye... there'll be loads of proper polar bears outside your local."

That made him grin. "Don't think so... cos they live up in Canada and the Arctic... I know things like that. My local pub was near to a zoo a hundred years ago... that's why it's called 'The Polar Bear' cos they had a proper polar bear living in the zoo. And another pub 'The Botanic' just over the road was called that name because it was beside the botanic gardens... I know that an' all. Ohh aye and something else, d'yer know there's a pub in Beverley called the Drum and Monkey but there's not?"

"Ehhh... what?"

"Yehh that's what I used to say... it makes you confused cos you're sitting drinking in a pub that everyone calls the Drum and Monkey but the sign outside says it's the Royal Oak."

I didn't know where the conversation was heading and I wished I hadn't started it off, "Wow... that's really interesting. I didn't know that."

"Yeh... just one of the things that I know. People think that I'm slow on the uptake but I'm not, I'm just a bit slower than fast folk. My brainbox just takes longer to put things away in the proper place. That's what Frances says anyway and she knows just about everything."

He wasn't far wrong there, "She sure does... she's a smart cookie."

Joss gave me a funny look, "Cookies aren't smart... cos they're just American biscuits... that's another thing that I know. Custard creams are probably just as smart as cookies."

"It's just a turn of phrase... it doesn't..."

"And another thing... when Frances asked me to help out with the frilly thing that you're both doing she told me about a man she knows who keeps touching young lasses when they don't want him to. That's why she wants me to be there to protect the girls. But I said to her that the man might be different now... you know... like he might have changed and he might have stopped doing those bad things. Frances doesn't agree though cos she said, 'a leopard never changes it's socks'. I had a right good laugh at that... not in front of her of course. But how silly was that? Can you imagine a great big cat like that trying to put socks on when it hasn't even got any hands? And folk say that I'm not bright."

I didn't know how to reply to that and I didn't dare laugh. I was sitting with another Albert but this one was solid and muscular with hands like shovels. I was very aware that I needed to choose my words very carefully and make sure that none were misinterpreted.

I was sure Joss had misheard Frances but nonetheless I said, "That was a strange thing for Frances to say. Maybe she just doesn't know as much about animals as you do."

"Probably not... cos I know lots about frogs and ferrets and sheep... and I once had a pet rabbit until mam's bloke killed it for dinner."

I really felt for him in that moment... he looked so miserable, "Aahh that's awful... that must have made you feel sad."

"Yeh I suppose it did... for a little while, but it tasted alright."

I made no comment and silence took over for a few minutes. I lit up a cigarette and we both paid great attention to our pints. Joss finished his first.

"Same again Mr Bates?"

"Aye... please."

Joss toddled off to the bar and was back a few minutes later with pints and crisps. It felt as if we had reached an understanding. Not quite friendship but a mutual acceptance... and we chattered on for a good hour or so. To be honest it was mainly Joss who chattered on and I found myself sitting back and listening to the contents of his weird and wonderful mind.

I found out during that interlude that Joss was actually called John but he had reluctantly adopted the nickname because of the constant Joskin taunts. It was easier he said to just accept the insulting name instead of constantly fighting the tormenters and then being arrested. He'd been arrested a number of times and had done a stretch of 6 months in Armley prison for abh before Frances entered his life and gave him a different life focus.

The most surprising thing about Joss though was the fact that he was married and happily so with a young son who had made his first appearance the previous year. He told me his wife was a teacher and way smarter than him. I didn't comment. And he was grateful to be able to do some paid work for Frances and myself because he found it difficult to hold down a regular job. Apparently, during the week he was a house husband looking after his young son. He told me that most mornings would find him pushing a buggy around Pickering Park and taking care of his child until his wife came home from school. Apparently he also did most of the cooking and he'd become something of a dab hand at it... or so he told me. I was quite amazed to be honest and it reinforced that old adage about not believing everything your eyes tell you and using your ears instead to find out a person's real story.

"Wow John... you're one surprise package."

"Why?"

That one-word reply meant I was skating on thin ice. I didn't know how to respond without causing offence. The information about his wife and child was what had really thrown me... it was so unexpected but my 'surprise package' comment had taken me to a cliff-edge moment and he'd asked a question that needed a response. I certainly couldn't go with, 'Sorry Joss but a daft bloke like you isn't the kind of fella I thought would be married'... I couldn't possibly go down that route. What could I say...honestly?

I suddenly thought of a way out.

"I just meant that I can't imagine a big bloke like you doing the cooking cos I'm rubbish at it... I have great difficulty just making beans on toast," was my escape from the predicament.

He seemed satisfied with that and grinned, "I do baking as well. I'll bring you a Victoria sponge when we do the Priory on Tuesday."

"That would be kind of you John... thank you."

"Call me Joss like everyone else... I'll know that you're not being nasty... we're pals now".

"Okay Joss it is.... nae bother. And by the way just to clarify when you were going on about being married I thought you were going to tell me that Frances had a fella."

Joss laughed out loud, "No chance of that Mr Bates... she don't like men very much. She once said to me that 'a woman needs a fish like a man needs a bike'...' or something like that. He'd got it wrong again... I think... but I didn't care... why would I?

We both smiled... and we were both comfortable. Our evening together had forged something of a bond between us and I was happy with that.

CHAPTER 5

No Expectations

———————————◼———————————

O
ur first lingerie event at my local pub 'The Priory' was
something of a wake-up call for both Frances and myself
and also something of a huge shock to me when I heard Joss
stand up and recite a piece of poetry that I'd always thought was
the dominion of intellectuals and at a stretch old Grammar
school lads like myself. It was also the evening when after
the selling had been done and the stock was boxed back up
that I stood up and sang a parody song about my old football
club 'Sunderland' but with most of the words pinched from
the Hull RFC song 'Old Faithful'. The song I sang that night
would be something of a 'Ouija' board moment because it
would be another ten years or so before Roker Park bit the dust
and became a bunch of houses... strange ehhh?

"Old Roker we saw some games together,
Old Roker in every kind of weather,
When your big match days are over
And the pitch is growing clover...
You'll still be that faithful pal of mine."

Okay my singing career never actually took off after
that evening. I could tell from the pained expressions of the

folk listening to me that maybe the lovely melodic notes I imagined were coming out of my mouth weren't the same ones that those people were hearing. Perhaps it was sensible to put my shot at vocal stardom on the back burner... so I did, and there it remains to this day.

We'd called an early halt to proceedings that first night because it suddenly dawned on Frances and myself that there was no way we could carry sufficient stock to fulfil all the potential sales. The function room was packed that evening... mainly with locals and regulars but it soon struck us that there were so many differing sizes of ladies that it would be impossible to carry the many different and varied garments we needed. We had all sorts of folk wanting to purchase that evening... from size 6's up to size 18s and beyond. Bust measurements from 32a to well up into the 40s. Petite ladies, large ladies, tall ladies and short ladies. Men buying for their womenfolk. and on almost every occasion they would underestimate their wives and girlfriends sizes... because to be fair most of them were just guessing.

What we swiftly cobbled together was an order and deposit scheme. Name, address and products ordered... written into the back of the accounts book that Frances carried with her religiously. 25% deposit required with the balance to be paid before delivery in seven days' time. Deposit to be non-refundable if the balance hadn't been paid before delivery or the purchaser had a change of heart. Strangely enough this went down well and although the evening was somewhat curtailed it was nonetheless lucrative... and we learned some important lessons from that run-through.

I also learned that Frances could be very caustic if not indeed cruel when it came to interacting with folk she was unable to gel with. She excelled with the finance and figures side of the business but she didn't have the friendly personality to rub along with folk when faced with a selling situation. She could be really acid and spiky and she almost caused an altercation which opened my eyes somewhat. The situation that evening was eminently avoidable had she possessed a smidgeon of tact, but unfortunately that wasn't the case.

To be honest we were rushed off our feet for one intense half-hour period. I was busy with two customers one of whom was quite tasty and unattached while Frances was being hassled by a middle-aged bloke who was somewhat the worse for wear. A drink or two too far. I could tell she was struggling and Joss was hovering but I couldn't leave my customers.

"Scuse me... scuse me can I get a bit of service here?"

"Be with you in a sec," Frances replied.

"You said that five minutes ago."

"What do you mean? you've only just arrived."

"No I haven't, I went away and came back... and you're still writing in that book. I've got cash to spend. Do you want some of it or not?"

Frances was looking red and flustered. Dealing with a constant swarm of buyers was not her forte... and it showed. She smacked the book down on the table then turned and faced the man.

"How may I help you sir?" Sarcasm dripped from her mouth with a huge emphasis on the 'sir'.

The man seemed not to notice, "I'm after one of those Basque things, the white one not the red and black."

Frances stared brazenly at his stomach, "I'm not sure that we'll have one to fit you... 'sir'.

Now the man had picked up on the sarcasm but he wasn't fazed at all, "It's not for me actually, but to be honest I'd probably look better in a Basque than you... 'madam'." He laid the emphasis on the 'madam'.

Frances was not a happy bunny. Being reverse insulted by a man was not in her playbook even if it was deserved. She took a huge breath and seemed to be pulling herself together before replying.

"My apologies... we've been rushed off our feet," then she forced a smile, "Who is it for?"

The man seemed pacified, "For my wife... over there beside the juke-box," he pointed.

I was just about finished with my two customers and I looked over to where the man was pointing. His wife was one hefty lump of female. I sort of knew what was going to come from Frances.

"Which one's the jukebox?" she asked innocently... as if butter wouldn't melt.

The comment was uncalled for and the man was now riled. I watched his cheeks turn red and noticed his hands clenching and unclenching. Had he been faced with a man I'm sure his next words would have been 'right... outside now' but it was a woman he was facing and he couldn't hit her... surely.

Just for a brief moment I thought the guy might plant her one but with an almighty effort he seemed to pull himself together. "You remind me of my sister," he gave Frances a rancid smile. I didn't know what that comment meant but the man did and I was sure it wasn't complimentary.

"So do you have a Basque in my wife's size?" The man continued... no doubt expecting a caustic comment in reply.

"I don't think so," said Frances diplomatically, "we only stock up to size eighteen, and that's not going to be enough."

He accepted the response without question as Frances continued, "I could ask of course if our supplier can possibly source the next size or maybe two or three sizes up."

"No... no don't bother I'm sure that would be far too much trouble for you. Is there anything else that would fit my wife?"

I'd finished with my customers and stepped in smartly at that point because I could imagine Frances coming out with something like 'we could order a marquee and cut the guy ropes off.' She didn't seem able to restrain her rudeness compulsion. I was annoyed with her that evening because if Joss had somehow become involved we would have had a pub brawl caused by her crass stupidity.

"I'll order something in for your wife," I said and gave him a big smile as I stepped in front of Frances at the same time as I gave Joss the eyes... which he immediately realised meant 'get her away from here'... and he did so. I continued the conversation with the fellow. "I'll order a playsuit maybe or a negligee in size twenty... I'm sure we can manage that."

The guy still seemed annoyed, "But will a size twenty fit her?" He looked rather doubtful.

The honest answer would have been 'not in a month of Sundays,' but the diplomatic answer was, "It will be nip and tuck to be fair but when your wife sees what you've bought she'll be so pleased that she'll want to shed a few pounds to fit into her new lingerie. So it's a win-win. You'll end up with a slimmer happy wife with a goal to aim for and she'll be chuffed that you've bought something romantic for her. Everyone ends up happy... myself included because you'll have made me a tiny profit."

The guy laughed at that... "How tiny?"

"Extremely tiny... barely enough to buy me a new Mercedes."

He laughed again. The heat had been taken out of the Frances situation. "Okay, order something for me... whatever you think will be best. Can I buy you a pint?" he asked.

"Nah," I replied, "But I'll spend my tiny profit on buying you one." Difficult situation now staved off. After I'd written out an order for a negligee and taken his deposit we moved over to the bar for a pleasant half-hour. I offered him an apology of sorts by saying that although her behaviour was unacceptable Frances was having an awful time with arthritis and had just received some bad family news. A huge lie but he accepted that.

Frances kept well out of the way for the final bit of the evening... contrition being the order of the day. She even helped the girls with the packing away and believe me that was the first and last time I ever saw her do that. Joss hovered around and about just in case anything kicked off... but no, peace and love reigned supreme and everything settled into something of a pleasant end of evening.

Until the spontaneous karaoke broke out... and that would turn out to be an eye-opener. Alan the landlord must have noticed that boredom had surfaced now that the fashion show was over and our scantily clad models were now back into their normal attire. He didn't want punters drifting away... so he kicked off proceedings by going over to the little raised stage, plugging in a microphone... giving it a 'testing... one-two, one-two' to make sure the equipment was working. Then when folk began to turn their gaze to the dais he began to theatrically stamp his foot in a regular rhythm to attract further attention. Finally... grinning like a Cheshire cat he burst into song without any intro or indeed any backing music. He began by destroying an old Frankie Vaughan song I remembered vividly from my junior schooldays.

"If I were a tower of strength, I'd walk away
I'd look in your eyes and here's what I'd say
I don't want you, I don't need you, I don't love you any more
And I'd walk out the door
You'd be down on your knees
You'd be calling to me
But a tower of strength is a-something
I'll never be."

The thing is... he knew all the words and he carried on to the bitter end. The initial catcalls and boos ended up with everyone clapping in time to the words and quite a few of the folk who remembered the song joined in. Emboldened by his initial success he then introduced song two... something by the Four Preps called 'I Was a Big Man Yesterday'. To be fair he wasn't too bad and he certainly livened up the audience. Folk who'd been about to leave sat themselves down again and more drinks were ordered. When song two ended he grinned elatedly whilst accepting the sporadic applause before calling for volunteers to continue with the singing but there were no takers. After a minute or so of zero response and obviously disappointed he looked around the room and then pointed as he fastened his eyes on me.

"Jim'll do it... he's made a heap of money tonight. Let's hear what a rich Geordie sounds like."

'Aarrggh'... I wasn't best pleased. I certainly wasn't rich and singing wasn't something I was good at. I could have happily given him a swift foot up the jacksy but I had to accept the invite and smile as I walked over with reluctance to take his place and continue the entertainment. I would have seemed like a real killjoy if I'd refused... bugger-bugger-damn.

Before I got to the microphone he announced, "As you'll all be aware Geordie Jim is from the part of the country where they hang monkeys as French spies." That comment was my inroad... because he'd made a blooper. Folk were laughing at his French monkey comment.

I walked up to the little stage... reached out and took the microphone with a big smile, "Hi all you generous folks... thanks to each and every one of you for your custom this evening... it's most appreciated. I'll be keeping an eye out in nine months' time to see if the lingerie has worked its magic," that elicited a few knowing chuckles, "And also a big thank you to landlord Alan for use of the function room this evening and also for the introduction. Truth is he's not wrong you know, we do indeed hang monkeys in my corner of the world... and that explains why he looks so nervous every time I pop in for a pint." More laughter followed... Jim (1) – Landlord (0). Until I began to warble of course. Without further ado I did the foot-stamping thing before breaking into song and murdering my version of 'Old Faithful'.

It didn't go down well. I can't remember any actual boos but there were catcalls a' plenty. "Gerroff... my eardrums can't take it. Come on Jim... give over you sound like a horse fartin'. We want Bob Dylan not Bob dildo."

My shot at stardom was over. After squawking out the final line of the song I gave an embarrassed bow. Standing down to muted applause and dodging a whizzing beer-mat. I happily handed the microphone over to Liz... one of the lingerie models who... having now changed into skirt and jumper proceeded to give me a rueful grin before facing the audience. She introduced herself and her song before beginning to belt out Anita Ward's hit record... 'Ring My Bell'. She sounded light-years better than my meagre offering. I slunk sheepishly back to the bar while everyone joined in with the 'Ring My Bell' chorus.

My new-found pal was still sitting at the bar when I returned.

"Good try Jim."

"No it wasn't."

"Aye fair enough it was pretty naff."

"Thought you'd be with your wife now. Where is she?"

"With my sister... still beside the jukebox."

I looked over and sure enough his wife was still in the same seat but now with pint in hand.

"My wife's the one in the dress... not the one with all the records inside."

My new-found pal had a sense of humour. I gave that comment a chuckle.

As the evening wound down to last orders the spontaneous karaoke was just about finished. Quite a few folk had decided to brave the microphone after my pathetic attempt. No doubt they'd been thinking... 'well I'm not very good but I can't be half as bad as Jim'. To be fair a good night was had by all.

Then surprise upon surprise... a request was made for Joss to have a bash. He was very well known in the local area and most folk gave him a degree of tolerance if not respect. He wasn't best pleased to be called up for a turn at the vocals but thankfully he didn't shirk the invite.

He wandered over to the stage and took the microphone from where it had been laid on a table and tapped the top before proceeding to blow into it causing some screechy feedback. Then an embarrassed apology as he brought the microphone up to his lips, "Ermmm... sorry I can't sing cos I don't really know any proper songs all the way through except 'twinkle-twinkle little star,' but I can say some poetry."

"Go on Joss give us a poem lad... there was an old lady from Lincoln," shouted a wag from the back of the room.

"No... not that one cos it's dirty. I know a better one though."

"Come on then... get on with it Joss... stop fannying about," shouted the mouthy wag again.

Joss gave a sickly grin and looked totally out of his depth. He kept his eyes down... not looking at the audience as he cleared his throat. "I learned this one years ago at university... it's called Ozymandias and it's by Percy Shelley." There was a gale of laughter at the university statement. Joss looked both embarrassed and annoyed at the same time but soldiering on he gave his throat a second clearance and began anyway.

> I met a traveller from an antique land
> Who said: Two vast and trunkless legs of stone
> Stand in the desert. Near them, on the sand,
> Half sunk, a shattered visage lies, whose frown,
> And wrinkled lip, and sneer of cold command,
> Tell that its sculptor well those passions read
> Which yet survive, stamped on these lifeless things,
> The hand that mocked them and the heart that fed:
> And on the pedestal these words appear:
> "My name is Ozymandias, king of kings:
> Look on my works, ye Mighty, and despair!"
> Nothing beside remains. Round the decay
> Of that colossal wreck, boundless and bare
> The lone and level sands stretch far away."

The silence that followed when Joss finished was profound. I think everyone in the room was stunned... more so the folk who had maybe encountered that poem in their learning days. I remembered it from my English lit class but couldn't have spouted anything more than 'my name is Ozymandias, king of kings' and maybe the next line. It went over the heads of the other people in the audience but even so they realised they'd heard something special and completely unexpected.

The stunned silence continued for a good ten seconds until it was broken by the noisy wag from the back of the room who stood up and began a lone clap. Then after a second or two someone else joined in... then someone else clapped and stood up and before you knew it the entire room followed suit and they were up on their feet clapping, whistling and cheering and shouting words of encouragement. "Brilliant Joss... brilliant. Go on Joss lad you're a star. Bloody hell where did that come from?"

Four or five people moved forward in a noisy cluster to stand right in front of Joss on the stage and clap even louder. Joss looked completely shell-shocked and kept his eyes down on the floor... his face reddening as he did so. I was aware that he was struggling with the adulation in his bemused state and I was worried how he might react. But Frances sorted the problem before it became one. After a minute or so of the noisy reaction she walked to the little raised platform and held out a hand. Joss took it and followed Frances like a lamb as she led him out of the room.

That protective interlude told me that Frances did indeed possess empathy... when it suited her. The applause and shouts of encouragement had been heartfelt but also overwhelming for someone like Joss and luckily Frances had averted anything bad happening.

Ten minutes later the bell rang for 'Time gentlemen please' and I went to look for Joss and his lady minder. They'd gone... but the events of that evening would be talked about for weeks to come.

CHAPTER 6

Everybody Was Kung-Fu Fighting

―――――――――――――――――――■―――――――――――――――――――

The low down on Joss was that he had truly been to university in Hull, studying history, and had graduated with a 2:1 before joining the army. Two years into army life found him in the Falklands conflict and less than two years after that a medical discharge because of injuries. Serious head injuries received in the Falklands hadn't finished him off but they'd left Joss as we knew him now with learning or comprehension difficulties. An Argentinian Pucara ground-attack plane had done for him. His life was on a downward spiral until Frances appeared in his life... and that's all I ever found out about Joss apart from the fact that his wife had been one of the people involved in his rehabilitation. Anything else I could tell you would just be pure fiction or repetition of rumour. I began to look at Frances and Joss with different eyes when all that information came to light and my demeanour towards them both changed somewhat.

Anyway... after our eye-opener of a night at The Priory life moved on and Night Shadow zoomed in an upward trajectory. We began making money hand over fist. Our routine quickly became imbedded as we arranged fortnightly fashion events... using the same criteria we'd hit upon at The Priory. The girls modelled... the captive crowd oohed and aahed and Frances, myself and later in the evening one of the girls would write down the orders in our little books and relieve the buyer of 25% of the total. They'd be given a receipt of sorts with the no refund policy clearly visible in case of non-payment before the seven-day deadline.

Events were always held midweek... a Tuesday or Wednesday and I would keep off the alcohol at one event and then Frances would do the same at the next. This was so we could take turns at sharing the driving home. On the morning following an event the order would be phoned through to Bradford and every Sunday following a fashion night we would take our bundle of cash... meet up with our supplier at a transport café somewhere on the M62 and return to the shop with another load of stock. The following week we would drive back to the event location on the seven-day deadline... usually in Frances' car to save on the petrol expenses. We'd collect the payments that had been made then hand over the nicely packaged orders to the host landlord. One of us would drink... the other wouldn't as we waited until closing time for any last-minute payers. Then we'd drive back to Hull, usually arriving well after midnight and count the cash at Frances' house. We insisted on cash but we did receive the occasional cheque which we then had to filter through the shop accounts and on one occasion we were paid our 75% balance with a crate of beer and two bottles of spirits. We didn't refuse.

We were coining it in but unexpectedly the no-show payments became really important. We found we were pulling in buckshee cash from the second-thoughters and the non-payers. Their 25% non-refundable deposits were invariably enough to cover our petrol expenses and payments to the girls and as a bonus we still had the uncollected garments for resale. We began to look forward to having a good few of those non-paying folk who'd changed their minds when the event was over and the drink had worn off.

Of course we were occasionally lumbered with an item of stock which was virtually impossible to shift because of the outrageous size that we'd ordered for a prospective customer but after a while we even found an outlet for those items via newspaper adverts. After our first advertising success mail order also became a sideline... not lucrative because of the postage or delivery costs and the initial cost of the advert but more often than not it was enough for us to turn a small profit.

The furthest west we ever evented was Liverpool, the furthest north was Durham and the furthest south was Peterborough. We did however have a four-day roadshow which took us to events in Carlisle and Glasgow but that was a one-off trial which was never to be repeated because we lost a chunk of money on that one and the girls didn't like being away from home. Joss didn't accompany us on that occasion because he refused to spend a night away from his wife and bairn. Anyway... Glasgow turned out to be a rowdy event and we quickly realised our limitations when our minder was absent. We had to make a swift departure from that one... escaping from the Partick venue by the skin of our teeth and with a smashed window on the campervan. We'd all have a chuckle about that night later... but at the time it was one scary evening.

The only serious altercation apart from the Glasgow escapade was at a pub in Mansfield. It was the first and last time that I ever saw Joss called into serious action and at the end of that evening I was glad we were on the same side.

I'd thought the entire event was progressing smoothly... with just the occasional lewd comment directed at the girls and a few loud punters who had obviously overdone the alcohol intake. Just another lucrative noisy evening I thought. It was heading for closing time and the girls were now back into their travelling clothes and sitting together in the 'snug' area of the pub. The orders and cash deposits had all been collected and noted down. Then I noticed that Joss seemed to be on edge.

"You okay Joss?"

"Aye."

"Doesn't seem like it to me."

"Just keeping watch... that's all."

Somehow he'd sensed something that I wasn't aware of. He was alert and sweeping his gaze around the room. He seemed coiled for action. Joss put his orange juice down on the bar and moved out a few feet.

"So who are you watching?"

"Big bloke with the tattoo on his neck. Far corner with the other two guys. They came in a few minutes ago and the landlords have been moving away from them. They must be well known in the area. There's a few nervous people in the pub now."

The three blokes he'd indicated had moved away from the corner and were laughing and joking as they headed towards the bar. Other folk in the room were vacating tables and moving quickly out of their line of travel.

"D'yer think there's gonna be trouble?"

"We'll see."

"What do you want me to do Joss?"

"Make yourself scarce and keep out of my way."

"But there's three of them."

"Two and a wimp. Just do as I say Mr Bates and keep out of the way."

I wasn't about to argue and moved away about four seats down the bar. I'd done as told but I was ready to do my bit and jump in if required. It had been my turn to have a drink and completely sober I was a right pussy but after four or more pints I turned into a Geordie Henry Cooper... in my head at least. So I held myself ready for action.

I saw that one of the approaching morons had barged an oldish guy out of the way and caused him to stumble into an adjoining table... knocking a beer glass to the floor. It hit the ground at the same time as the man but no-one went to help. I eased myself off my bar-stool.

Then it kicked off.

Caroline one of our models had picked that moment to emerge from the side room and swan up to the bar. She was completely unaware of any tension in the room and I saw her give the barmaid a big smile as she said, "Three packets of prawn cocktail crisps and three Bacardi and cokes please... they're the free ones for the models."

The service area had thinned out considerably as the stooges reached the bar and tattoo neck... now with his hand on the bar-rail said in a loud voice, "We'll have those drinks darling."

Caroline half turned to face the voice still blissfully unaware of the rancid atmosphere, "Aahh... sorry no they're not for you. We get the drinks for doing the lingerie modelling." The drinks and crisps were by this time appearing in a row on the bar top.

"Free drinks for taking your clothes off."

"Excuse me... what?"

"Taking clothes off for payment isn't called modelling here darling... it's called something else," he grinned at Caroline then reached over to the bar picked up one of the glasses and drained the contents all in one swift movement. Before Caroline could react he'd picked up a second glass and drained that one too.

Licking his lips he said, "So what do you say to that?"

Had Caroline ignored the provocation and turned away and left at that moment the situation could maybe have been averted or at the very least smoothed over. The lady however was not for turning... she'd been insulted and that wasn't on.

"Oink-oink-oink," grunted Caroline as she reached for the remaining full glass standing on the bar and drained it in one... before turning back to tattoo neck and giving him a smirk.

"Ehhh?"

"Oink-oink-oink."

"Are you stupid... what's that supposed to mean?"

"Dunno... it's just what I usually say to ugly ignorant pigs."

The guy's face turned purple and his expression changed from mockingly sarcastic to enraged. He seemed to stare at the floor for a second then quick as a flash he grabbed Caroline's breast and squeezed three times... "Oink-oink-oink," then gave a snorting laugh.

Caroline drew her arm back to give the bloke a slap but in an instant her arm was grabbed by Joss who pulled her backwards out of the line of fire. He spun her around and whispered...

"Into the van... you and the others... don't argue, don't look around just get out and take Frances with you... just do it!"

"Hey, you," tattoo neck shouted at Joss, "what the hell do you think you're playing at pal?"

Joss turned back to face him, looked him up and down then said, "You meaning me?"

"Aye you."

Joss took a second to reply and seemed to be steadying himself.

"Well I'm not playing at anything and I'm not your pal." I noticed that Joss had half turned so that he was standing sideways to tattoo neck. Then it all happened in a flash.

"You're looking for a smack in the mouth," growled the man as he drew back his arm intending to hit Joss with a huge punch.

'Bang... crackkk,' Joss threw a lightning left jab... it didn't seem hard at all but it connected with the man's nose and sent it pointing off in a different direction. The guy clutched at his face as Joss swivelled and aimed a kick at the kneecap of number two bloke who'd dived in to the attack. He went down bellowing in pain and number three took a straight knuckles to the throat as he attempted to join the fray. Three seconds at most and three downed pseudo hard men. Tattoo came back for second helpings with his wonky nose covered in blood but one swift punch to the groin downed him and he gave a strangled screech as he hit the floor and rolled about.

Joss surveyed the scene quickly then turned and ushered me out of the pub as a matter of urgency. "Quickly Mr Bates out you go... don't want them to spot the van registration."

We hurried outside and jumped into the camper. Frances was doing the driving and already had the van ticking over as we jumped in. Then as we slammed the doors shut behind us she shot out of the pub carpark like a female Stirling Moss. Five minutes later we were out of Mansfield and on the main road north. We all breathed a sigh of relief when it became obvious that we'd made good our escape and weren't being followed. Truth is I'd been mightily impressed with Joss so after a few minutes of silence I asked...

"Where did you learn that stuff Joss? You've got faster hands than a Newcastle shop-lifter."

Joss shrugged, "Where doesn't matter... but I wasn't that good. It's just that those three were useless. Pretend hard-cases who've probably acquired their reputation by picking on lasses or bullying blokes they know can't fight."

"Aye but the hand speed?"

"You saw it Mr Bates... the big bloke with the tattoo didn't just telegraph the punch... he could have sent me a postcard it was that slow. I didn't need to hit him hard... just in the right place with sufficient force. A broken nose will heal in two or three weeks. Second bloke may have more of a problem if his kneecap is dislocated. Third bloke... the wimp, will have a sore throat for a week or so but I didn't use enough force to cause serious damage. They'll be as right as rain in a few weeks with the only permanent damage being to their egos and local hard-man credentials."

"Thanks anyway Joss," chirped Helen... one of the models. "You're our hero now... isn't he everyone?"

There were four definite yes's from the females in the van and I reluctantly added my affirmative. I was a little miffed because I hadn't got in on the action. I'd had a few pints and I'm convinced I could have seen those three off without breaking sweat. 'Aye Jim that'll be right!'

A few minutes later and still with a long hour or more to endure in the back of the camper Frances chirped up from the driving seat, "If you lot look in the hamper basket under the seat you'll find some cold cooked sausage and a big pork pie... ohhh aye and a bottle of gin. Help yourselves, I think you all deserve it. There's some plastic cups up in one of the net holders and paper plates in the hamper side pocket."

"Nothing for me," said Joss from the front passenger seat.

Sally took over the organisation and began passing out the food. She was the oldest of all the models... twenty-six and a few years over the Frances age parameter. Helen sorted the plastic cups and the pouring of the gin. She was nineteen and saving the modelling money for her upcoming marriage.

"Anything for you Frances?" Sally asked.

Frances took a second to reply. "I'm driving Sally... so no gin obviously, but you can pass me a sausage."

"A stiff one or a floppy one?" chuckled Sally and everyone including Joss had a laugh at that.

"You're a cheeky mare Sally," said Frances over her shoulder but she too was enjoying the exchange.

For the next few minutes we relaxed into chomping and slurping. The food was going down a treat and the gin was beginning to work its magic. Tongues were being loosened by the alcohol but also because of the relief that came from escaping unscathed from an ugly situation. The girls were doing girly banter and I kept out of it as much as possible... I was feeling somewhat superfluous to requirements. I'd become nothing more than an unwanted eavesdropper... and listening in on private conversations that I shouldn't have been privy to. But they were enjoying themselves and that could only be a good thing. They were talking time of the month things and boyfriend interludes.

Sally reached for the last sausage.

"Let me have that one Sally," Helen said.

"What for... you should have been quicker."

"Aahh come on, you've got one waiting for you at home. I haven't."

"Ehhh?"

"A sausage... at home. You're married and you get sausage whenever you want one," she giggled.

Sally frowned and handed the last sausage to Helen, "You've got a lot to learn young lady. It only lasts for a year or two."

"What does?"

"The sausage thing... the sex... that's what you mean isn't it? It tails off. It doesn't last."

"What are you talking about?... you can do it whenever you like. Not like me in the back of Bob's car."

Sally gave a rueful smile and shook her head. "I've been married seven years and that itch, that desire or excitement...

call it what you will turns into endurance. It becomes boring, but boring becomes okay because you realise it's better than giving up and starting over. You just decide to put up with all the little niggly things that have surfaced over the years. Your knight in shining armour turns into the rapidly ageing bloke lying on the couch in his boxer shorts with a beer-can in his hand watching Match of the Day. That fresh baked bread eventually becomes stale."

"Yeh... but you still do it when you want."

Sally gave another head-shake, "Is that what you're really expecting? If sex is the only reason you're getting married then you need to wise-up girl because marriage isn't like that. My Trevor's dick has turned into a semi-colon. I can't remember what it's for and I never use it anyway."

Helen frowned, "So you don't have sex?"

"Of course I do... occasionally, but only if I don't have to move around too much or take both legs out of my pyjama bottoms."

Everyone in the van laughed out loud at Sally's comment but I could see the questioning look on Helen's face.

Then most surprisingly Frances joined the fray, talking over her shoulder as she drove. "Girls... many-many years ago I had a fiancé... a lovely-lovely guy who looked like Adam Faith, and he once told me that sex was so much better on holiday," to be honest we were all a little shell-shocked in the back... because Frances didn't normally join in. There was a long, pregnant silence before she resumed. "I never want to get another post-card like that one." Everyone in the van laughed like crazy at the Frances input. It was funny... but afterwards I wondered if there was also an element of truth in it.

Then before we knew it we were back in Hull. Frances drove the girls to their homes and we waited in the van until they'd gone into their houses and shut their doors behind them. Then Frances, Joss and myself headed to Frances' house for the reckoning up and the money counting. It was the final act in what had been a very strange day.

CHAPTER 7

Return to Sender

———————————■———————————

The next twelve months flew by. We managed lots of events and made a stack of cash. Then Frances disappeared to Australia to see a son I didn't know anything about... a child born out of wedlock presumably. Joss proudly announced the coming of a second child and I sold the 'Night Shadow' business. It was almost immediately after selling the business that the tax-man made an unwelcome appearance. A huge demand landed on my front-door mat one morning and the massive assessment they'd worked out made me realise I needed to make myself scarce. I panicked because I didn't have the kind of money they were saying I owed and Frances had emptied the building society accounts that we kept our secret cash in. It was then that I took the opportunity to head off for my final get-together with Charlie.

Charlie had written to me in the hope that I might be able to make the short crossing to Belgium for a meet up. He was on an end-of-life journey trying to find information about the extended family of Jesus. That morsel of information gave me immediate flashbacks to that time in Charlie's front garden in Cowpen with the Bates pit bloke. What did Charlie suspect that I didn't know?

I'd arranged the giving up of my Hull flat. I'd put in my four-week notice. It was time to make the move back to Blyth in order to give the tax folk a body-swerve. Surely they couldn't follow me all the way to Blyth? But first I arranged a trip on a ferry called the Norstar in order to make a night-time sailing from Hull to Zeebrugge. Charlie wanted us to meet up in Bruges and to introduce me to his family.

I'd been looking forward to it. A bit of a jolly and a catch up with my old mentor before having to come back to England for the sorting out of life.

Now for those of you who are fond of the occasional few quid on the horses this next bit is in no way a criticism, but my gambling days had always been sporadic and more or less confined to history. I've never been a gambler per-se. It's never been one of my must-do vices ever since I lost a week's wages in the space of four hours in a betting shop. I'd been a very naive and silly young man and had to tap my mam for the week's rent on my flat. I'd seen early on in my life the misery a gambling compulsion could cause and decided never again to be sucked into that downward spiral. I'd very rarely touched drugs either but I did smoke cigarettes and I liked the occasional good old drinky-poo so two out of four wasn't too bad.

However, on my boat trip I'd changed a chunk of money into Belgian Francs on the night crossing but being bored and drinking alone I thought I'd risk ten pounds of my remaining English money on gambling chips and sat myself down at a Blackjack table. The lassie doing the dealing was attractive but showed no interest so I didn't bother going down that route. I didn't even know what I was doing... not really... Blackjack was a pirate in Treasure Island as far as I was concerned. But after half-an-hour or so at the table I found myself almost fifty pounds to the good. I'd been making daft bets on turnovers and doing doubling up or something but everything I did had been paying off and my initial tiny pile was now a decent pile. The guy sitting next to me was winning a little bit too and he seemed incredibly surprised when I picked up my chips, thanked the dealer and stood up to walk away.

"Ere myte wotcha doin' yer on an 'ot streak?" A cockney fella.

"Quitting with my winnings."

"Doan be a mug... follow yer luck myte... fill yer boots."

"Thanks for the advice but I'm done. You crack on fella if you're feeling lucky. Hope it goes well." Then I left him to go and cash in my chips and then sit at the bar for a bit of a chat with the pleasant serving bloke.

I watched from my perch as the cockney guy sat for the next hour turning cards and moaning. After a while he held up a hand to admit defeat and stood up before looking around the room and seeing me. He must have lost well over a hundred pounds. He came over and sat beside me.

"You toddled off with me luck me old cock sparra."

"No pal... I toddled off with mine while I was winning."

"Nah... you're takin' the Gypsy's... I doan Adam an' Eve it... you could've won a ton me old China... maybe a monkey."

He was irritating the life out of me. Cockneys always seemed so full of crap with their daft rhyming slang. But

I decided to endure his banter because he was just a lonely bloke wanting to impress. Apart from that he'd just lost a tidy packet and I'd won enough to cover a good drinking session so I stood him a lager and a rum. My good deed for the day. Nevertheless I was looking forward to tomorrow. It came around quickly.

I met Charlie at Café Vlissinghe in Bruges the following day. Reputedly the oldest pub in the city and it was busy when I arrived. I'd been dropped off from a cab which seemed to have taken a roundabout route to transport me to my meeting place. I didn't make an issue of it. Weather wise it was quite a pleasant day and I spotted Charlie almost immediately sitting at an outside table. I was surprised because he was alone and I'd been expecting to meet up with his nephew and the other members of the family.

"James, at last," were his first words when he spotted me as I walked towards the table. I noticed immediately that his voice had lost a lot of its authority. Somehow weaker and unsure. His facial hair was now sparse and neatly clipped and his clothes were all smart and fashionable. No combat jacket. Not at all like the picture of Charlie I carried around in my head.

"Hi Charlie. All on your lonesome? Where's the family?"

Charlie eased himself out of his seat with the help of a walking stick and grasped my outstretched hand. It still felt a firm handshake, "Boat tour with the girls. Then they're off to do some research at Basilica of the Holy Blood... but you'll meet them tomorrow." he gave me a smile as we shook then we sat down opposite each other. It felt really easy this time. He was different.

"Drink James?"

"Just a beer Charlie... no shorts. Had a bit of a night on the ferry."

Charlie smiled then turned and gestured to the waiter. An oldish fellow. Charlie ordered in a foreign language.

I was a little confused, "Don't they speak English Charlie? because I don't know any Belgian."

He grinned at me, "Nobody speaks Belgian James... there's no such thing as such. And yes almost everyone speaks English but that waiter is one of the older generation and I was practicing my Walloon."

I gave him a big grin, "Yeh I used to practice my Walloon at school cos I hated the recorder."

That made Charlie chuckle, "Yes very funny James. But Walloon is one of the old languages and to be honest I don't speak it fluently, but it's made one old waiter guy very happy that someone is making the effort. Belgium is a country of many languages and dialects. In some parts of the country they speak French... others German... some areas speak mainly Dutch and there's a whole host of other dialects and old Romance languages. It's fascinating."

It wasn't fascinating to me but within a few minutes we had two tall glasses of Belgian beer put in front of us. "Merci tot'd'bon," said Charlie as the waiter put them down.

"I gn'a pon d'mô," the old waiter replied then turned and left with a smile.

"What was that all about?" I asked.

"Just simple etiquette James... a 'thank you very much' from me and a 'think nowt of it bonny lad' as a reply."

"What?... you mean the bloke replied with a Geordie phrase in that Walloon thingy?"

Charlie rolled his eyes, "Of course not James... for heaven's sake it was just a thank you and a polite reply to the thank you. You should study some of these languages. You'll find they mostly have the same Latin or Greek root... even some of the Romance dialects."

I was out of my depth with the linguistics thing. I spoke German to donkey level and French to schoolboy level although I had progressed somewhat during my enforced library period with Charlie in Hull so I changed the direction of the conversation as a matter of urgency. "So what's all this Jesus stuff you were referring to in your letter Charlie... what's that all about?"

Charlie took a mouthful of beer then reached into his jacket pocket and produced a packet of Gauloise cigarettes and offered me one. I'd always thought that French tabs were smelly and effeminate but I took one anyway. We both lit up and began puffing.

"I'm doing a final research project before I head off to meet my maker,' he paused and puffed out a smoke ring. It reminded me of Tug, another old fella from my schooldays. He'd always been good at those. Charlie continued, "I'm wanting to know if there is actually a maker to meet. I have my own ideas of course but I've been looking for confirmation."

Something fundamental had changed with Charlie and I wasn't quite sure what he was aiming for on this quest so I said, "And you think you're going to find that out in Bruges?"

"No James of course not. Bruges is just a handy stop on our way back home to Sweden and an easier place to meet up with you. We've been down in Cathar country for a few weeks trying to make sense of the story that followed the crucifixion and the escape of the Jesus family to France."

So that was it... Charlie's quest. I'd done a fair bit of reading during my recovery phase when Charlie and I were last together in Hull. That story or legend about the escape of Mary Magdalene to the south of France after the death of Jesus was compelling and mighty interesting.

"So what's your conclusion Charlie?"

"There is no conclusion James. I have only a feeling, and that feeling tells me there is some substance to the legend."

I thought those words over for a few seconds... then, "So... do you believe that Jesus was married and had children... with Mary Magdalene?"

Charlie glanced around the other tables then frowned, "Keep your voice down James. This is a Catholic country and opinions like that are not held in high esteem. Old men in black dresses who can recite the old testament word for word are the important folk in Belgium. What Charlie believes or doesn't believe is rather beside the point. In my opinion every man or woman should have the freedom to make their own minds up about things which will never have a definitive answer. Reaching back two thousand years is a virtually impossible task and one should rely on the heart and the gut in such situations. It is the time to form your own beliefs without feeling the need to force them down the throats of others like the organised religions do."

"But what do you think Charlie. Was he married or not?"

Charlie hesitated... then, "He was referred to as rabbi."

"What?"

"Rabbi James... Jesus was referred to as rabbi in some of the scriptures. Now you think it through from there. You don't need me to lead you through the thought process. You have a brain."

I mulled that over for a few seconds, "Babies have brains too Charlie but they don't know anything. Not until they're taught and given guidance from grown-ups with knowledge and experience."

Charlie laughed out loud, "How old are you now James? Thirty-seven? Thirty-eight? For heaven's sake it's a bit late for me to be potty training you or showing you how to tie shoe-laces."

We grinned at each other, "Fancy another beer Charlie?"

"Of course."

I held a finger up in the air then swiftly put it back down again. "How do you ask for two beers in Walloon?" It was time for me to ingratiate myself with the old waiter fella.

"Dji t'veû vol'tî."

"Ehhh?... Jee terview volty?"

"Almost James... well done but the middle word is pronounced ti ver like in the French word blue... blerr' bleu."

Cracked it. I was feeling chuffed with myself. I held up a finger and the waiter appeared as if by magic. "Right bonny lad... two more beers... Jee t'veû volty... sil vous plaît." I chucked in a bit of Charles Aznavour just to show off.

The waiter laughed then bent over and kissed the top of my head before shooting off for the beers.

"Whoa fella... what was that all about?" I rubbed at the top of my head where the kiss had been planted and watched the retreating back of the waiter, then glanced at Charlie, "Is that bloke a bit ac/dc."

Charlie was creased up and I thought he might choke. He was guffawing and gasping for breath but it was sheer rapture not a bad turn. He belly laughed and slapped the table. "Gotcha."

"Ehhh?" ... then it dawned on me. I'd been stitched like a kipper.

"What did I just say to that bloke Charlie?" I was having a chuckle to myself by this time knowing that the old bugger had blindsided me.

Charlie could hardly get the words out... "I love you... if you please."

The waiter returned at that moment and I was feeling silly as he put the two beers down. I was still chuckling as I tried to get some words out, "I errrmm... didn't errrmm... mean..."

The waiter winked and blew me a kiss. That started Charlie off again and we had a giggle-fest for a minute or so. He might have been ancient but there was still a lot of kid inside that old body.

We spent a pleasant few hours that day putting the world to rights. I did ask Charlie about the Bates pit timberyard Jesus. Whether he really believed that Jesus had returned. He was very vague in reply merely saying that Jesus had returned many times and was terribly concerned about the future of the human race. We were destroying ourselves. I tried to question him further but he would say no more other than, "Make up your own mind James. Do you believe that our species is the pinnacle of creation? Do you think that maybe there are too many humans on this planet? Or what? do you think that self-destruction will be our contribution to evolution... our fingerprint left at the scene of crime when the succeeding species forensic team arrive and humans are extinct? Are we to be the next dodos or dinosaurs? for that's the way I believe we're headed... think about it."

I left Charlie's speech without a response hoping that we'd maybe discuss it at a later date. We never did.

We were joined by the old waiter after his shift finished and he spoke English fairly well. Certainly not fluently but well enough to make himself understood. His name was Toby and he was an interesting old fellow. He managed to give me a toothy grin as a sort of half-hearted apology for the wind-up from himself and my old mentor. He was a little younger than Charlie but nevertheless they seemed to have forged a bond... a generational thing and I felt a little bit of an outsider. Moreso when Charlie practiced his Walloon and they conversed in a gibberish way beyond my understanding. It did throw up one entertaining moment though.

The pair of them were jabbering away in their Walloon mumbo-jumbo with myself as a bored spectator when suddenly I saw Charlie's face change from happy to one of shocked. His mouth dropped open and he was shaking his head slowly from side to side. He looked stunned.

"No Toby... surely not," Charlie had reverted to English.

Then I saw Toby frown and they both began talking Walloon again before Charlie and Toby both burst into laughter... with a slap on the table top from Charlie and a huge hoot of merriment.

"So what's that all about Charlie? I asked. Something weird had just happened and they were both still chuckling.

"My Walloon isn't as good as I thought it was," said Charlie. "Perhaps we should continue in English."

"Ehhh... what?"

"Sorry James... sorry. I've been rather rude leaving you out of the conversation. We've just had a right old cock-up in the understanding of Walloon verbs and tenses and placement of nouns and pronouns."

"What?"

Charlie chuckled as he spoke, "I thought that Toby had just told me that his father had beaten his mother to death. You know? like a violent attack. But it was just my mental translation going wonky."

I heard Toby give a snort.

"That's why I looked shocked. But all that he'd actually said was that his father died before his mother... and I understood it all wrong. Perhaps this old brain of mine isn't as sharp as it once was."

I couldn't argue with that although I still felt in awe of Charlie. We spent the next hour or so chatting away about everything and nothing. Toby left us on our own for that last hour and it was a most agreeable interlude. We arranged to meet up the following day... same place. I was about to meet Charlie's blood family and I was looking forward to it. We took leave of each other and headed off in separate taxis and in different directions. I was booked into my room for a full four nights and tonight would be the first. Seeing Charlie today had been so exhilarating and I was feeling happy.

CHAPTER 8

We Are Family

———————————————■———————————————

Charlie's family turned out to be incredibly nice and welcoming. Jerzy and his wife Ursula and their two grown-up daughters Astrid and Ebba. Neither of the daughters were married although Ebba was living with her long-time boyfriend. Astrid was the elder of the two… in her mid-thirties and she'd taken a shine to me but I wasn't up for any foreign shenanigans and I certainly didn't want to upset Charlie and his new-found family so I laid off. Astrid was twice divorced which didn't give me any good vibes. We did hit it off though and I still get a regular Christmas card from herself and husband four… or maybe five. I can't remember the sequence.

We spent a pleasant interlude that day and Charlie and myself delved into the past and brought out many a morsel for their delectation. We laughed about things that had once seemed so embarrassing and insurmountable and Charlie's family were fascinated. We had them laughing at some of the stupidity of my schooldays and my early encounters with Charlie and I didn't care how ridiculous some of those memories now seemed. They had happened and they were true so that was enough. I told them about my Hull days and how meeting up with Charlie had given me a new direction in life after the mentally down phase I'd gone through. They were extremely supportive and in no way judgemental. I think Jerzy's tale which was to follow would make my life progress seem less than epic and more mundane.

Then the big story emerged. After a while the conversation turned more serious and Jerzy's story came out. It's not a story that I could repeat with any degree of accuracy and to be fair I wouldn't want to. It was personal and harrowing and told to us that day with a certainty which made the entire tale believable, true and irrefutable. A young boy's precarious journey through war-torn Europe having suffered the loss of his immediate family at the hands of the Nazis. Then his final escape via the Baltic sea to Sweden hidden in the bowels of a trawler beneath coils of rope and netting in case of any search by the Germans. It made the telling of my own life tribulations somehow pale and pointless.

We spent a whole day and early evening together but that was the last time I was to see Charlie. I'd receive the occasional letter from him over the next few years. Then they stopped coming. Eventually I would receive a letter from Ursula informing me of Charlie's passing. That day was a bad day.

They left that same evening... choosing to drive by night and miss the worst of the traffic. Charlie and I did a few arm punches when we parted... neither of us realising that this would be our last meeting. The whole family invited me to come for a Swedish holiday and I was eager to do it but life eventually took over and did its own thing and I wouldn't see any of them again. But who knows what the future holds? Jerzy passed four or five years ago and I was invited over by Ursula but couldn't make it for various health reasons and also because Lorraine and I won't put our dogs into boarding kennels. That sounds daft... I know but we've had two bad experiences with supposedly caring kennels and both times we were shocked at the state our dogs were in when they emerged. Never again... our dogs are family, not possessions. I won't name the kennels... but it was while we lived outside of Tain.

I spent the next few days in Bruges on my own. I hadn't expected to be on my lonesome but that's the way it turned out and to be honest I quite enjoyed it. A did a fair bit of sightseeing and general mooching around bars. I also hired a bike for a day and only occasionally forgot to ride on the silly side of the road... much to the consternation of the swerving car drivers. I heard 'merde anglais' a few times but hey I'm from Blyth... did they really think I'd be upset by words shouted from a car window?

I was even abused in German... 'Englischer Scheißkerl' but I couldn't understand what on earth that bloke was on about. I knew it was German because it sounded arrogant so I shouted back 'Zeig Heil' and put my finger over my top lip to do the Hitler moustache thing and the hand up in the air waiting for a Nazi high-five. The car screeched to a halt and four Waffen SS guys leaped from the car and began spraying me with machine-gun bullets. Nah... only kidding... they just stopped and shouted, 'Englisher bastard', which was fair enough they'd got one out of two. I cycled away singing 'Hang out Your Washing on the Siegfried Line' while they searched for stones to chuck at me. Apart from that my Bruges sojourn was quite a pleasant affair but I was ready for my return to England and some British sanity.

On my return it took me a week to sort out my affairs in Hull. I sold my camper and bought something less ostentatious. It was an estate car and a right old heap but I needed to downsize for my upcoming confrontation with the tax guys. Charlie had given me advice about acting dumb in order to escape from their clutches. I took his advice and remembered it well.

Then came my Blyth return and a brief interlude with a bloke called Cecil.

CHAPTER 9

Take Me Home Country Roads

———————————■———————————

Blyth felt so different that November 1988. The life seemed to have been sucked out of the town. When I'd left ten years or so ago Blyth was vibrant and constantly busy. The mines were churning out record amounts of coal... factories were buzzing with activity and the shops were crowded and prosperous. Now it seemed flat and gloomy... with hopes for the future in short supply. Even the pubs and clubs were now suffering the constant onslaught on the working classes and the Saturday market had visibly shrunk too with empty stalls and spaces. The only thing showing growth was the dole queue. Maggie was having a field day.

So it was a return to a somewhat strange-feeling Blyth for me. And my first port of call on the evening I arrived was to Gladstone Street. I was to lodge for a number of weeks with my old childhood acquaintance Cecil. It was strange how that came about because just by chance we'd bumped in to each other when Night Shadow had been eventing in York. We'd recognized each other immediately. I had no idea why Cecil was watching scantily clad lasses when I'd assumed he'd have been watching scantily clad folk of the male variety. However, after the 'Eeeh aah thought it was you' greetings I'd mentioned that I would be returning to Blyth in the near future. To cut a long story short he offered me a place to stay until I could fix myself up with something permanent. I thanked him and the rest as they say is history.

Cecil and I had never been really good friends. He was a year or so younger than myself and as eight and nine-year-olds our gang of six called the Geronimo's would let this little ginger chubby lad tag along with us. He didn't have any friends his own age as far as we could tell and we felt sorry for him. His home life wasn't good and he'd had some medical problems which made his family decide that he was something special. He wasn't... he was a prat... he knew it and we accepted it.

We talked about our younger days on the second or third evening of me bedding back into the Blyth way of life. Strange how we all remember things differently but the conversation that evening was about our early years when our Geronimo camp was an old gnarled tree that stood beside the track that led from Newsham to Bebside at the side of Buglass's farmer fields. It was easy to climb and we Geronimos' could all make it almost to the top... so the base of that tree became our camp.

Those were the days before Sid Brown appeared in Blyth and we were all just little Blyth folk who understood Blyth-speak. We were a proper little gang and we did all the proper little gang stuff that kids of our age were supposed to do. We'd spend hours playing hide and seek around the huge expanse of colliery waste we called Red-Rock canyon. We'd climb to the top of the Bella pit heap for no other reason other than to say we'd done it and had survived being sucked underground like that entire family from Newsham... their bodies had never been found and their ghosts roamed the Bella heap every night... but were we frightened?... 'aye a bit'.

Usually though we'd just do the mundane stuff like nicking bagies out of Buglass's field and then pretend to each other we liked eating them raw. We'd go out doing the knocky-door ginger and enjoying the chase on a dark evening when we couldn't be recognized. On boring days we'd hide behind trees and then jump out and try to hit spuggies with our catapults... but we called the catapults 'gats' and spuggies were actually sparrows and we never did get to hit one. And on those rare occasions when we made it as far as Blyth beach beside the concrete ship and swings we would chip in with our pennies to buy an ice cream to share... but only if it had been squirted liberally with monkey's blood. We were a genuine gang.

One of our gang was a girl. Okay it wasn't the accepted way of the world at that time. Boys had their own secret societies and brotherhoods and strutted around with toy holsters and six-shooters while girls did skipping and chucks and played with dolls. That was how it was. But we were different because one of our clan was called Carol Watson and she was okay. She refused to do the blood brother ritual though. We lads had all used a penknife to make little cuts on our palms and then clasped hands to mix our blood in the time-honoured ceremony before swearing undying devotion to our little tribe. All for one and one for all as the musketeers used to say.

Carol however was a law unto herself and she refused. She hated the sight of blood and she told us about a lad who'd done the palm-cutting blood-brother thing and had died the following day from screaming leprosy after both of his arms had dropped off. That made us think. I remember for almost a week after that morsel of information I would wake up in the morning and nervously waggle my arms about to make sure they were still attached to my shoulders. But all-in-all it was a good time for most of us. Cecil not so much.

We were sitting one evening in Cecil's front room after having a good old chortle at a video. We'd been watching 'An Audience With Billy Connolly' the uncut version and we'd laughed ourselves silly. Then we settled down with our tabs and beers. Cecil produced a spliff he'd knocked up himself but I wasn't happy with that. Mind bending stuff wasn't really my thing but how could I refuse. I had a drag before Cecil suddenly asked.

"Can ye remember Jim when Wilf made me do that arse-smackin' dare?"

Aye I could, and it raised a smile. A memory from so many years ago when we were all kids and life was somehow more sensible. There was no forgetting that particular gang dare. Wilf was the oldest in our group and because of his age status he was also our leader. We were in our camp that day at the base of our gang tree... and we were all a little bored. The dare he thought up on that particular occasion seemed silly even then but looking back it was completely stupid. Wilf had turned up that day with an old table-tennis bat. The pimpled rubber had been removed and it was basically just a bare wooden paddle. Wilf informed us that we were going to draw lots for the dare that day. There were just six of us ... Carol was missing for whatever reason. So we ended up doing the penny-flicking heads or tails to find out the final three then onto rock-paper-scissors. I'd always felt guilty about that day because Wilf in his wisdom had decided it was to be Cecil doing the dare and he manipulated the competition to make it turn out that way.

"Cecil you're doing the dare today," Wilf ordered.

"Aye okay but aahh think ye were cheatin'."

Wilf looked angry... "You what?"

"Nowt."

"Good." Wilf continued with a hard stare until Cecil looked away.

"So what's the dare," Cecil ducked out of the accusation conversation because Wilf wasn't best pleased that his leadership had been questioned. We all knew it was fixed but said nothing.

"Arse smackin'."

"Ehhh?"

"Arse smackin'... Wilf grinned and the others in the group must have thought the same as myself... it was a dare too far.

"Whose arse?" asked Cecil hopefully. Maybe it would be one of us.

"First person that walks past on the track. You hide until they go past then you sneak out onto the track and creep up. Smack them on the arse with the bat... shout 'smacky-arsey' and then run like Roger Bannister. Divvent get caught."

Cecil looked shocked and terrified. We all thought this dare was too much but Wilf wasn't for backing down or being questioned.

"Not deein it!" Cecil squawked.

Wilf stood for a while, head down and thinking... then, "Yer oot the gang then, haddaway yem," Wilf wasn't pleased.

"Aahh done skinchies... me fingers were crossed."

"Tha's nee skinchies man... we've aall got ter dee dares. If ye cannit dee it then join a gang of bubbly bairns yer own age."

"Still not deein it."

"Ye'll dee as yer telt or ye'll gerra gud howkin'.

"Nah... aahhmm gannin yem."

"Haddaway then... we'll get somebody else in the Geronimos." Wilf turned his back in disgust... refusing a dare wasn't in the rulebook.

Cecil walked off about ten paces then stopped. He was obviously thinking out the options. He was the little fat ginger lad with the foul mouth who no-one liked. Walk away and he was on his own... stay and at least he had pals of a sort.

"Worrif aahh get caught?"

Wilf grinned, "Jail... but not fer lang."

"Me mam would gan daft."

"Divvent get caught then."

"Aahh knaa but me mam's in a reet fettle just now cos her brother... me uncle didn't even tell her that her sister... me aunty had died. He didn't have the guts but me mam thinks he was just fiddlin' the will cos he was executa' or summat like that and he was really just a sad man."

Wilf shook his head, "Naebody would dee that man... he'd have to be a reet gutless coward. Anyway what's that got ter dee with...?"

"And my cousin thinks he's deed hard and spits on the floor a lot to show how tough he is... but he's a sad little idiot... and he got a right good fillin' in at the funeral cos he's soft as shite."

"Cecil... you really swear a lot... but what's all that got to do wi' the arse smackin?"

"Errr... nowt?"

"So are you in or out?"

"In."

"Good."

It would be a half hour or more before we saw Cecil's intended victim. Two men had passed by in the meantime but Cecil wasn't up for doing a gadgie. Then we saw an oldish lady walking along. Cecil gave the okay with his eyes to Wilf. This was the one.

Wilf gave out the orders, "Reet everybody, doon on yer hunkers or else we'll get spied." We all shrunk into the undergrowth. Cecil was handed the bat.

The old lady couldn't have been more than late thirties... but that was extremely old to our gang. We kept our heads down as she went past but there was so much giggling and squeaking going on that she must have been aware of a bunch of kids hiding... but she said nothing as she walked by.

Our heads popped up as Cecil sneaked out onto the track behind the woman. We were all waiting for the 'smacky-arsey' and the sounds of pursuit with Cecil outrunning the woman and making good his escape. What we heard was a growl, a bark, a scream and a 'shit the bugger bit me... gerrim off,' We hadn't spotted that the lady was walking her dog and said dog wasn't best pleased with Cecil and his smacking bat.

We Geronimos did the sensible cowardly thing and ran away over the railway line into Red Rock canyon and abandoned Cecil to his fate.

Cecil ended up in hospital that day having stitches. Proper hospital too. We heard he'd received a good hiding from his mam and he never returned to the Geronimos. That was no problem for the Geronimos because none of us had really liked the little gobby ginger lad. But quite soon after that the gang disbanded and we all moved on to other things. Carol however would continue to be my pal at Grammar School and we'd often walk home together when we were pupils in the Tynedale school. She was nice.

"Aye Cecil I remember that day but what's yer point about the arse smackin' thing? Cos we couldn't help with a big dog there."

"Ye all buggered off and left me."

He was right of course... but nowadays he would be called collateral damage. I had to think for a moment or two. Remember I'd had a drink or two and a drag on one of Cecil's spliffs. "Naebody really liked yer so we weren't bothered."

"So what are ye deein here then?"

I realised for that brief interlude that I'd gone too far. Someone was giving me lodgings but I'd just told him he was unliked. Honestly I didn't know how to respond but the spliff had transported me into the 'don't give a toss about the consequence but I'm going to tell the truth' mode. I took a deep breath, looked him in the eye... and said...

"Aahh was just readin' through yer blokey ginger-beer mags and decided maybe this place wasn't for me." Quite by accident I'd found a stash of magazines featuring scantily clad men in various poses.

"Ye've been gannin into me private black box... and anyway they're not even mine. Aah've been keepin' them for me mate."

"Aye right... and aah borrowed me lugs off a cocker spaniel."

"Then bog off then!"

"I am, next weekend."

"Ye'll gan tomorra."

"Right."

"Right." End of conversation. I couldn't argue. Tomorrow I would be on my travels again and looking for a place to lay my head. I was quite happy to be honest. No more nights lying awake in case the bedroom door opened. My sojourn with Cecil was at an end and would be the end of our relationship... thank heaven.

CHAPTER 10

Whisky In The Jar

∎

My immediate problem was to find somewhere local to use as a base while I planned out my next career move.

It turned out to be easier than I'd imagined. I'd bumped into my cousin Carol Meins and she'd given me the name of a person to contact whom she knew let out rooms. It was good advice and I found a place to stay within a matter of hours on the day following my retreat from Cecil's gaff. A room in a shared house in Shankhouse of all places. With the taxman hot on my heels I thought it would be ideal. I'd be paying room rent in cash and my name wouldn't be appearing on any tenancy documents. Apart from that I found my next watering hole... 'The Folly'. That wasn't its proper name of course it was the nickname of the Albion Inn. Why that nickname? I never did find out but it really wasn't important. It did however became something of a hideaway for myself during the following period and before the tax folk finally tracked me down.

My cash stash would need some attention soon. Frances had salted money away in various places but she wasn't for returning until she'd played out her Australian exploration gig. I reckoned that wouldn't be for a heck of a long time so I needed to earn while she was missing in action. I still had a decent amount of money from the shop sale to see me through the next few months or so but I had visions of it dwindling away. I didn't want to sign on the 'King Cole' because my insurance number would show up and I'd be captured. But what to do? How to earn and still slip under the radar of those official fellows? I didn't fancy starting up the lingerie business again... so what to do?

The answer came to me one Saturday afternoon... 'books'.

The Folly was my hangout for the entirety of those first weeks in the small village of Shankhouse while I was trying to get my head around what my next move should be. The pub was usually deserted on an evening and there were several times when I just sat alone with my drink... and reading. Jim the bearded old chubby landlord would make conversation for a while then leave me alone as I began to devour some of the classics I'd missed out on. Catch 22 had an airing and I had a bash at the Russian authors... first with Crime and Punishment which was passably okay then a crack at War and Peace which was complete rubbish. It was like reading the telephone directory. If anyone ever tells you they've read War and Peace all the way through then believe me... they're lying, or at the very least they're one of those boring folk who'll occasionally bend you're ear whilst telling you about the history of knitting yarns... or mud and straw brick production during the Inca Empire... 'get a life you people'.

The Folly to be honest was on its last legs. The toilets were disgusting... the pub felt permanently cold and the number of punters who used the pub had dwindled to a handful of daytime diehards. It wasn't a pub which offered entertainment and it wasn't a place to take your girlfriend for a pleasant evening. Even the dartboard looked like a burst couch with the bullseye ring missing. It was a pub in terminal decline. But it did have its afternoon coterie of sad folk who congregated for their daily bout of moans-groans and falsehoods. I began to think of it as 'deadbeat corner'.

Afternoons would quite often see a table with five folk sat around it. One was an old retired bloke from Bog Houses called Fred who was still mobile enough to be doing bits of casual work, and the second one was a full-time benefit fiddler from High-Pit whom we called Bob the Knob but not to his face. Another afternoon regular was a guy called John who had a milk business around Cowpen and Bebside and the fourth was a bloke I'll call Chunk who was perhaps late forties or early fifties and a reputed hard-case who worked sometimes as a builder's labourer but usually did a bit of protection work in pubs and restaurants. The fifth and final attendee at the Folly table was myself whom the rest of the group had nicknamed 'Jim the Book' which was a way of distinguishing myself from the landlord 'Jim the Pint'.

Chunk was as thick as they came and told lies as a matter of course. You could generally tell when Chunk was about to lie because his lips would move and his mouth would open. But I'd been warned by landlord Jim never to laugh when he was talking rubbish and never to question him. He was prone to losing his temper and had apparently done a seven-year stretch in Durham prison for involuntary manslaughter...

having killed a sailor during a pub brawl. I never did laugh at his stupidity... well maybe only on the inside.

The benefit fiddler always seemed to have more money than he knew what to do with... especially on family allowance days but that was his business and none of mine. Fred the old retired guy would sometimes pop in with something to sell when he was short of spending cash... sometimes a chicken, still feathered, and sometimes fresh fish but where they came from was a mystery. There'd be other offerings for sale too... usually nick-naks from his house... an occasional ornament... or a bag of sea coal which he'd trundle to the pub in an old bogey with pram wheels. Jim the Pint usually bought the coal. One day Fred turned up with a tailor's dummy and Jim the Pint's wife bought it from him. He was a constant surprise.

John the Milk was different because he was permanently depressed about his lot in life and could quite quickly turn a decent afternoon session into a drab and gloomy affair when he was on one of his downers. He'd more or less given up on his milk round and had two idiots running it for him but he couldn't seem to grasp the fact that they were taking his eyes out and robbing him blind.

"Nah it's not their fault," he would wail, "the customers have stopped paying their bills and even refusing to hand over their milk tokens... I don't know what to do... it's all a mess."

"Perhaps get off your backside and go out on the milk yourself for a week to see what the real crack is," I said to him one day.

"Nah... can't do it. Not just now anyway cos my head's all over the place and our lass isn't too clever at present. Nah definitely can't do it but I'll pay you to go and do the collecting for me if you fancy doing it on Friday."

I didn't think about it for too long. I wasn't actually awash with employment opportunities and I wasn't about to look a gift horse in the mouth... so I took him up on that offer. The following day he supplied me with a customer address book... having told his two stooges that he'd be doing the collecting himself. They weren't too happy about it apparently and the reason for that would soon become obvious.

Most of the addresses were on Cowpen Estate. A nice little stroll around my old stamping ground and a tenner in my pocket to boot can't be a bad thing I thought to myself. And it wasn't. It was so easy that it made me wonder why John wasn't doing this himself. The story about his wife's health just didn't ring true. Perhaps nowadays we would see his problem as being a mental health issue... but this was 1988 and mental health was never mentioned.

That Friday I began the collecting early and proceeded to knock the same doors as the two blokes who'd told John that folk had stopped paying. Tynedale, Briardale, Ravensdale, Chasedale and a dozen other streets in that vicinity were on the list. There were very few houses where folk were out... and all in all it was an easy collection day and I bumped into a few folk I'd known from my schooldays. I asked at a number of doors that had been marked down as previous non-payers whether they paid weekly. The answer was always 'yes, we pay every week'. Just as I'd suspected and the cash mounted up swiftly.

It was too late to return to the Folly when I'd finished collecting that Friday afternoon so it was Saturday lunchtime when I finally met up with John the Milk. He looked extremely surprised to see me as I walked into the pub... almost as if he'd been expecting me to do a runner with his cash takings and milk tokens.

John seemed to jerk out of his seat as I fixed my eyes on his gloomy face and he shot over to the bar and ordered me a pint of lager while I took my coat off. I shuffled into my usual place and placed the cash bag and payment book in the middle of the table. John returned, handed me the lager and sat down.

He seemed to weigh up the situation for a few seconds before beginning, "Well... what did I tell you?" he said, depression lacing his voice as he eyed the leather money bag but didn't touch it.

"What?"

"You know... the shitty folk in Cowpen who won't pay up."

I reached for my pint and took a mouthful. John was getting on my wick with his constant downers. I gave my head a little shake.

"Which shitty folk would they be?"

"All of them."

I thought about that for a moment, then... "Humour me John, how much money did those two blokes tell you they'd taken last week?"

He replied with a round figure, keeping his voice low, "And that was just enough to cover their wages for the week.

I'm going to be bankrupt shortly and lose my business... ohhh shit."

I realised then that John was a lost cause. He'd fallen too far down the black hole to be able to climb out again. He was actually needing some professional help for his mental state but perhaps I could put a little smile back on his face when I told him the running total from yesterday.

I pushed the bag over to him, "Count that John... there's three times what you said was taken last week together with a bunch of tokens to cash in. Everyone paid up apart from half a dozen houses where there was no-one in and two who said their husbands hadn't been home with the wages yet. That should tell you something. Ohhh aye and there were two houses in Devonworth that hadn't been knocked on for weeks and they both paid up their back money."

John looked shocked as he lifted the flap of the bag and spied the little mountain of cash. Realisation seemed to hit him full on. He glanced at the bag then at me then back to the cash. He rummaged around in the bag and emerged with two fivers and some pound coins.

"Thanks Jim," he said and shoved fifteen pounds across the table."

"We said a tenner John."

"I know... but I didn't expect..." then he looked me full in the face and began to cry... and it was uncomfortable. Fair enough I felt sorry for the guy but bloke cuddling wasn't a thing then and I certainly wasn't about to be the trailblazer. I just sat there being very embarrassed until he pulled himself together. It took him a minute or two but the sobs stopped after a while and he wiped at his eyes with the sleeve of his jacket... then he grinned.

"Must stop eating onions," he joked and I gave him a supportive smile back.

"You've got to get rid of those two cowboys John. They're taking you for a ride and your business will be down the pan if you don't."

He nodded, "I know... I know but I'm not up for going out every morning at five o'clock. My wife's in a bad way at the moment." Then he looked at me hopefully, "Don't suppose you could do it for the next few weeks until things improve and I get my head together?"

"John man..."

"Okay, okay... you can't do it but I don't know what to do. If I tell them they're finished those two will kick off and do a few nasties to the milk float or put the windows out at my house or something. I've heard about other stuff they've done to folk. I'm not up for fighting with them, they're a couple of radgies... and I'm no fighter anyway."

Then a voice from nowhere, "I'll see to them for ye Johnny Milk."

That statement came unexpectedly from the pub doorway where Chunk had been standing unseen... and eavesdropping. We both turned to face the voice.

"Ehhh...?" said John, looking up, "Hiya Chunk... what d'yer mean?"

The voice walked over to join us at the table, "What I just said... I'll have a quiet word with them for you."

John gave him a doubtful grin, "Thanks Chunk but I don't think a quiet word would do the trick."

"Then I might have to raise my voice a bit."

"They won't listen man Chunk."

Chunk didn't look best pleased as he shuffled into his usual seat and parked his backside, "Aye they will. It'll cost ye twenty smackers and I guarantee you'll never be bothered by them again."

John's face changed swiftly from doubtful to hopeful, "What are you goin' ter do Chunk... kill them?"

Chunk shook his head and growled, "Best you don't know milkman. You can't tell what you don't know if you're ever asked. Anyway... get the beers in and find twenty quid in that bag of yours if you're wanting it sorted. Unless you're not up for it of course."

John by this time had a worried look written on his face but he did as he was told and ferreted twenty pounds in coins and notes from the bag and stacked them on the table before sloping off to the bar. Chunk who was now sitting beside me pocketed the cash pile with a grin, "Easy money that."

"How easy?"

"Ten years in the SAS easy."

"SAS?... I didn't know..."

"I don't tell folk cos they get scared," then he turned his head and gave me a look which told me not to question his word. I didn't know how to respond. I was a little wary of giving responses to Chunk's proclamations.

"Did ye ever kill anybody?" was all I could think of.

"Course I did." he was enjoying the spotlight.

"How many times?"

He glared at me with the strangest expression on his face, "Ehhh... you only need to kill somebody once man... cos then they're dead and don't need killing again. I done it loads."

Old man Tug had once told me that big lies were the best lies but I had to smile at that effort. The question needed refining somewhat. I took a mouthful of lager before continuing, "Where did you kill them?"

Chunk continued looking a little confused... he glanced up as John returned to the table with the drinks before answering, "Wherever they were standing."

I almost snorted at the reply... almost but not quite. I remembered Jim the Pint's warning. "Nah Chunk I meant where in the world?"

"All over the shop man. You name it and I've probably killed somebody there. Loads of places."

I was trying to think of recent conflicts and the Falklands came into my head... "Port Stanley?" I ventured.

He seemed to be struggling with the name and took a big mouthful of beer before replying... a lightbulb suddenly sparking up in his head, "Nah... not there. I never killed anybody in County Durham."

I knew better than to crack a smile and could see Jim the Pint giving me the eyes from behind the bar... a warning signal, so I let it lie and tried to change the direction of the conversation.

"So you reckon you'll be able to sort those two out?"

"Aye... I'll see you all in here tomorrow dinner-time. It'll all be done and dusted," said Chunk with ultimate confidence.

John didn't look convinced. He must have been thinking he was being fleeced yet again. His poor money bag was now thirty-five quid lighter plus whatever he was spending on drink. I didn't hold out high hopes for his future business prospects.

At that precise moment old Fred stumbled through the doorway, a bulging carrier bag in hand.

He looked to see who was present and spotting the usual suspects he asked, "Anybody want to buy a bag of veg?"

None of the table trio showed any interest but Jim the Pint asked, "What ye got like?"

"Taties, carrots, cabbage and a load of sprouts," Fred offered.

"Let's see."

Fred walked over to the bar and handed the bag to Jim who proceeded to have an expert rummage and give various bits of the veg a squeeze. "How much d'yer want?"

"Three pints," grinned Fred.

"Two and a bag of scratchings... final offer."

"Done," agreed Fred with a smile on his old face so huge you'd think he'd just come up on a six-horse accumulator.

Fred waited for his pint to be pulled before coming to claim the chair next to John. He plonked his drink down with a bit of a wobble. Some splashed out onto the table and Fred used a beer towel to mop it up. "Bliddy shaky hands man. Doctor says I got them from somebody called Parkinson." Then he grinned and gave us a thumbs up before finally sitting and having his first mouthful, "Aahh that's better... nectar of the gods." The tremor in Fred's hands suddenly became noticeable. It was a shame for the old guy.

Then in came Bob the Knob. The quintet was complete although to be perfectly honest Bob was a bit of an outlier.

We sort of looked down on him because he was constantly trying to fiddle a system which didn't have much more to give him. That day he told us he'd just got a bedding grant and he was boasting about it. The money he'd drained from the Social to finance new sheets and blankets for his kids was now being spent on lager and crisps. We weren't impressed but we said nothing. That was how he and his wife lived their lives so that was their affair and it wasn't our business. Anyway it was time for a game of shilling dominoes. Five new pence per game.

I played dominoes but I couldn't be bothered with the whole concept. Even though I shielded my dominoes from view somebody would always be telling me which tile I should have laid. "What ye doin' man Jimmy ye should have laid the five blonk then Fred would have been knockin' man." I utterly hated all those folk who had x-ray vision... they knew what dominoes I was holding in my hand without seeing them...the Geordie supermen... cheating buggers. I didn't manage to win a single game and must have lost a whole 75p. Finally we played a game called last man standing for ten bob... or fifty new pence in newspeak. I was first to bite the dust swiftly followed by John the Milk. We left the table together... not unexpectedly I have to say and we ambled over together to prop up the bar. Last orders was being called... not that it mattered in the Folly. John bought me a pint.

The beer must have gone to my head because after a moment or two I said, "I'll do the milk round for ye John but just for one week, definitely no more." I'd given John's offer some thought and a week's wage paid in cash wouldn't go amiss although I had no secret longing for the early morning starts. "D'yer think ye can find somebody else to do it for the following week... not the two goons but somebody ye can trust?"

I thought John was about to start crying again but he managed to control it. "Aye... there's a lad lives beside me who I think will do it after his holidays. They call him Tony. He's back on Friday. So are you saying you'll do the round next week... and the collecting?"

"Aye."

"Aahh bliddy hell that's brilliant. D'yer want a whisky?"

"Aye... but make it a big'un."

He grinned and ordered just as old Fred came and joined us. John was so happy that he bought Fred a pint as well. I don't think I ever saw John with such a huge grin on his face... either before or after.

Jim the Pint looked at the clock and said, "If you're wanting service after time ye'll have to put three quid each on the bar top. I can't take money after time... it's illegal... but I can give ye free drinks at my discretion."

An afternoon lock in had just been offered and Jim the Pint was covering his back in case the police knocked. Not that they ever bothered the Folly of course but who knew what those boys in blue would think of next. John, Chunk and I put our money on the bar top and the three of us put down an additional quid each for old Fred. He gave us a thank-you wink. Chunk had won the last man standing round and was in happy spirits... he paid his quid for Fred with two fifty-pence pieces. Bob the Knob wasn't up for it... his cash must have dwindled and no-one offered to slip him the lock-in money. He finished his pint and left... saying he had a bit of business to attend to but would see us all the following day. Business... what business? the bloke had never struck a bat for years. He thought manual labour was a Spaniard. I think we were all relieved when he departed because we didn't like him much. Jim the Pint picked the cash up from the bar top and squirrelled the cash away into a tin under the counter... not the till. That must have been his keepy-backs.

"Okay lads three pints each but I'm wanting ye out afore tea-time."

Four nods of agreement.

We were all quiet for a little while, engrossed in the supping of sneaky pints. John the milk was first to chirp up.

"Are ye doing the round tomorrow Jim?"

I didn't manage to reply because Chunk jumped in, "Nah He's not doing tomorrow John... cos I'm needing to have a word with your two blokes when they've finished delivering. So let me know where the last deliveries are and I'll sort the rest."

"But you don't know who..."

"Aye I do. I know them idiots very well. Believe me Johnny Milk you'll not hear from them again."

John was looking worried now... probably thinking he'd just paid a hit-man twenty quid and he'd be arrested as an accomplice. "You're not goin' to..."

Chunk chuckled, "Calm yersell doon man John... they'll do as they're told and I probably won't even need to give them a slap. I've had dealings with them two before man. And they know me... very well." He chuckled again.

I piped up next, "I'll take over on Monday John if ye fill me in on what I have to do and where to load up." John nodded and for the next five minutes he proceeded to fill me in with the details whilst the other two made small talk with Jim the Pint.

A pleasant afternoon took us all the way to tea-time and the cut off for our beer session. It was a bit of a laugh to be honest... but a disguised laugh because Chunk proceeded to tell us how he once met Sitting Bull when he was in America and the old chief had made Chunk an honorary member of the Apache tribe. It was John, now worse the wear with drink who pulled him up.

"Chunk man... don't you mean the Sioux?"

Chunk stared hard at John... not amused, "Nah John I know what I mean. Anyway Sue was Sitting Bull's squaw." John shut up, dropped his eyes and tackled a mouthful of beer. I don't know what age Chunk actually was but he was definitely not in his eighties or nineties which he would have needed to be to have met Sitting Bull... even as a bairn in arms.

It was time to go but just before we abandoned the Folly old Fred gave my sleeve a tug.

"You're always into books Jim," he opened his oilskin jacket and produced a leather-bound book from a big inside pocket, "D'yer want to buy this?" He thrust the book into my hands.

I was tired by this time... wanting something to eat and then to get my head down, "Not really Fred," I said... then had an immediate change of heart as I handled the book and opened it up. It was stunning. Page after page of woodcuts. Beautifully drawn birds with their English and Latin names side by side with a description of their preferred habitat and breeding season. I tried to look uninterested but I had the weirdest feeling as I handled the book. Even the tooled leather spine with gold lettering was in good nick.

"Aye it's all right Fred but not really the sort of stuff that I read."

Chunk had picked up on the conversation and was peering over my shoulder. "I'll give ye a quid for it Fred."

"Pffft... aye that'll be right. Nee way man Chunk, I want a tenner for it at least. Wor lass told me to get what I could for it. It used to be her dad's book but he sold the other two volumes and he got a fiver for each of them and that was yonks and yonks ago."

"But it's just an old book man Fred with some birds in. Tell ye what I'll give ye two quid just to help ye out." Chunk was just being a pal to old Fred I think but I had a good feeling about the volume... I don't know why.

"Nah Chunk... thanks for the offer but the missus would gan spare," then he grinned, "I need a tenner so I can tell her I got a fiver and then I'll have enough beer money myself for tomorrow and Monday."

We all had a chuckle at that. Old Fred liked his little bit of wheeling and dealing. It probably kept him young... at least in his head.

I pretended reluctance as I said, "Fair do's Fred I'll give yer a tenner but you might end up having to buy me a pint next week." Fred looked grateful but I paid up and made his day. That afternoon cleared out the fifteen pounds I'd just earned and a bit more but I had a really good feeling about that book as I headed back to my rented room... and that feeling was spot on.

CHAPTER 11

This Little Bird

———————————————— ■ ————————————————

It was almost two weeks later that I stood beside Grey's Monument in Newcastle waiting for Chunk to return from Steedman's Antiquarian Bookshop at the other end of Grey Street.

During those two weeks I'd done my duty on John's milk round and made myself a tidy wedge for a week's work. Then I'd picked up a few shifts behind one of the bars in Newcastle... which shall remain nameless because it was notorious as a gay bar... but I escaped unscathed with cash in hand, having had lots of drinks bought for me. It must have been because of my affable manner and stunningly good looks. 'Aye Batesy that'll be right'. Then I decided to cash in on the book I'd bought from Fred.

It turned out to be a Thomas Bewick and volume two of a two-volume set. I don't know why Fred had thought it to be a three-volume set. The one I'd bought was 'History and Description of Water Birds' and had I possessed the first volume I could have made a killing. However the volume I did have was in immaculate condition with very little in the way of foxing or fading and the leather work and gilding was almost pristine. The date on the title page bottom was 1804.

I'd persuaded Chunk to come and do the dirty work for me because I'd once worked in Steedman's and had been sacked when I was fresh out of school and all because I'd taken some books home to read without asking. Anyway I couldn't face going back into the shop in case I was still recognisable as that callow young upstart. I'd promised Chunk a third of any profit and a few pints at The Blackie Boy in the Groat Market. He was at a loose end that day and up for something different so he agreed. I told him to refuse to accept anything less than £50 and definitely no cheque. I'd done some research at Blyth library and thought we'd make at least that amount.

Chunk was away for ages and I was becoming worried that maybe they'd offered him something stupid and he'd kicked off and planted someone. He hadn't... but it was more than an hour later when I felt the tap on my shoulder. I don't know how he'd managed to sneak up behind me because he was a tall, thick-set bloke... distinctive and easy to spot. I didn't ask.

"Time for a few jars at Blackie's Jimmy Book." He was grinning like a Cheshire cat.

"Did ye sell it Chunk?"

"Aye... but I had to wait while the bloke went and drew some cash out at the bank."

"Ehhh... how much?"

He reached into his coat pocket and shoved a pile of fives and tens into my hand. "You owe me thirty smackers... easy money. We'll have to do this again it's like tekkin bullets off bairns."

"Thirty... but that means...?"

"Aye they offered fifty and I said no and walked away. I was a bit worried that I'd blown it but one of the customers who'd been mooching around in the shop followed me out and asked to see the book. When he saw it and had a quick skim through he asked how much I wanted for it. I just thought a number up and said a hundred. He didn't bat an eyelid. He shook my hand and said, 'Done'. Then he had to go to the bank to get the cash out and I was hanging around for ages. Felt a bit conspicuous... you know... like I was doing something illegal. But fair do's he came back with the spondoolicks. He said it was the best condition he'd ever seen for a Berrick... or something like that. The bloke looked really happy anyway."

"Bloody hell Chunk... that's brilliant."

"Aye... well divvy up and you're buyin' the beers." He had a huge grin creasing his face. Feeling somewhat proud of himself he gave me a slap on the back which would have downed a lesser man. "Howay... we're missing drinking time man Jimmy... get yer skates on."

We put a fair few jars away that Day in the Blackie Boy and I paid but it was a worthwhile excursion which fired up my enthusiasm for doing the same again. I'd had a good little earner. Job's a good'un.

The next few weeks were busy to say the least. I'd managed to get myself a stall on Blyth market but it was at the top end... standing with its back to the toilet block. Not the best place to do business but it was a start. That stall was only operational two days per week so that left plenty of time to get the other elements of the book business up and running. I'd had something of a brainwave.

I'd been diagnosed with a type of arthritis called Ankylosing Spondylitis which really affected my spine. It was controllable with tablets and exercise but it was a real pain at times. I wasn't a kick off forty years old but I was making old man noises when trying to get out of a seat or bending down to lift something. "Aiyhhaa ooff yer bugger." It was embarrassing... but that's life.

Anyway I'd had a thousand leaflets printed for an outfit calling itself Arthritis Help. I was the outfit and it was myself who would benefit from the help. So in effect it was true... ish. The leaflets asked folk if they had any spare books lying around the house which they could donate and which could be sold on to benefit individuals suffering from arthritis. If so could you please bag them up and leave them outside your front door and your donations will be collected tomorrow. Thank you for your kindness.

It worked a treat and there were hundreds of books left for me to collect after leafletting the private areas of Whitley Bay initially, before moving on to other nice areas. But people weren't just leaving bags of books. There were magazines and vinyl records and the occasional decent ornament... which was very nice of people but it was really the books which whetted my appetite. The ordinary paperbacks were sold on my stall... you know, the Catherine Cookson's and suchlike which as it happened turned out to be very popular during those stall days. Most of the donated vinyl records I managed to sell on to various dealers but not for a great deal. Initially I took a pile of records to an old shop from my schoolboy days... 'The Trade in Store'... but like a lot of other businesses in Blyth it had disappeared and was no longer trading. I couldn't even find the place where I'd remembered it to be. There was just an empty space. Anyway, those were the days when vinyl was dying the death and cassette tapes were all the rage so after finding some alternative outlets the records went for a pittance.

It was principally the specialist books that I was on the look-out for. The hidden golden nugget glistening in among the gravel on the riverbed. I found a fair few over the following few months and they financed my lifestyle pre-taxman.

The biggest early hit was eight volumes of Hume's History of England in beautiful condition. Printed in the early 1800s and leather bound with gold lettering to the spine and face of each volume. I can't even remember whereabouts they came from but the day that they turned up I recall that my heart almost stopped when I pulled the volumes out of their Hessian bag. Their value turned out to be nowhere near the thousands that I'd imagined but I still scored big style. I cashed in at a book-dealer's in one of those rickety Tudor streets in York and walked away with £250.00. A week's wage in one day. Unfortunately I had no option other than to be paid by cheque... and that transaction would ultimately lead the taxman to me.

Chunk was with me once again and was chuffed with his forthcoming cut but we drove home to Blyth before we went out on the pop. I was driving so drink was a no-no. Chunk paid that evening and we had a good old session doing the rounds of some of the Blyth pubs. I was a little short of ready cash so Chunk wouldn't receive his percentage until the cheque was banked. By ten o'clock though we were back at the Folly but we were the only two in the pub. I think Jim the Pint was glad of the company.

CHAPTER 12

Donkey Serenade

∎

It would be a little while before I was confronted with my tax and VAT responsibilities and during that interim the book business moved on apace and life settled into something of a routine. A routine which did throw up the occasional blip. None more so than when an old pal from the past made an unexpected appearance.

I'd been out in the car that day picking up donations of books around the Gosforth and Ponteland area and it had proved to be a little goldmine. A quick glance told me that there were a few promising book pearls amongst the offerings. It was a Saturday and I'd left Blyth to do the pick-ups after setting up the stall and the stock. My dad was looking after the stall until I returned and he was happy to do it. He knew so many people and on other occasions when he'd helped me out the takings always seemed to increase.

After unloading that day's donations into the side room I use for storage at the Folly I head back to Blyth. It's well into the afternoon when I return to pack the stall stock away for the day. I'm heading from the bottom end of the market... the Regent Street end towards the top end just before Church

Street where my stall is located. I'm having a good look around the other stalls to see who is doing well and what is selling. I'm not overly impressed. Blyth market has lost a lot of its oomph and is no longer the vibrant place of ten years ago. To be honest it now has a gloomy kind of air hanging over it and I reckon it's only a matter of time before it gets even worse and fades into obscurity.

Then I come to a halt. I stand and stare for ages before my head can make sense of what I'm seeing. I'm staring up the right-hand walkway towards my stall which seals off the top end of the aisle like a cork in a bottle of wine. What I'm seeing is Albert... if I'm not mistaken of course. The same Albert who worked with me perhaps twenty years ago when we sold potatoes from an old blue wagon. The same Albert who'd become so upset when he'd carried a bag of potatoes into a Cramlington property and discovered the lady of the house was walking around topless. The Albert whom I'd eventually liken to Forrest Gump even though we ended up as pals. Surely my eyes were playing tricks. It couldn't be him could it? If indeed it was Albert he hadn't aged well. His hair was now almost completely grey and sparse to boot. He was standing beside my dad on the selling side of the stall and they were both busy with a couple of lady customers. Here was a turn up for the books... pardon the pun. What on earth was Albert doing there? I needed to find out.

It turned out that Albert had spotted my dad and he'd remembered him from all those years ago. If I remembered correctly he'd only seen my dad on one occasion when I was being dropped off after a tatie selling day. Remembering like that was impressive on Albert's part. Perhaps his brain power had increased somewhat over the years. I would soon find out that wasn't the case.

I veered off to the right between two stalls in my journey up the market and headed over the road towards Woolworths. Then up past the Market Tavern and the wet fish shop. I crossed back over before reaching the church and stopped to make essential use of the gent's toilet facilities. It was there I found out that apparently... and according to the writing on the wall, someone called Kilroy had recently visited the toilet too... and had for whatever reason left the premises broken-hearted after having paid his penny.

Leaving the toilet block I quietly approached the rear of the stall and stood for a little while watching the pair of them... Albert and my dad, as they worked away serving or tidying the book display. There was no question now that the bloke with my dad was none other than my old workmate Albert. I was pleased but I don't know why.

I walked up behind the pair of them... quietly, then reached out and gave Albert a hefty smack on the shoulder.

"What the bloody hell you doin' nicking my books?"

Albert almost jumped out of his skin. He swung around to face me and he looked terrified. Then when his eyes had made sense of who was standing in front of him his face broke into the biggest lop-sided grin I'd ever seen. He looked happy and relieved at the same time.

"Hello Jimmy Bates."

"Albert my old mate, long time no-see. What on earth are you doing here working on my stall?"

He broke into a laugh, "I was just looking around the market for some comics and I spotted your dad. I thought

I remembered his face from all those years ago," he paused and took a packet of sweets out of his pocket. He offered me one and I shook my head... they were dolly mixtures. My dad refused too. Albert took a small handful and stuffed them in his mouth. He chomped a while before resuming the conversation.

"I live in Blyth now... over Crofton... Woodbine Terrace. Mam was left the house by my dad's uncle. Not that I knew my dad's uncle... or even my dad come to that... but it's all right I suppose and it'll be mine soon my mam says, when she's finished dying."

That piece of information wasn't a brilliant beginning. For evident reasons I wasn't even aware that his mam had begun dying. "Sorry Albert. I didn't ever meet your mam... so obviously I didn't know she was so ill," I paused... not sure how to continue, before saying, "I realise it's not a nice question mate... but has she long to go?"

Albert thought about that for a second or two before replying, "Dunno really cos she's been telling me she's dying for years and years now and it never happens but I'm ready for when it does."

"Ready?"

"Aye you know... mam's got everything written in a book for when it does happen. Solicitors and savings account things and the coffin. The headstone from Bart Endean's and doctor's certificates and that. There's loads more other things you have to do when somebody dies. It's lots harder than being alive. Anyway that's why I was around the shops and the market today cos me mam's diabolic and I had to come into town. She needed her prescription filling for her insulation injections from Boots."

I saw my dad turn away when he heard that. I didn't hear him laughing out loud but I saw his shoulders moving. For my part I just looked at the ground and tried to appear sad. Not a single chuckle escaped my lips.

But time was marching on and the number of folk around the market was dwindling, so after another half-hour of catch-up chat and the occasional straggler sale we began the packing up. Albert helped me load.

Dad was on a keeping healthy kick and he decided he was walking home. Mam and dad were living in Gareston Close by that time and waiting for the council to offer them a bungalow. I tried to argue by telling him he was knocking on eighty and should accept the ride home. But he told me in no uncertain terms that eighty was just a number and he wasn't going to let that bother him. You don't keep getting older by sitting on your backside he informed me. He won... and I gave in. We settled up, said our cheerios' and dad walked home.

Albert however was glad of a ride. He had to direct me because I couldn't quite place Woodbine Terrace in my head. The Crofton side of town hadn't been part of my old stamping ground. But it didn't take us long and in a matter of minutes I pulled up in front of their house. I wasn't impressed... but who was I to judge... living in a rented room in Shankhouse.

"There ye go Albert. Thanks for helping out on the stall and it was good to meet up with you again. Hope your mam gets better." By this time I was ready for the off and looking forward to some food before a quiet night looking through my latest pile of books in the Folly. I was sure I'd spotted a couple of promising juicy donations.

"D'yer want me to do some more work on your stall Jimmy cos it was really good and I liked it... and I'm good with numbers now... you know for giving change and that?"

To be honest I wasn't over-excited at the prospect but put in that position I couldn't really say no without giving my old pal a knock-back. I wasn't up for looking at his disappointed face.

"Aye okay Albert... sounds good. I can't pay you much though."

"That's okay Jimmy. I just want to help you out and anyway my mam's got loads of money. My dad died. The real one... not the other one and not the uncles who kept changing over all the time. He left my mam lots of dosh and the house. I know I told you my dad's uncle left it to mam but he actually left it to my dad and then dad left it to mam when he died. That was strange cos I didn't even know that he liked my mam. He never came to see me anyhow... not even once and I don't know what he looked like cos mam burned all of his clothes and photographs."

After that long winded explanation I was lost for words.

"So is it okay then Jimmy?"

What could I say other than, "Yeh Albert... glad to have you on board. My dad's getting a bit too old to still be working."

Albert grinned, opened his side door and began to clamber out... then paused with his back to me. "D'yer fancy goin' for a pint tonight?"

Now here was a surprise. All those tatie years ago Albert had been terrified of going home and smelling of drink. His mam kept him on a tight leash... for obvious reasons. I think she was afraid that Albert would do something stupid if he had booze in his system. He wasn't the brightest spark and I believe she must have been trying to keep him safe. Alcohol had been a big no-no.

"Aye alright Albert. But won't your mam give ye grief?" Albert... still with his back to me, laughed out loud, "Jimmy man I'm forty-five. I'm a grown-up now. I can do what I want. I had two pints last week at that pub they used to call The Thoroton. Don't remember its new name. Ohh aye and I had a game of darts with two blokes. I'm canny good actually... cos I scored fifty-two on one of my turns. Anyway when I went home mam didn't say anything because like I said I'm grown-up now... well, actually she did say 'hope ye enjoyed yourself drinking beer,' so that was quite nice wasn't it?"

I don't think Albert understood sarcasm... not from his mam anyway. A night out with Albert wasn't a joyous prospect so I attempted to put him off, "I'll be in the Folly tonight Albert and that's a fair bit out of your way. I'll be having a shufti through some books and having a few jars. So maybe best some other time ehhh?"

"Nah Jimmy, that's all right. I know where the Folly is. I know lots of places now. It's the Albion isn't it? I'll get a taxi over there and I'll get a taxi home."

It would have been ignorant and unkind if I'd refused... so I didn't and we arranged to meet up around eight o'clock.

So that evening... after a cup of tea, a brace of pasties and some mini cheddars I was in the Folly before seven o'clock and spent the first half an hour going through the latest batch of collected offerings. Most of them were run of the mill but when sifting was complete I'd rescued three promising hardback volumes from their donation bags. I left them well wrapped up in a safe place behind the bar with Jim the Pint before having a welcome wind-down and murdering a packet of crisps. Then I ordered my first beer and downed it almost in one. I ordered a follow-up and a wee whisky and carried them over to our usual meeting table. Bob the Knob wouldn't be out on a Saturday because it was his wife's bingo night. I wasn't expecting John the Milk to make an appearance either. He was a daytime only drinker but it wasn't too long before Chunk showed his face and came over to join me. We did the hiya thing, mouthed the expected pleasantries then had a bit of a chinwag for a few minutes before lapsing into silence.

Silence didn't really suit us and it didn't take us long before we noticed the only other customers in the pub. A well-dressed chap perhaps in his late forties with his arm around the waist of a younger woman who, from a side view led us to think she was middle thirties. They were standing at the bar with their backs to us and we saw the guy occasionally allowing his hand to drop lower and give the lady's bum a squeeze. We grinned at each other.

"Playing away?" I commented.

"Sugar daddy," Chunk replied.

We weren't quite sure which one of those statements was accurate but we reckoned it was one or the other. We were keeping a close eye on 'bum-squeezy' when Albert suddenly stumbled into the pub. He'd tripped over something when coming through the door... probably his own feet and he'd grasped the side stanchion for support. He wasn't in the least embarrassed as he looked around to get his bearings then spotted me.

"Hi Jimmy... told ye I'd come," he said and threw me a huge smile.

I smiled back and he went off to stand beside the bar couple. While Albert was busy ordering his drink I said to Chunk, "He's an old pal I used to work with and I felt a bit sorry for him. He's going to do some work on the stall for me for a few weeks... but go easy on him Chunk cos he's not smart and streetwise like you and me."

Chunk seemed pleased with the smart and streetwise comment, "Nee bother Jimmy... I'll be the soul of destruction."

I didn't know if he'd just got the wording wrong or if I should start to be worried. I decided it was the wording... and kept my fingers crossed.

Albert still had the big smile on his face as he put his drink down on the table and took a seat next to Chunk. That was a surprise in itself... what was wrong with sitting next to me? I'd even put some Brut on. Splashed it all over.

I waited until he'd made himself comfortable... then introduced them, "Chunk this is Albert and Albert this is Chunk," they both half turned in their seats to face each other and shook hands.

"Y'all right mate," said Chunk.

"Aye... canny man... and you?" Albert replied.

"Aye canny an' all," and that was it... social niceties dispensed with.

There was an awkward silence for a long minute so all three of us gave great concentration to our beers and the production of cigarettes. Not Albert with the tabs because he didn't indulge but Chunk took out a packet of Senior Service and I rolled myself quite a fat fellow out of my baccy pouch. We both lit up and gave one of those 'God I needed that' sighs.

It was myself who kicked off the conversation having been uncomfortable during the chat hiatus, I began but kept my voice low, "What on earth is that wifey doin' wearing a mini-skirt like that? Them teeny things died the death in the seventies." Both Chunk and Albert shuffled around in their seats to look at the bar lady's legs.

"Bloody hell man... have ye seen them thighs? She must play rugby or summat cos they're huge. She's got more muscles than North Shields fish quay." Chunk had great difficulty keeping his voice low. He was a shouty person at the best of times.

"Shhh man Chunk... they'll hear."

"So what?"

I was sure I'd seen the bloke at the bar glance over at us out of the corner of his eye. I wasn't fancying any confrontation... but it wouldn't have bothered Chunk in the slightest.

"Could be a man with a skirt on," volunteered Albert.

Chunk turned to face Albert with a puzzled look on his face, "What ye on aboot... are ye daft or summat?"

Albert wasn't fazed by the comment, "I was watching something on the telly," then he paused and thought for a second, "Naah... maybe I was reading it... or somebody told me... I can't remember which. But anyway there's some blokes that get dressed up as women and they go out on dates with other blokes. They call them transistors... I think."

I would normally have chuckled at that but I was struggling to keep myself out of the conversation because it wasn't being held in hushed tones anymore... and I knew for certain that the bloke at the bar had overheard. He'd half-turned and glared in our direction. I dropped my eyes and fiddled about with my baccy pouch. Not to roll one... cos I was already smoking. It was more to demonstrate to bar bloke that I certainly wasn't engaged in the silly talk. Not that he looked like a hard-case or anything. He was wearing a decent suit with a collar and tie and had shiny shoes. He looked more like an accountant or a civil servant... but you never could tell nowadays so I was being somewhat circumspect. That's a better word than cowardly isn't it?

Chunk had taken ample time to think over Albert's words and came back with, "Albert aahh divvent want ter piss on your chips or nowt but that's nuts what you're talkin' man," he'd lapsed into Geordie street talk, "Fellas prancin' aboot dressed like tarts isn't normal man. Not here aroond Blyth... London mevvys or in Scotland cos they dee it all the time up there and it's like God bless ye to the Jocks. Anyway the gadgie in the suit is wearin' a weddin' ring. So if what you just said was right that would mek thon fella at the bar bifocal... and aahh cannit stand them blokes."

At that moment I felt like an Arab thoroughbred in the company of donkeys. Their banter would normally have given me an inward giggle. But not at this juncture because I needed to halt the flow and to do it pretty quickly. This line of conversation was heading in the wrong direction... downhill, and the voices were becoming louder. Even Jim the Pint was looking concerned now and gave me a quizzical look from his perch behind the bar. I gave Jim Pint a reassuring wink but I didn't know how to divert these two from their chosen path.

Fortunately that decision was taken out of my hands. The two folk at the bar had finished their drinks and the woman had picked her coat up from an adjoining bar stool and was struggling to put it on. They were about to leave. The guy helped her with one of the sleeves and then, when said coat was in place she began to button it up. Strangely though as the man headed for the exit the woman paused, then turned and walked over to our table. Up close she was actually very attractive with a cracking figure, and her legs, meaty though they were, went all the way up to her armpits.

She stared at us... and spent a second on each face in turn and I thought there was a glimmer of recognition when she looked at me. But the eyes moved on and finally came to settle on Albert. "All woman I'm afraid guys, and I play hockey... for England as it happens. I can't stand rugby or funny shaped balls... although I'm sure three sporty fellows like yourselves play with them all the time." Then she turned and left without further comment and not so much as a backward glance.

Chunk snorted as the door closed behind her. I'd expected some sort of a reaction from this big man and he felt my eyes on him... querying. Kicking off was his standard response to spiky situations... but not on this occasion. It wasn't normal. He could feel the question in my gaze.

"I'm on my best behaviour Jim Book cos believe me aahh fancied stickin' the heed on her nose-end like."

I could do nothing else but nod an agreement. I'd been concerned that Chunk might have jumped up and removed a few of her teeth. He was certainly playing Mr nice guy this evening.

"But you couldn't bash a lass could you Chunk?" chirped Albert.

"Course aahh could. Ye knaa, equality an' all that?"

Albert didn't seem impressed. He was a bloke with a weird and wonderful code of conduct. A product of a domineering mother.

"Have you ever bashed a woman before?"

Chunk shrugged, "I'm not proud of it or nowt. But aah've clagged a few when they needed claggin'. Mind you aah've killed a few an' all."

That comment stopped Albert dead in his tracks for a brief second, "Ehhh? What d'yer mean killed a few?"

"Ye knaa... when aahh was in the parachute regiment."

I butted in and immediately regretted it, "I thought ye were in the SAS Chunk if I'm remembering right."

Chunk gave me a look of disdain, "Ye might knaa a lot Jimmy but ye divvent knaa much. Ye hev ter be in summat else afore ye gan in the SAS man. Ye cannit just roll up ter the recruitin' office and say ye want to join the SAS. They'd just laugh at ye."

That shut me up quickly but it also made me think. I'd believed in my own mind that Chunk was just spouting off and manipulating the truth when he boasted about his army exploits but now I wasn't so sure. Perhaps it wasn't all just porkies and bravado. There again maybe it was. It makes you somewhat uncomfortable when you aren't sure what's going to come next from a person you're close to. It can be most unnerving... and annoying. That's how I felt every time I was in Chunk's company. Trying to get honesty from Chunk was like peeling an onion... there was always another layer to be peeled and before you got anywhere near the truth the effort had you in tears.

Not so with our other pal that evening. Albert was like a dog with a squeaky toy and he wasn't about to give up on the conversation no matter where it was headed. He was just one of those folk who can't sense personal danger. Not that he was in any danger with us two. I'm sure Chunk wouldn't have turned psycho with anyone like Albert... but there again...

"Did you kill them women around here in Shankhouse... or Blyth?" Albert needed answers. I was keeping well out of it now so I stood up and sauntered over to the bar and sat my backside down on one of the stools before ordering another drink. I could still hear the back and forth of the conversation. They were both so loud.

Then I heard the bar door open, I had my back to it but didn't turn around. Maybe it was that couple returning. Jim glanced over.

"What d'yer want," he boomed towards the door.

"A pint of beer," a voice replied.

"How old are ye?"

"Eighteen."

"No son I meant how old are you now... not how old will you be in three years' time." Jim growled.

No reply. The door closed and the voice disappeared. Jim smiled then pulled me another pint before asking, "Owt decent in them books?"

"There's three might do the trick but definitely one there that should turn up trumps. It's by Harrington – The Commonwealth of Oceana."

"What's that all about then?"

"Buggered if I know Jim... but it's real old and in super nick... and that always seems to be the main thing... you know, condition?"

"Aahh well let me know how you do with it."

"Will do Jim."

"Anyway what's those two up to?" he nodded towards Chunk and Albert.

"Talkin' bollox Jim... and doin' my head in." He laughed, and we listened in. They were still going at it... hammer and tongs.

"No man Albert aah'm tellin' ye it was Colombia."

"Aye but that's in Canada?"

"Albert man will ye listen, aahmm tryin' to tell ye... it was proper Colombia... not British Columbia. They're different and they speak foreign in proper Colombia. It's where all the drugs come from man."

"What... like paracetamol and Benylin and stuff?"

A shrug from Chunk, "Errrmm... I don't know about them but probably. I just heard about cocaine and heroin and things like that."

"So why did ye kill a woman in Colombia?" Albert paused and took a mouthful of beer before continuing, "Was she being cheeky?"

Jim the Pint and I were smiling at each other and raising eyebrows at most of the overheard chatter. But we kept our own counsel.

"Aahh told ye man Albert. I never done any killin' in Colombia. Well not women anyway. We just found three bodies in the jungle. They were like guerillas ye knaa. Probably from one of the drug cartels. They have lots of women with guns oot there. Them cartels keep killin' each other so aah'm not sure what we were supposed to be deein' there. Anyway two of the deed women had their hands tied behind their backs. They were covered in blood and snot and were face doon in the river. But the other one didn't have any clothes on and she was sitting with her back against a tree... sprawled out. And she'd had her head blown off."

"Bliddy hell... it must have been really windy?"

"Ehhh?"

"If the head had blown away how did ye know it was a woman?"

"Cos she had nee clothes on."

"Ohh aye... that was rude of her wasn't it. She should have put her clothes on, especially if it was windy like that."

"Ehhh... am I hearin' right?" I think Chunk had met his match... at daft talk anyway. There was more to come as they bantered away but I'd reached my limits. My head was totally frazzled listening to those two.

Entertaining it would have been for a casual observer... and Jim the Pint and I certainly had a few chuckles too... but I was mighty glad when that evening came to an end.

CHAPTER 13

Money For Nothing

◆

As it happened the Blyth market stall chugged along nicely and for reasons unknown Albert turned out to be quite popular. Takings were always decent enough although there was an occasional poor day, due mainly to the weather. We also had brilliant days even though the stock was always much of a muchness. I also managed to find a few nuggets of pure gold amongst the donated books and the cash from those fellas came in very handy.

Fortunately or unfortunately... cos there's two ways of looking at it, the tax folk finally caught up with me. I knew it had to come sooner or later and when it did happen it became something of a relief... no more dodging. They'd traced me via my bank account and insurance number. Paying in cheques to my bank account had lit up a beacon for those fellows and I found myself having to attend magistrates court in Hull. Not attending would be a non-starter I was informed. If I attempted to give the court a body swerve then a warrant would be issued for my arrest.

So it was several weeks later that I found myself standing in front of a courtroom bench with three magistrates looking down at me. I wore a suit that day with an open necked shirt. A collar and tie might have made me look a tad more affluent than I really was.

Without boasting I have to say I played a blinder that day even if that does literally sound like boasting. In fact for a while afterwards I thought it may be a good idea to become a full-time actor. My dummy act in the magistrates' court that day was perfection. Oscar material I thought.

The first ten minutes in court however were boring and taken up by the tax people laying out their position to the magistrates. They seemed calm and assured and armed with a pile of folders and ring-binders. So initially there wasn't much I could do other than listen and fix my attention on some points they were stating as fact. Those facts seemed, in my opinion anyway, to be on wobbly ground. After another few minutes they wound up their presentation and sat back in their seats which were off to the right of me across an aisle. My turn came next.

One of the three wise folk sitting in front and above me spoke, "So Mr Bates we've heard the presented evidence concerning your tax liability calculation. Do you have anything to say in response."

The big chunky taxman had managed first dibs with the magistrates which was fair enough and that was how I wanted it anyway. He had set out his brief and the longer he'd talked the less I recognised. Some of the figures and totals he'd been spouting were completely alien to me. Were they honestly talking about me and my business affairs... or were they just blagging it? Where they'd found those figures and those sums of money from had me baffled. To be honest

I wasn't completely baffled but that was how I was going to play it for the three folk who held my destiny in their hands. "Mr Bates... your response. Do you have one?" I certainly did. It was time to go into dumbo mode. Charlie had briefed me on the stance I should take some time ago. I remembered it well and I was hoping it worked. "Your lordship I can't..."

The magistrate in the middle immediately held up a hand to stop me and smiled, "Sir will be sufficient in your responses today Mr Bates... I'm not your lordship." I knew that of course but I'd reeled him in with an old salesman's trick. I'd just bumped his ego up a notch.

"Sorry sir... I wasn't sure what your title was... sorry."

He smiled again and that was definitely a sign of some sort I thought to myself. I didn't know if it was a good sign or a bad sign. Perhaps he was on my side and feeling sympathy for the little man. There again maybe he smiled at everyone before he handed down the ten years hard labour sentence.

"Carry on Mr Bates," and there was that smile again. I was encouraged. Maybe he liked me. The lady magistrate to his left (my right) wasn't smiling at all. She had a countenance like one of my not-so-nice aunties. Her face held the sourest of expressions and she fixed me with a bitter gaze through jam-jar glasses. She wasn't impressed by me in the slightest. I needed to soften her up a touch and call her your ladyship if I got the chance. However she was looking concerned for some reason and leaned over to whisper something to the chief magistrate. He glanced over towards me. Then he beckoned the usher fellow to the bench and whispered to him in turn. The usher gave a smile to the bench before

132

approaching me and beckoned just like the magistrate had done. I needed to bend forward so he could whisper to me... he was really short. He put his mouth to my ear.

"You've got egg on your chin."

"What?"

"Your flies open."

"Ehhh?"

"Zip yourself up... dirty Gertie can't keep her eyes off your pants."

Ohh my God... I glanced down and it was right enough. Both of my hands did the protective thing to hide the offending gape from view. The tail-end of my shirt was sticking out of my flies. I turned my back to the bench, tucked the shirt tail back in and waggled my zip up. I was so embarrassed. I gave a half grimace half smirk towards the magistrates as I turned back to face the bench. Then there was a moment of silence but I'm sure I heard a snort from one of the tax guys. I was as nervous as hell and shaking inside and I remember thinking that maybe I'd blown it... and that isn't a double entendre. It had been the lady magistrate who'd noticed... and I found that strange. Why on earth had she even looked down there in the first place.

"Everything ship-shape and Bristol fashion now Mr Bates? would you please carry on," the chief gave a wave of his hand and another half-smile.

I nodded my agreement, gave an embarrassed grin, then cleared my throat, sucked in a breath and began.

"Sir, sir, madam," I addressed the three magistrates, "I've worked hard all my life and never once thought about loafing about and costing the country money. I think I've only ever claimed dole money for about ten or twelve weeks in my entire working life... I imagine the tax people will be able to verify that with their documents." I paused.

The chief magistrate looked over to the gruesome twosome sitting behind their pile of folders for confirmation. Those two looked at each other and began to rummage through various bits of paperwork. After a minute or two, the chunky chap who was presumably the most senior of the pair turned back to the magistrate and gave a shrug. "Unfortunately I don't have that information to hand sir."

"Hmmm that's not ideal is it?"

Chunky taxman grimaced, "No sir... my apologies."

Big magistrate looked away then back at me, "Continue Mr Bates."

"I'm not well-educated sir. I mean my English is alright... it's passable apart from my spelling. I've never been able to get the hang of numbers though and the percent thing is a complete mystery, so other people have usually helped me with that. I have something like dyslexia but with numbers instead of words... it's got a proper name but I can't remember it. I know how to buy something for one price and sell it for a bigger price but I don't have much idea what to do after that. I do know that I've never had the kind of money that those tax people are saying. I know they're just doing their job but some of the things they were presenting just weren't right."

"Hmmm, what things are you referring to Mr Bates?" The big magistrate did sound friendly... I was sure of it. The reference to number dyslexia had softened him even further and apart from that I don't think he liked the tax folk.

"Well I don't have a Bedford van worth three thousand pounds sir like they've just stated. I have a twelve-year-old estate car worth about two hundred pounds if I could find anyone daft enough to buy it."

The magistrates smiled... even sour puss. I felt like I was on stage in a little play and working the audience.

"I must interject there sir... with your permission," said the chunky tax guy. I was happy that he did, because I knew what was coming next. We were all mere actors in this production and he was taking the role of the pantomime villain. Chief magistrate nodded his approval.

Tax guy continued, "We have it here in black and white concerning the details of that particular vehicle."

Then I jumped in without asking, "Sir, one of the things I remembered to keep hold of was the receipt for the sale of the vehicle." I indulged in a pretend rummage through various pockets before producing it and sticking my hand up in the air. Said receipt had been lurking expectantly in my jacket... anxious for its entrance into our little courtroom drama.

"The engine blew up and I couldn't afford a new one. I had to sell the Bedford for scrap, eighty pounds."

I passed the scrapyard receipt to the little usher fellow who walked over and took it from me. He in turn passed it up to the magistrates and they all had a good look at it. I owed my contact at Hanratty's scrapyard a huge debt of gratitude and a good night out on the tiles. Chunk had put me in touch with the guy and that bill of sale had been written out a mere two days ago... but the date would show six months ago.

"May we see that document sir?" asked the reserve tax guy.

"Mr Bates do you have any objection?" asked chief magistrate.

"Yes sir I do. That's my evidence. If I'd forgotten to bring that today they would have ploughed on whatever the facts were and given me grief about a vehicle I no longer have. I don't think they're telling the truth at all and I don't see why I should be doing their work for them."

The magistrates had a little pow-wow then big magistrate said, "Fair comment Mr Bates." Then he turned to the taxmen, "Sorry but the document belongs to Mr Bates and it's a proof of transaction. You may wish to ask him afterwards if you can make a copy."

I resumed as soon as he'd finished, "Sir I told the MHCC about it when they first got in touch but they never got back to me. The insurance wouldn't pay up because I was only insured for third party fire and theft. I've given them this information. They must have that in their records over there," I pointed over to the two tax department people, "But if they have then they've just told you something that's not true," I gave a brief pause after that statement to let the idea sink in, "And if they haven't then they must be working with out-of-date information," I paused again, "Because quite honestly sir I don't know how in a million years I could be owing twelve thousand and something pounds. I wish I did though because then I'd have a big fat bank account."

"Yes-yes Mr Bates," said the chief magistrate. "And by the way it's HMRC," he smiled at me again... 'yeeha'. Then he nodded towards my opponents, "Do you have any record of this in your documentation?"

They scrunched and scrabbled around in their sheets of paper, their official documents and their manila folders. They came up empty once again. "Sorry sir we have no record of that. But shouldn't Mr Bates have ensured he had fully comprehensive insurance for a business vehicle which was used exclusively for carrying stock and passengers?"

I butted in, "Yes I should have and I know it's probably breaking the law but I couldn't afford fully comp."

"Enough... enough," came the cry from the bench. I dropped my eyes because I could see big magistrate was becoming irritated. Sour-puss leaned over and whispered something in his ear. I checked my flies again. No... she wasn't whispering about that.

"Do you have anything further to add Mr Bates?"

Of course I did... the clincher, "Well your worship," he didn't stop me this time... he must have liked it, "I'm just baffled as to how they've arrived at that total of twelve thousand and something. None of the paperwork that would help me out seems to exist in their folders, even though they took what records I did have away with them... when they came to my door. All I've got is this huge demand. It's like big lads against little lads in the playground. Anything they say is going to be right because they're bigger and stronger than me. It seems to me they've just thought up a number. They've already informed me that it's my responsibility to prove that I don't owe whatever total they come up with. They know I'm no good at sums and stuff so how can I prove anything. Shouldn't they have to prove what I actually do owe cos they might as well have thought up a bigger number. A hundred thousand or something... or a million. There you go mister little man prove you don't owe a million." At that point I shrugged and held my hands out... palms up. I stared at the floor with my face sporting my best downcast look. I stopped talking.

"Is that it Mr Bates, are you finished and do you concede the point that you may owe some of this money?"

I shrugged and gave him my best 'resigned to my fate' expression, "Yes sir... I do agree that I must owe a bit of tax... a little bit... but that amount? You might as well throw me into jail now sir and get it over with because I know for certain that those figures just aren't right. I'd like to know how they arrived at that total." With that finishing comment even sour puss magistrate smiled at me, the presentation was working. She must have been incredibly impressed. She gave me another glance then she leaned over and whispered in big magistrates ear once more. I think she must have been saying something like 'there's no way we can send a lovely looking bloke like that to prison'. But there again maybe not.

"Yes-yes, good point, I agree," said big magistrate. "Knowing how those figures were arrived at would be most informative," he looked over at my two enemies. "Can you enlighten us as to how you've actually arrived at this total?"

There was a few long seconds of huffing and puffing and paper shuffling before the chunky chap stood up. He proceeded to give a long-winded explanation about how, using well tried and tested formulae they would calculate expected profit from a business of this size and use similar businesses as a yardstick. They would then project expected profit and work backwards from that to arrive at a figure they considered reasonable. Where paperwork hadn't been presented by their target business they would sometimes inflate the total in order to hurry along the production of said accounts and other relevant documentation... or he used words to that effect as far as I can recall. I remember plain as day however that he did use the word inflate.

The three magistrates went into a huddle. It was make your mind up time. They looked like a little gang. Who's going to give the verdict... I thought to myself. I hope it's old sourpuss cos she seems to have taken a shine to me. After a few minutes of discussion I wouldn't have been surprised if they'd started doing rock-paper-scissors. They seemed to take an interminably long time to come to an agreed decision.

Ten minutes later it was all done and dusted. The upshot was that the twelve thousand had now been whittled down to twelve hundred, much to the chagrin of my two adversaries but a most gratifying outcome on my part. Not so good however was the time frame for paying up. I had twenty-eight days to stump up otherwise it was the gallows for me... a custodial sentence not out of the question. The final verdict though hadn't been so gratifying for my opponents. They actually went out of their way to collar me on the steps outside the court. I think in all honesty they were trying to play it like nice guys at that juncture and tell me there were no hard feelings. I wasn't in the mood for new friendships that particular day. Bravado aside I'd been terrified in there. Clean underwear desperately needed.

Big tax dog spoke, "You definitely got away with one there James... I wouldn't mind a quick look at that sales docket though. Nevertheless it's been a good result for you... kosher or otherwise."

Under normal circumstances I would have put the bloke in his place with a scintillating witty reply but my head was all over the place. So I turned and looked him in the eye and zonked him with the most imaginative retort I could conjure up… "Fuck off."

Truth is I was mightily relieved after going through that wringer and it took a while for me to calm down and chill out. I spent the next few hours in Hull after the court appearance. It was just for a final look around really. The city had consumed ten years of my life and there was a feeling of regret that my time there hadn't worked out more favourably. I didn't expect to return any time soon. In fact I didn't expect to return… full stop. I decided to call in at The Priory, my old local and I received a warm enough welcome, but it felt ever so weird. I felt like a tourist must have done… an interloper. I bought myself a couple of pints and a cheese toastie… then a few games of pool with a beefy bloke called Taff before taking my leave of that pub for ever.

On the journey home I decided to take a picturesque drive over the top route via Wetwang and the moors, then to head for Sutton Bank. That was a steep and winding old bugger to navigate down, but fortunately my brakes held up okay on the descent. I eventually made my final stop off in Thirsk to have another feast on anything edible and another jar or two of beer. I was aware I was over the limit when I set off again to drive the final leg of the journey. I was breaking the law so to speak but I didn't care a jot.

CHAPTER 14

Homeward Bound

———————————————————■———————————————————

It was late when I arrived in Shankhouse and I didn't bother with the pub... I was knackered... and happy... and sad all at the same time. I parked outside my lodgings and stared at that front door for ages. I realised in that moment how my life was needing some serious changes made. Before I got out of the car I decided there and then that it was time for moving on. It was time to stop playing silly buggers and allow my life some breathing space.

When I gave it some thought I realised my life had taken a turn for the better. I'd sorted my serotonin levels with those magic tablets and that was good. I'd dodged a bullet from the tax people and that was brilliant. Apart from the spinal arthritis thing I was in relatively good health so that was fine too. What I didn't have in my life were two things. The first of those was direction... because books weren't going to be a long-term project, unless of course I wrote one. I needed to find something which would to all intents and purposes be substantial and fairly permanent. The other thing was female company. It was many weeks... months in fact since I'd had any of that... and I realised I was missing it. I did appreciate however that on this occasion I'd need to be more circumspect and choosy. Now was definitely not the time to just become involved with the first person I met who was wearing a skirt. Over the years I'd experienced more than my fair share of disasters.

I slept soundly that night. My head that evening was like a Tetris and all the blocks were falling neatly into place. I felt invigorated.

Invigorated I may have been but certainly not expecting that the following afternoon at the Folly would produce some welcome news from half a world away. In addition I'd also receive information about a surprising phone-call which would point my life in a totally unexpected direction. A direction which in retrospect I've never once regretted. I'm sure my old pal Tug must have been looking down on me... shaking his head, tutting... and constructing another one of those life-change moments.

I was up and about in a much-improved state of mind the following day. I was feeling chipper in the extreme. That afternoon I was first man into the Folly... which to be fair wasn't too unusual. First to buy a pint and first to make short work of the two pork pies which I'd rescued from a shop in High Pit that same morning.

Also I'd managed to get right up Jim the Pint's nose after I'd ordered my first pint of beer and he'd stood it on the bar top.

"There ye go Jimmy... that's 96p."

"Aahh divvent want that one Jim man. It's been standin' in the pump all night. Aah'll hev number two though."

"Yer a right cheeky bugger Jimmy... I'd already pulled the first two through and swilled them afore I opened up. That one in front of ye is the third one. I knaa how to run a pub ye cheeky get." He wasn't best pleased.

"Aye righto... just checking. Ye cannit be ower careful." I smiled but he didn't smile back. He was not happy. I'd questioned his professionalism. Time for some ego stroking.

I looked him up and down... then, "Mind that's a lovely jumper yer wearin' Jim... the colour doesn't half suit ye. Looks like your lass has been to Marks and Sparks?... is it new?"

"Fuck off."

We both laughed at that. Jim's repartee was somewhat limited in scope. He grinned... and with his profusion of black and grey facial hair he looked for all the world like a friendly hedge."

"Anyways Jimmy ye got a phone call yesterday from Australia. Now what did aahh tell ye about using the pub phone for your own personal number?"

"Ehhh... Australia? Sorry about that Jim. It must have been Frances or somebody with news about Frances... and my missing money. I rang the number she'd given me for emergencies and spoke to some Australian chap and I left the pub number with him in case she called."

"Aye, Frances that's the name. She said she had to be brief cos the phone call was costing her an arm and a leg but to tell you she'd be back in England sometime in late April. She said you'd remember the usual Hull address and phone number."

That was welcome news but April was another five months away. five months before I would be able to get my hands on the cash she'd salted away from the lingerie business... my share of it anyway.

"Did she say anything else?"

"Nah... other than she'd visit if ye happened to be in prison."

"God... did she say that?"

"Nah, aahh med that bit up." He laughed at his own humour... and why not indeed, because no-one else ever did.

The Frances news was welcome and it suddenly struck me that I didn't need to be dodging the tax folk any longer. I could sign on the dole now if I fancied. Not that they'd be throwing up enough money to settle that looming bill. Twelve hundred pounds to find in twenty-eight days. Twenty-seven days now... and my bank account was currently hovering around a few hundred pounds. I was going to have to come up with something creative.

I was sitting there pondering the money problem when Jim chirped up again... and once more he wasn't a happy chap.

"By the way... there was another phone call an' all and aahmm bliddy annoyed about it. What de ye think we are here ehhh? we're a pub man, not a bliddy hotel or your personal answering service. Aah'm tellin ye for nowt... if it happens again there's gannin ter be murders on."

"Another phone call?... For me?... can't have been Jim, I've only given the number to Frances... and that was only until I got fixed up with my own gaff."

"Aye so ye say... but apparently not cos there was another woman on the phone for ye."

"If that's right then I'm sorry about that Jim... a woman, I can't remember giving anyone else this number. What did she want?"

"Buggered if aahh knaa Jimmy. To meet up with ye or something." He paused while he searched under the bar, then having come up empty-handed he searched through his pockets before producing a crumpled bit of notepaper. He unfolded it and continued, "Somebody called..." he struggled for a few seconds, holding the paper at arm's length... then put on his glasses in an attempt to decipher his own handwriting, "Somebody called Lozenge or Lazarus or somethin' from Walker... and she says ye'd asked her on a date. Here, she left a telephone number for ye," he passed the piece of paper over to me, "And divvent even think aboot usin' my phone to mek a call."

I scanned the note. It was just a name incorrectly spelt by Jim of course... but I couldn't quite make the scrawl out. Surely it must be Lorna or Lorraine or something similar. The name was accompanied by a Newcastle phone number. For some reason the name Lorraine rang a small bell somewhere in my head. I wasn't sure if I just liked the name or if I'd remembered it from somewhere... maybe from that quiche I'd eaten in Thirsk... but the memory wouldn't surface so I was none the wiser. I couldn't remember asking anyone out on a date. Not for a few months anyway.

"Well-well-well Bonny lad I wasn't expectin' ter see you. Well mevvys through bars in Durham nick." Chunk was making an entrance... shouting the odds from the front doorway. "Aahh wouldn't care aah've just gone and bought ye a packet of Scott's Porage Oats." He guffawed loudly at his own humour... and why not, it was actually quite funny.

"Hi Chunk."

"Hi Jimmy Book. Ye bamboozled them buggers then?"

"Aye summat like that."

He came and stood beside me at the bar. "Pint Jim please," he ordered his drink before continuing, "Did ye shit yersell?"

"Just the twice."

"Ha-ha-ha, them places are scary man," he paused to take his pint from landlord Jim... then... "Did ye hear aboot Johnny Milk?"

I looked from Jim to Chunk, "What's he gone and done... somethin' stupid I bet. Got them blokes back workin' his round or summat?"

"Nah... he went and got his jaw smashed."

"Ehhh... how did he manage that?"

"Apparently he was workin' his ticket in the Indian restaurant in Newsham. Shoutin' and screamin' they hadn't paid their milk bill and hoyin food aall around. Ye knaa... rice and them pancake things and curry and stuff. Them claggy things mek a hell of a mess on carpets."

"So how did he break his jaw?"

"Somebody broke it for him. Gave him a reet crackin' wallop."

"Who was it?"

"Divvent knaa... he won't say and he's told the police he can't remember but I reckon it must have been one of the hard lads from aroond there. I've got my own ideas about who it was. Anyway, if it had been one of the Indians they'd have belted him with a tomahawk or summat."

That one made me grin, "Where is he now?"

"He should be home by now. Their lass said his jaw was aall wired up. She's up in the air of course. She was callin' him aall the daft prats under the sun. Ye should have heard the language man... it was choice."

"Hello Jimmy Bates. You've escaped." Another voice from the doorway interrupted us as Albert made his usual trippy entrance. He knew there was a tear in the canvas... so why didn't he lift his daft feet up?

"Hi Albert. You're gonna break your neck one day if you don't learn to bend those knees and lift those plates of meat."

He laughed before giving his greetings to Jim Pint and Chunk. He ordered his pint, I ordered another and then the three of us toddled over to our afternoon sanctuary table in the corner. Chunk and I lit up cigarettes.

"Did Jim Pint tell ye about that woman who phoned up cos ye'd asked her for a date or something?" queried Chunk.

"Aye but I can't remember askin' anyone."

"Are ye gonna go out on a date Jimmy?" asked Albert.

"Dunno... maybe."

"Ye'll be getting' married soon then."

Chunk jumped in, "Last thing he wants to be deein'."

Albert pulled a face and gave Chunk a questioning stare, "Why's that, are you not married then Chunk?"

"Of course I am Albert, happily for three years."

Albert seemed confused, "But you're older than me and you're telling me you've only been married for three years?"

"Course not Albert, I've been married for twenty-five years... but the first three were happy."

Albert was normally slow on the uptake but even he found the humour in that pearler from Chunk. We all laughed.

Albert and Chunk via some unexpected and remarkable twist of fate had struck up a friendship which hadn't seemed remotely possible. They approached life from diametrically opposed ends of the pal spectrum yet they had gelled and took pleasure in each other's company. It was weird.

Those two were gabbling away with their usual life rubbish so I left quietly and went to sit at the bar with Jim Pint.

"What's those two on about?" he asked as I ordered another pint..

"The usual."

"Done your napper in has it?"

"Aye... summat like that." I paused for a second, "Don't suppose you've got a spare twelve hundred smackers kicking about... you know... to lend to your best customer?"

My pint appeared in front of me and I paid up. "Just put the change in the Sooty spastic box Jim." He did.

"Twelve hundred quid... aye that'll be right. The profit from my permanently packed-out to the rafters pub? We're on our last legs here man Jimmy. The brewery won't pay for any improvements and we're just hanging on by our fingertips. I'll give it another year... maybe two and then they'll be pulling the plug. Goodbye Albion... and that's a shame with the new houses they're talkin' about building."

"Just thought I'd ask... I wasn't being serious anyway."

"What about that book you said was a bobby-dazzla?"

"Aye the Harrington. Sold it in York on my way down to Hull. I got seventy-five quid for it. Better than nowt but I was expecting more."

"That's a shame… but ye could just gan ter jail and get it ower with. Aah'll visit ye and fetch a cake in with a file inside."

We both smiled at the thought of it, "Think I'll give that one a miss Jim. I'll think of something before then," I said that without any confidence. Then we took a talk break and listened to Chunk and Albert instead.

The voices from the table had notched up the volume. Chunk was spraying out advice like a garden sprinkler.

"So where is it yer thinkin of gannin' on holiday man Albert? Ye cannit just say abroad cos that's a big place."

"Aahh don't know. Just somewhere that's not here."

"Are ye daft or what? everywhere else is not here man… Ashington's not here… Morpeth's not here, you've got to pick a proper place that's abroad. Just ask me cos aah've been everywhere."

"Okay Chunk, where would you go?"

Chunk didn't hesitate, "Neewhere… not me, I'd just stop here. Abroad is just like Britain but the folk aall speak foreign… not English like us. Abroad is full of ignorant folk. We've got mountains and rivers and animals here. What's the point in gannin and spendin' loads of money so ye can see somebody else's mountains and rivers and stuff?"

Albert thought about his reply, then, "What about Japan? That seems canny."

Chunk frowned, "Nah not there, it's aall rubble and deed folk man. The American's dropped that fat-lad atomical bomb on them and med a reet mess. They'll be busy buildin' their hooses back up again. If ye gan ower there Albert it'll probably be just a load of cement mixers and lots of little blokes wi' slanty eyes pushin' wheelbarras aroond."

"China then?"

"Nah not there either, they're communists and it's really hard to get in. Anyways there's millions and millions of them and they're aall starvin'... they'd probably kill ye and eat ye when they see that belly of yours."

"Aahh divvent knaa man Chunk. Yer makin' it seem difficult."

"Look Albert... divvent bother with them faraway places man. Honest ter God and straight up... nee crossed fingers or nowt but aahh was in Burma for six months deein some killin' an' that. The whole country was full of baldy blokes in yeller dresses, bashin' tambourines and singin' aboot some bloke called Harvey Dishcloth or summat. It was mad oot there."

"Chunk man aahh just want ter gan somewhere that's not called local. Aah'm forty-five and aah've never been out of Northumberland."

"Aye Albert, aah get yer point." Chunk seemed deep in thought for a good few seconds before holding a finger up, "If aahh was you then aah'd gan ter Scotland. They've got canny big mountains and the world's best whisky. Another thing... most of the Scottish folk can understand English but fair do's they're not so good at speakin' it. And ye'll see loads of blokes wi' checky skirts on and wi' little black and white handbags boonsin aroond their clems. Some of them even stick cutlery doon their sock cos they aall eat this mince stuff

call'd haggis so they need to carry their own knife and fork...
cos things like cutlery are considered jewellery up there. Aye
Albert lad... that's where I'd go if I was you... and tell yer what
aah'll even come with yer if ye like."

On hearing that Jim and I looked at each other...
grimaced and then shrugged in unison. Now there was a
turn up for the proverbial book. Chunk and Albert indeed...
going on holiday together... naah surely not.

As it turned out they did go on holiday together. Not that
I was around when it happened because my life was about
to change big-time. When I left the pub that day I wasn't
to know about the forthcoming life change... and I wasn't
to know that apart from three or four further visits I would
abandon the Folly for ever. That was a shame because it had
become a hideaway for me and given me succour at a time
when I desperately needed it. I'll always remember that old
pub with great affection.

Anyway... enough of the girly stuff. It was time for moving
on. Back to the future. I had the second half of my life to
live and I was looking forward to the journey. It was a new
beginning and a time to consign the bad bits of the past to
the first handy dustbin.

CHAPTER 15

Gonna Send You Back To Walker

———————————————— ■ ————————————————

So to be perfectly honest I'd never been to Walker in my entire life. I'd heard about it of course in the Animals song and I sort of knew it was a depressed area of Newcastle out towards Wallsend way. Now that shipbuilding had more or less disappeared from the Tyne during the current Thatcher reign... Wallsend, Walker and Byker had become yet another depressing Tory wasteland... resembling many of the other North-East communities which had mines, shipbuilding, fishing and factories ripped out of their lives. What Hitler had failed to do had been accomplished instead by a self-righteous woman and a cabinet of wimps... or so I'd been led to believe. The truth of the matter of course was more complex than that.

When I left the Folly that afternoon I had no intention of making a phone call to that mystery woman... none at all. But I began churning over things in my own head... and mysteries once discovered tend to suck you in like quicksand. That one was no exception... and I was hooked. I still managed to put off the inevitable for a few hours but eventually I knew I had to find out who that Lozenge or Lorraine person was.

Ring-ring-ring... I was calling from a public phone box beside Blyth market place. As for the call itself... I'd been intrigued, so I decided to dive in and lance the proverbial boil before moseying along to the Oddfellows pub for a few flagons of nectar. I'd left the car in Shankhouse and on a healthy living whim had walked into Blyth down the Laverock then on through New Deleval and Newsham before the long trek down Plessey Road. I was knacked. It would be a taxi job for the return journey... definitely.

Ring-ring-ring... nothing, ring-ring-ring... nothing. I was about to give it up as a bad job when... ring-ring... "Hello."

I pushed my ten-pence into the slot and another straight after. My mouth was dry and my tongue felt as if it had knots in it, "Ermmm hiya, hello... I err... could I speak to Lorraine... I think."

The reply was instantaneous, "This is Lorraine-I-think speaking." Humour indeed... that was promising. "Sorry I took so long to answer I've just got out of the shower." I wish to God she hadn't told me that... my mind was immediately conjuring up visions that it shouldn't. Far-far too early of course to reply with 'so what ye wearin' like?'.

"Aye... err, sorry to disturb you but you left a message for me. My name is Jim and you... err, well... you left a message."

"Ohh yes... I remember. The intriguing advert in the newspaper. Blyth based businessman, nearing forty, would like to meet attractive female with good sense of humour... age range 18 to 80. Must have own teeth and no moustache. Is that the one?"

Ohhh God no... now I remembered. I'd been a wee bit drunk one afternoon and penned a silly advert for the lonelyhearts column thing. I'd forgotten all about it and the regret didn't kick in for a few days. I tried to cancel it but I'd posted it off and paid for the insertion with a postal order and it was too late to stop it. Bugger, I shouldn't have used the Folly phone number... what if loads of women replied and phoned up the pub. Jim Pint would go absolutely mental and I'd probably be barred.

"Aye that's the one. A bit daft I know?"

"No... I found it really funny. It stood out for me. It's the first time I've ever thought about replying... well even looking actually."

"Yeh... well, I've never done an advert in those columns before. I tried to stop it from going in."

"What for? It was a laugh... do you want to meet up?" she asked.

I jumped right in because I liked the voice on the other end of the line, "Yes... why not, okay."

"I'll have to go soon... I'm going to have to go and dry off. Are you free tomorrow? I'm living in Walker... so somewhere half-way say?"

Immediately my mind is imagining the drying off and it's myself doing the towelling. I was making a good job of it an' all. "Aye okay Lorraine. What about the Rex at Whitley Bay."

"Righto, what time?"

"Seven-thirty," I replied.

"Okay... how will I know you?"

I hadn't thought it through... so, "I'll wait outside the main entrance until you turn up. Can't having you walking in on your own. Just so you'll be extra sure it's me I'll be wearing a lettuce in my buttonhole."

I heard a chuckle, "Thank you... got to go. See you then."

"Right... good night."

"Good night Jim." Bzzzzzzz... the phone went down.

She probably won't turn up I thought to myself. I was hoping she would though because she sounded interesting. For some reason I wasn't feeling so knackered now as I headed off towards the Oddfellows.

There wasn't anyone I knew in the Oddfellows pub that evening. Although that's not completely true... because as I sat on my own having a quiet pint and a read of a newspaper, some bloke perhaps in his early thirties walked past the table and he was eyeballing me. I didn't feel uncomfortable because I thought I recognised the face but just couldn't place where I'd seen it before. He walked past again and cracked a smile... and I smiled back. I was rummaging around in the memory banks but they were empty and before I knew it the bloke had left with two male friends.

"Another pint please pet... and have a drink yourself," I smiled at the barmaid as I walked over and stood my empty glass on the bar.

"Thank you, I'll just put 50p in the tip box," she said as she pulled my pint and then put it on the counter before whisking away the empty one.

"If you don't mind me asking... can you tell me who that bloke was who's just left with his two pals. I just think that I should know him from somewhere but I can't place where. It must be ten years at least since I was last in here."

"Aahh... you mean Toss. He's on his best behaviour tonight."

"Toss?"

"That's not his proper name. It's John Meins. Lovely lad and he'd doing anything for anybody... sober. But he can be one heck of a handful when he's well served."

"John Meins... ohhh my goodness. That's my cousin and I didn't even recognise him or try to talk to him."

"We all change when we're growing older," she offered, "He mustn't have been sure about you either... cos he didn't speak to you."

"Aye aah suppose. Any idea where he might have gone?"

She shrugged, "Haven't the foggiest... sorry."

"No matter... but can I pay for a pint of his favourite tipple and leave it in the pump for him? Let him know it's from his cousin Jim."

"Yep... I'm sure he'll appreciate it especially on one of his hard-up days. Does cousin Jim have a surname?" She grinned.

"Bates... Jim Bates."

I paid up for the pump pint and then enjoyed another pint of my own and a finish of the newspaper. I left the Oddfellows shortly afterwards... thanking the barmaid as I left. I decided to have a wander across town to explore another old haunt... The Joiners. One pint there and then another at the pub opposite... The Masons Arms before a swift phone call for a taxi and that was it... the end of my solo night out. However, I now I had a date to look forward to the following evening... at least I thought it was a date. I wasn't so sure... because I was badly out of practice.

My thoughts that night were thankfully all positive apart from the looming sum of twelve hundred pounds which needed finding sharpish. I have to say that life was taking on a calmer and more radiant hue (I put that in because it sounds better than 'life was geet muckle canny').

Rex Hotel – December 15th, 1988. Still ten days to Christmas and two-and a-bit weeks to go until next year makes an appearance. I'm standing outside the front entrance of the Rex, all done up like a dog's dinner. I'm wearing my best suit with a white shirt (bought that morning) ... my other ones needed washing, shoes polished and glinting in the light from the lamp-post. I'm sporting my best double-breasted top-coat with the fake fur collar. The coat was a bit dated to be fair but I thought that turning up in a cagoule might make me look like a trainspotter or a twitcher. First impressions count because you can only make them once. My hair had been neatly trimmed, my face had just been scraped hairless without a single nick to hide and I'd splashed on some expensive after-shave I'd bought on Blyth market... 'aye that'll be right'. My pits and nether regions had been Right-Guarded... my underwear was passably cleanish and decent enough in case I was knocked down and had my trousers cut off in hospital. All bases covered and everything tickety-boo... so there I stood ready to go and primed for action.

It had crossed my mind that I didn't know how old Lorraine was. She hadn't said and I hadn't asked. All I knew for certain was... if she'd read the advert properly... that she had her own teeth, a hairless top lip, and she was somewhere between eighteen and eighty. With that thought I took a step further back into the hotel doorway. If I saw any female approaching with a hopeful look on her face and she looked anything like Hilda Ogden... then I would be offski... like the proverbial rocket... goodnight Vienna.

I'd noticed a little red Daihatsu car drive slowly past about five minutes before and there had been a nice-looking woman peering out. I'd sort of hoped that it might be her but if it was she was taking a mighty long time. Maybe she's looked at me and thought 'Pffft... no way bonny lad'... or not so bonny lad possibly. There again perhaps she'd driven past and couldn't spot a lettuce. She may not have picked up on the humour. Shut up Jim she's only a few minutes late... or not coming at all. Anyway... if she doesn't turn up you can have twice as much to drink because you won't be paying for someone else. Every cloud has a silver lining... except of course those long wispy cirrus ones you sometimes see because they're not fat enough to have a lining. They're like normal clouds but with an eating disorder. For God's sake Jim shut your brain down and give it a rest.

"Hello" a voice from the side I hadn't been scanning. I'd been looking in the other direction that the Daihatsu had travelled. I turned and saw a bonny face. She was wearing one of those belted white raincoat affairs. She looked really smart and attractive.

She spoke again, "I've had a heck of a job getting parked. So... are you Jim?"

"Err, yeh errrmm yeh."

"You don't sound too sure?" she smiled.

"No-no, sorry errmm it's definitely me. I've been me for most of my life... well, all of my life actually." I smiled back.

"No lettuce then?" she pointed towards my lapel.

I held my hands out... palms up, shrugged, and gave her an apologetic look, "I did have... honest, but I was attacked by a rabbit."

That reply was the best ice-breaker I've ever used. We were both still chuckling even after we'd made our way into the lounge area and had taken our seats. I ordered our drinks. A pint for me and an orange juice for Lorraine. She wouldn't risk alcohol because she was driving... although she did tell me that her usual tipple was whisky and lemonade. Ehhh?... She was obviously not a malt aficionado... lemonade sploshed in whisky for the love of God... yuk-yuk and thrice yuk.

Apart from her whisky foolishness that evening went down really well. Lorraine was forty-three... five years older than myself. She worked in the chiropody department at Sanderson hospital... wherever that was because I hadn't heard of it. She'd worked most of her years in the NHS. Divorced with two grown up and left home offspring and a couple of grandkids. She had a flat in Walker... and a mortgage and had recently moved from West Denton. The chat came easy and conversation motored along as if we'd known each other for months instead of minutes. She'd gone first with the potted life history and then there was a period of silence.

Then the bit I'd been dreading. It was my turn to do the life-story thingy... and therein lay the conundrum. Should I go with the... 'I'm working undercover for MI5 trying to infiltrate an international crime syndicate who are flooding the country with counterfeit Revels'. Or do I just go with the truth and hope for the best? She'd been so honest with me... so truth it was which won out.

My potted history didn't sound too clever to be honest. Nevertheless I soldiered on through all the relationships... and the bipolar serotonin episode. The family history and my two daughters. Then on through the working life and job history which must have sounded more like a weekly shopping list. I left a few out but that was primarily to stop boredom setting in. Charlie, Tug, Sid and Frances figured prominently in my discourse and there were more than a few humorous moments discussing those four. Finally I gave the rundown on the lingerie business and the tax-man fiasco. I'd been unsure as to whether I should include the court appearance and the current financial problem but for some reason I felt comfortable with this lady and I let it all hang out. I finished with my last few months in Shankhouse, the Folly, and my stall on Blyth market. There was no more to tell.

There wasn't a hint of judgement in her response, "Wow... you've had one interesting life. Much more interesting than my feeble offering," she said.

"Believe me Lorraine feeble would do the trick for me. I wish my life had seen more feeble and less chaos."

"You've been very honest Jim. I like that."

I gave a shrug, "There's not much point in beginning a relationship with a string of porkies."

"So we're beginning a relationship are we?" She smiled as she said it.

"Dunno... it's not up to me. It has to be unanimous."

"Well it gets my vote."

"Aye... mine too," I agreed.

"There you go then... sorted. Do you fancy meeting up in Newcastle at the weekend? All the girls from work are meeting up for our pre-Christmas jolly."

That was when my first untruth of the evening surfaced. Walking into a Newcastle bar to meet a bevy of females wasn't high on my list of 'favourite things to do'.

"Yeh... sure if I can make it. I've some loose ends to tie up in Hull. If I get back in time I'll definitely pop in." I think she believed me.

"Good... I hope you can. Give me a call to let me know either way. The girls will be letting their hair down and will be dying to meet you when I tell them all about you."

That comment put the final kybosh on any chance of me turning up. Drunk women indeed? I had an instant vision of the evening. It would be like walking into a sozzled Tupperware party with the women all showing off their fancy boxes. Body swerve required... absolutely.

"I've got to go now Jim," Lorraine said as she glanced at her watch, "Do you need a lift?"

"Thanks for the offer Lorraine but I've got the taxi booked for quarter to eleven. Can't let them down cos I use them regularly."

With that we said our goodbyes for the evening. A helping on with the coat and a swift peck on the cheek and then she was gone. It had been a good night I thought to myself. Whether it would go any further I wasn't sure. I stayed behind and had another pint before leaving.

CHAPTER 16

Walk Of Life

———————◆———————

Shamefully, I did give the girl's night out a miss. I honestly couldn't face it. Male cowardice was rearing its timorous head. Instead I spent that particular day and evening at the Folly. I rang Lorraine around about six o'clock, apologised and told her I wasn't going to get back from Hull until the early hours. She seemed disappointed. I felt guilty about the lie but also relieved. I promised to phone in a day or two.

As predicted Jim the Pint went through me like a dose of salts when I showed my face in the Folly that morning. I thought I may as well get it over with, so I went to face the music early doors. I was waiting outside when he opened up at five minutes before eleven.

Seemingly there hadn't been too many phone calls from interested women he informed me but there'd been a few who'd given him grief about the wording of my advert. No doubt toothless ladies without a sense of humour and sporting profuse facial hair I remarked.

His extreme grumpiness only lasted for fifteen minutes before he calmed down and lapsed into his normal level of grumpiness. When he did we sat and chatted. There were only the two of us in the pub at that time and it became the most strange and confusing half hour. We didn't talk about the normal men things... football, booze and boobs or the price of tabs and petrol. No sir, Jim Pint was on some sort of a mission and he began philosophising. About weird and wonderful things like the meaning of life... and is there a God? and what happens to an idea when no-one's thinking it anymore?... Ehhh?

Jim was certainly acting a tad quirky that morning. All I could do was sit and listen... he was on a roll and coming out with thought provoking insights.

"Ye knaa Jimmy...every person alive today is destined to die... nee argument there... but then they'll be forgotten and eventually their houses will be lived in by complete strangers who won't know a thing about them. Complete strangers wandering about in the same rooms where those dead folk had lived and breathed, had fights and arguments... laughed and cried and brought up their families. Life will continue regardless only they won't be a part of it... not even a memory. So what is it all for? What's the point of it all?"

For the next few seconds Jim seemed to be staring out into a future that I couldn't see and wasn't a part of. He gave a shudder then suddenly came back to earth, giving his head a shake before finally coming out with...

"Jimmy, a bit of advice for ye. Divvent be so bothered about buyin' fancy things just to impress other folk... cos believe me... they won't be. I'm including that lass ye've just met. When you're gone naebody will remember your expensive possessions... and ye sartinly cannit tek them wi' ye. Honestly man, no-one truly admires anyone's expensive possessions other than themselves." Then he pulled his sleeve back and stuck his wrist in front of my face, "That's a Rolex Jimmy... a proper one, not a fake and it's worth a bliddy small fortune," he gave a rueful smile, "But if you ever talk about me in the future... when I'm dead and gone, I bet you won't say... 'Jim from the Folly... nah can't remember him... but I remember his Rolex... boy did we have some good times together... me and that time-piece. No, it's people Jimmy... it's people that make your life worthwhile... not fancy things." He pulled his sleeve back in place and lapsed into silence.

Bloody hell... what was that all about. Jim Pint had morphed into Confucius and to be honest it worried me. I thought that he may have been given some bad health news and he was attempting to make sense of his life before facing the end-game. There again perhaps I was overthinking the situation. Maybe he'd just been leafing through a Readers Digest and had remembered some of the quotations to show off with.

I wasn't to find out because just as I was about to ask Jim where all that philosophy had sprung from and was he okay health wise... Chunk came booling into the pub like a bull having spotted a field-full of cows. Some people can glide over the ground and some can tread softly. Chunk always crashed.

He came in loudly... as per usual and having spotted me sitting at the bar he opened up that huge gob of his and began singing the old Tottenham Hotspur 'Nice one Cyril' song with all the words changed around.

"Nice one Jimmy... nice one son... Jimmy took his pants off... to go and have some fun." He was grinning and laughing like a horse. So I told him precisely that.

"Chunk man... yer laughin' like a horse."

His grin was even broader now, "Mevvys so Jim Book, but it's you who's had his oats, not me."

"Howay man Chunk, give ower. There's a lady present."

That stopped him immediately and he glanced around the room. He couldn't spot anyone and gave me a puzzled look, "So where is she?"

"The owld woman wi' the beard servin' behind the bar." I nodded in the direction of Jim Pint. The comment fell on stony ground and I received a foul look from Jim in return. I had to turn away... but at least it shut Chunk up... almost. He ordered his pint.

"So Jimmy Booky... did ye get some nooky?"

"Chunk man, I only met the woman last night. And she's canny, actually."

"So nee nooky? Nae wonder yer a Sunderland fan."

That comment didn't make any sense, "So when's the last time Newcastle won the cup or the league?"

"Ehhh? aahh divvent knaa man. Aahh was just mekkin a daft comment. I follow Liverpool anyway."

That was a surprise, "Liverpool... yer kiddin' right... what d'yer follow them buggers for. Were ye brought up there or summat?"

"Nah... aah've never even been to Liverpool. But they win everythin' man. Nee point following a bunch of no hopers."

The conversation had found its way back onto dry land. Thankfully he forgot about my night out and we spent the next twenty minutes talking normal men things. Beer going up to a pound a pint and tabs to a pound-fifty... the Clapham

Junction rail crash and the mounting toll of fatalities. Margaret Thatcher... and what method of torture we'd use if we had her tied up with barbed wire in an empty mine-shaft. Then Chunk suddenly went into spitfire mode. One of his great pleasures was going to the pictures... and he spent the next few minutes enthusing about a film he'd watched called 'My Stepmother is an Alien' and describing Kim Basinger's breasts in great detail.

Just then Albert fell into the pub... which was a relief because I'm sure Chunk was working himself into an orgasmic frenzy with the Kim Basinger stuff.

"Bliddy lino," came the shout as Albert stumbled in through the pub doorway, bent over and trying keep his balance. "Somebody's gannin to set their neck if that's not fixed," he looked flushed and embarrassed.

"Aye Albert that'll be you man... cos every bugger else has the sense to lift their feet up," shouted Chunk, "There's a pint in the pump for ye... mek sure ye divvent trip ower and spill it."

Albert glanced over, grinning, and saw me sitting at our usual table, "Hi Jimmy Bates, you look happy. Did that woman show you her busters? And did ye do kissy stuff?"

That was a surprise intro from Albert. He'd certainly come out of his shell since palling up with Chunk. I wasn't sure if that was a good or a bad thing. Perhaps neither... maybe just a life thing. I didn't reply to the kissy question. I didn't fancy starting Chunk's motor up again.

Albert joined us and took his usual place beside Chunk. He didn't pursue the date question. We sat quietly for a while just comfortable in our collective company. It was myself who finally kicked off the chat.

"I'm thinking of packing the stall in Albert." I said, laying the information out there without preamble.

There was no immediate reply. I think that both of them were busy digesting that surprise pronouncement. It took a while before Albert spoke.

"But what about my job... ye know... if ye do pack in?"

"I know. Sorry about that Albert but there's not much I can do. It wasn't a proper job anyway. It was just helping out."

"Aye but I like it and I get to meet lots of people. Anyway... what are ye packin' in for?"

"Well to be honest Albert it's just time for me to be movin' on. The market doesn't make enough for a full-time wage and to be fair it's going slowly downhill. I just need to be doing something different. I don't know what yet, not precisely, but it feels like the right time."

"Is that cos ye've got that new bit of fluff on the go?" Chunk chipped in.

"Nah... honestly. That's got nowt to do with it. I don't even know if I'll see her again. No, it's simply because it's one of those times when I've realised a change is needed. My life needs a shake up, otherwise I'll keep on chugging along and then before you know it I'll be in a rut of my own making and sooner or later it'll be too late to climb out of it."

"Bloody hell," said Chunk, "Could ye not have just said that yer bored?"

I grinned, "Aye it was a bit long winded."

There was silence for a while... then, "Can I buy it off ye Jim Book?"

That was a surprise. I hadn't really thought the whole process through.

"What do you want to buy it for Chunk? You've got other irons in the fire for makin' money."

"Aye... well another one won't hurt will it? It'll be like another bow to my arrow string thing... ye know what I mean?"

"Ermmm, well to be honest Chunk I haven't given it much thought. It doesn't make a lot of money you know."

"As long as it makes some money then that's extra isn't it? Anyway Albert could keep on doing the selling. I wouldn't be doing much."

Albert jumped in, "We could go halfers Chunk cos I've got some money."

"Aye well that all depends on whether Jim Book is going to sell it and how much he wants." Chunk replied.

All eyes were on me. I could even feel Jim Pint's eyes weighing up the situation from behind the bar and his ears twitching.

It only took us a matter of minutes to come to an arrangement. We agreed that those two, Chunk and Albert, would take over immediately. All stock and the pitch would change hands. My shrinking pile of leaflets would be Chunk's responsibility to deliver and do the pickups. I gave him the details of the printer who'd done the work for me because the flyers would need replenishing fairly urgently. I also made out a list of the areas I'd already collected from. Jim Pint then weighed in and told the pair of them that they could carry on using the side room for the collection and storage of stock but he'd need to charge them ten pounds a month. They agreed. In return for my mini business I would receive a hundred pounds and all of my drinks would be paid for by Albert and Chunk until closing time that evening.

We shook on it. Done deal. A good outcome for me because I'd been going to pack in the stall without any cash changing hands.

Bob the Knob showed his face soon after our business had been concluded, followed shortly afterwards by John the Milk with his wired-up jaw. He spent the next few hours sipping beer through a straw. He'd had to bring his own straw because the Folly didn't cater for fancy stuff like that.

John became the centre of attention that afternoon and proceeded to tell us some cock and bull story about the jaw break incident. I listened but couldn't be bothered to become involved in the conversation. My mind was now working overtime. What on earth was I going to do next?

I left the pub that afternoon having had far too much to drink but happy enough. I had another free session to look forward to that evening. Getting shot of the stall and books had lifted one weight from my shoulders. Now there was just the looming tax bill to be tackled.

It was later than usual when I returned to the Folly that evening. I'd crashed on my bed after the afternoon session and had slept the sleep of the inebriated. When I awoke I was famished and wanted something substantial to eat... a horse would have done the trick. The nearest chippy would end up having a desperate visit but first I needed a change of clothes.

I realised that I had nothing clean to wear. My entire wardrobe was needing a trip to the laundrette. In fact I think some items of underwear had already walked off in that direction by themselves in protest. I proceeded to pick out the cleanest clothes from the growing grubby pile after having a quick sniff. To be honest they weren't extremely hacky but just to mask any hidden odours I gave myself a mammoth doosh of Brut aftershave and umpteen squirts of Right Guard. Job's a good'un... free pints time.

Fish and chips, two patties and a fishcake were nestling happily in my tum by the time I eventually made landfall at the pub. No Bob the Knob or John Milk present. It was just myself, Chunk and Albert in our little corner that evening. Down at the far end of the room two young blokes were playing darts on the monstrosity of a lumpy dartboard. They seemed not to care about that but they kept stopping and scanning the room. I watched them for a little while then thought to myself... 'if you're on the lookout for totty pal you're going to be mightily disappointed'.

The thought was no sooner out of my head when two bits of young totty walked in. Good looking lasses with cracking figures. The two lads spotted them, smiled and waved before turning back to the dartboard. Chunk saw what was going on.

"Couple of stiffies gannin on doon the other end Jimmy. What in buggery's name are young'uns deein' in a dump like this?"

"Leavin' it looks like Chunk."

One of the lasses who had given the pub a quick once over and was totally unimpressed, marched down to the far end and began making her displeasure known to the two lads. I couldn't blame the lass. Who on earth had arranged a date in a pub which was nothing more than a pigeon ducket with beer pumps. The lads looked sheepish as they struggled into their coats and headed for the door. The two lasses had easily beaten them to it. Not one of the four gave as much as a 'cheers' in Jim Pint's direction when they exited.

True to their word Chunk and Albert were keeping the drinks flowing. Not only that but Chunk handed over a hundred pounds in fives and tens.

"Is that a done deal Jimmy?"

"Aye Chunk thank you. The business now belongs to you and Albert."

"In that case ye can now call me Chunky Book and Albert will be Albert Dickens," Chunk chortled at his own attempt at humour and I grinned back. I didn't know if they'd make a go of it but I was certainly hoping so.

Then I was somewhat sidelined as Chunk and Albert began tossing names about for their new business endeavour. Daft stuff.

"What about Albert and Chunk's Books?" Albert offered.

"Nah... we need somethin' better than that... like World's Best Books."

"What about Paperback Writer? Ye knaa, like the Beatles song."

"Definitely not, aahh divvent like them Beatles. What about Rock Around the Clock by Bill Haley?" Chunk was being enthusiastic even though he was losing the plot.

Albert looked confused, "What's that got to dee wi' books?"

"Bill Haley must have read some books man."

I took the opportunity to slip away and sidle over to the bar and leave those two to their bizarre planning exercise. I sat myself down on a bar stool and ordered myself a large whisky.

"Who's paying for that one Jim?"

"Me... so don't bother them. It's like the Wizard of Oz ower there and they're both on the Yellow Brick Road... the tin man and the scarecrow."

Jim gave a snort, "Bell's do ye?"

"No Jim, give me a decent one... if ye've got a single malt."

"Course I have, cheeky sod." He bent down, his head disappeared, and after a few seconds emerged again. He'd produced a bottle of Macallan from under the counter. He opened it and proceeded to pour a glass for me... no optic required and it was much fuller than it should have been. I handed a fiver over and he produced my change from a tin, once again from under the bar counter. I didn't count the change... it would have been rude.

"Private stock Jim?"

"Aye... but keep it under yer hat." He grinned and poured a wee glass for himself. He was just about to wet his lips when the door opened. Kids again no doubt. I turned and was most surprised to see the hockey player lady breezing in with the older guy following her. That was strange. I thought they'd had their bellyful of Chunk's loud comments the last time.

"Evening."

I assumed that was directed at me so I replied, "Aye it certainly is."

The woman had a nice smile, "No flies on you then," she grinned.

Humour indeed. The older guy by this time was standing beside her and he ordered their drinks. In my head I'm thinking 'I hope he doesn't start with the bum squeezing again when I'm sitting here'. I didn't know whether I should move back to join Albert and Chunk. To do so immediately would look really iffy on my part... so I carried on sipping at my single malt.

Then unexpectedly the man looked directly at me and spoke, "It's a bit nippy out tonight."

I couldn't do other than reply, "It certainly is."

He pointed to my tumbler which I'd almost drained, "Can I stick anything in there for you?"

The mind boggled. I wasn't quite sure what the anything was that he wanted to stick in my glass... and would I want to drink from it afterwards. So I erred on the side of caution and politeness.

"I'm drinking single malt... it's a wee bit pricey. But thank you for asking."

"Then I'll have the same." He smiled at Jim, "Two single malts landlord and one for yourself if you'll join me."

"I certainly will," Jim grinned, "And what about the lady?"

"Just an orange juice for my wife. It's her turn to drive." He gave his wife a rueful smile and a pat on the shoulder.

Well that resolved the mystery that had us so confused during their previous visit. The husband wasn't in fact bifocal and his good lady wasn't a transistor. The fellow was within his marital rights to squeeze his wife's bum whenever he felt like it. I didn't blame him one iota.. it looked extremely squishable from where I sat... fortunately just out of reach.

"So what persuaded you to come back to the Folly?" I asked, "Most folk don't." I knew Jim Pint wouldn't be best pleased with that remark but I was merely stating a fact.

It was his wife who answered, "To see you actually."

"Ehhh... me?" Now I was worried. Maybe it was the tax heavy squad. Perhaps I should contort my features and attempt to look like someone else.

"Unless I'm mistaken and have lost my memory for faces, you sold me some lingerie in Partick."

I raised my eyebrows, "Partick... good grief that must have been two years ago... and not our finest hour."

"Yes," she replied and laughed, "I remember some of the pub regulars were a little boisterous."

I had to smile at that, "I'm afraid your idea of little and my idea of little are diametrically opposed."

She laughed again, "Ha-ha, yes it was over the top that night, Partick pubs and scantily clad girls are not a good combination."

"So how come it's taken you two years to track me down. If you're chasing a belated refund... you've got the wrong man... I just look remarkably like that lingerie bloke?"

She shook her head, "Refund?... no, I don't want a refund. The lingerie was quality... top class. It had this old duffer jumping around like a cat on a hot-tin-roof for weeks," she chuckled, taking hold of her husband's tie... pulling his head down and planting a kiss on his cheek, "Didn't it Casanova?"

Her husband gave an embarrassed grin, looked me in the eye and stuck out a hand, "My name is Roger... not duffer. Casanova maybe... on a good day."

I gave his hand a shake... the return pressure was firm and meant. "Pleased to meet you, I'm James... James Bates."

"I'm after some more lingerie," hockey lady elbowed in and continued, "That's why I'm here because I was sure I'd recognised you. I'm thinking that maybe you're here to do another of your lingerie shows?"

I held a palm up to stop her, "Sorry but no. I sold the business some time ago. I'm here because I'd had enough of Hull... that's where Night Shadow lingerie was based. I felt it was time to return to my roots, my home town. So here I am for better or worse."

She looked disappointed, but only mildly so. "My name is Becky by the way... Rebecca to my mother," she smiled and offered a hand. I took it and shook it. It was a typical woman shake... limp. I wondered if I'd been meant to kiss the hand. I decided that wasn't the case.

"So if you live local whatever were you doing in Partick?"

"We don't live around here. In fact the only reason we were in the pub the other night was because we'd taken a few wrong turns on our way back from Morpeth. Roger had been attending one of those boring business conference things for something or other. No, we actually live in West Kilbride. It was a licensee friend of mine who'd heard about your lingerie show and I went along with her that particular evening for a laugh. Roger of course found a reason to give it a miss."

We'd been overheard from the corner table and Chunk couldn't contain himself... and shouted. "Ask her if his name is Roger... or is that what he does?" Chunk guffawed at what he considered his witty repartee.

Roger grinned and to my surprise he shouted back, "Both actually. The name I've had for ever and the other one I'm getting better at." And that made Chunk chortle even louder.

"Sorry about that," I apologised, "He's a bit... you know?"

"Don't worry about it. I always think to myself... if you can't beat the buggers you may as well join them." Roger smiled and drained his glass. He held a finger up for a refill of all our drinks and even asked Jim Pint to send a drink over for the two reprobates in the corner. It was turning into an okay night.

The conversation after that was most interesting. Those two were really open and friendly and gave a potted description of their lives. Their house sounded as if it was really posh... and the area in which they lived even more so. They had two children both of whom were in boarding school in Yorkshire. Twin boys no less. Roger was some sort of a big-noise in a chemical and paper supply company. Becky had been his personal assistant and they'd ended up like most boss and personal assistant relationships do... they married. Becky had truthfully played hockey for England having been born in Shropshire but that had been in her pre-children days. Now she filled in her hours with charity work and a part-time job working with the National-Trust for Scotland. Eventually their revelations came to a halt and the spotlight turned onto myself.

"So James, what's next on the agenda for yourself now that you've sold up your lingerie business... another business venture perhaps?" It was Roger asking the question.

"Dunno precisely Roger. Funnily enough my time in Hull was spent producing chemicals. Then I left and went into chemical sales. After that a few temporary enterprises before noticing a gap in the market for quality lingerie. Ann Summers of course was on the go but I reckoned quality merchandise that was attractive as well as saucy would be successful. We didn't ever think of trying to go down the sex toy and wind-up walking-willy route and to be truthful the response was far greater than I'd expected."

Roger ignored the lingerie but focused on the chemicals. "Who were you with on the chemical side of things?"

"BP for four years. Most of the time spent producing phthalates for the paint industry and hospital grade alcohol for Distillers. Then I decided on a career change. I spent a while with Swan Chemicals selling a broad spectrum of chemical products to industry mostly... but hospitals produced a lot of lucrative orders too."

"Hmmm I know of Bob Tanfield at Swan. Kendal they're based isn't it? you've got a solid base in chemicals then James. Any thoughts about going down that route for your next adventure."

"Can't you talk anything else but business you old duffer?" Becky piped up and gave Roger a shoulder punch. She'd been chatting with Jim Pint but was now looking bored. "Anyway it's time we were going. Early start tomorrow. I have to take the hire car back before we go for the train."

Roger gave me a grin and a shrug. "Here James... take this." He handed me a business card. "Give me a buzz if you fancy going back into chemical sales. I've a small company crying out for new blood... if they're worth their salt of course. Company car is only a Cavalier I'm afraid."

Then Becky was tugging at his sleeve, "Come on Roger for heaven's sake before you bore the pants off all our new acquaintances." He shrugged, finished off his whisky, and did as he was told whilst she was giving a brief wave and smile to each of us in turn, even to Chunk and Albert. Then before we knew it they'd left... and after a minute or so came the sound of a car engine gunning outside the pub, and then a throaty whine... swiftly diminishing as they sped off south, heading towards High Pit and on to Newcastle.

The evening ended drama free but with myself somewhat sidelined. Albert and Chunk were now the book people and were engrossed in the mapping out of their business. I did mosey over in order to give Albert an old brooch which had turned up in one of the book bags. I thought his mother might like it. He thanked me but then immediately returned to his planning chat with Chunk.

Jim Pint and I had more or less concluded any meaningful conversation and as I sat at the bar the periods of silence were growing longer. I wasn't disappointed when last orders were called and no lock-in was offered. Time for bed and the beginning of another period in my life.

I lay awake for a while that night, mulling over the incidents of the day. The book business had reached a successful and unexpected conclusion. The job offer was also an unexpected development and I'd need to give it some serious thought. But first things first because while I'd been talking with Roger and Becky I'd suddenly thought of Lorraine and the untruth I'd presented in order to avoid a night out with her work colleagues. That wasn't a noble thing to do. I made the decision to give her a call the very next day.

Sunday morning, just after ten o'clock. I'd arranged to meet up with my dad at the Duke of Wellington club for a catch up and a game of bingo later on. But first things first... a phone call.

Ring-ring-ring, a pause, ring-ring-ring... "Hello."

"Oh, hi is that Lorraine?"

"Yes."

"Hi, it's Jim... from the Rex. The bloke with the missing lettuce."

"Ha-ha, hi Jim. When are you due back from Hull?"

Another lie, "I just got back half-an-hour ago."

"And your first thought was to call me?"

"Aye, sort of."

"Good... have you got a piece of paper and a pen handy?"

"Hang on a sec." I put the phone down on the shelf and gave my pockets a quick search. I did indeed have a notebook and pen in my jacket pocket. I made a mental note to hand the book over to Albert and Chunk. It contained the market payment details and a list of the pick-up areas.

I retrieved the phone and held it between shoulder and ear with my pen and notebook at the ready. "Yeh I've got them... all set."

Lorraine proceeded to give me her address in Walker and directions to transport myself there if coming from Blyth.

I scribbled away as she talked. "Right, got that... if I can understand my own handwriting."

"Ha-ha, I have the same problem. So I'll see you about two o'clock then."

"What... when?"

"Today for your Sunday dinner of course. We arranged it... on our night out at the Rex. I invited you for Sunday dinner if you'd managed to get back from Hull in time. You haven't forgotten have you?"

"I had actually... but thank you. The thing is I haven't anything decent to wear. I'm in need of a trip to the laundrette." I was trying to wriggle out of it.

"Pile your things into a bag and I'll put them in the wash for you."

"But we've only just... I mean... you can't be doing that for someone you hardly know."

"Why not?"

You can't send a shrug down a phone line, but I tried, "I don't know."

"Right then that's sorted. I'll have to go and start preparing. See you at two... and try not to be late. Cold dinner isn't nice."

"Okey-Dokey I'll see..." I didn't get to finish the sentence. The phone had been put down at the other end. By gum that lady was a bit pushy. So, like it or not it was to be Sunday dinner in Walker for me... and my life was about to change... big time.

CHAPTER 17

Go Now

———————————————■———————————————

So to be completely frank I hadn't expected my first meal at Lorraine's to be in the company of her mother, her daughter Ingrid and her two toddlers... Christopher and Emma. I walked in carrying a holdall of dirty washing which wasn't the best of entrances. I was somewhat gobsmacked... but nevertheless after the initial introductions I tried manfully to be on my best behaviour. The kids for some unknown reason made a beeline for me. So, trying to impress and show what a mighty fine fellow I was I made a great fuss of them. The kids were all for it of course and it seemed to go down rather well with the adult audience too.

The dinner was really nice apart from the broccoli and cauliflower. I wasn't into veg at that time... rabbits and dieting women ate vegetables. I was a pie and chips fellow. Nevertheless I managed to eat the green stuff and the cauli and the food filled a hole but I was anxious to be off after it disappeared. I was feeling as if I was under the microscope which made me uncomfortable and way out of my comfort zone. However it had already been decided that I was staying for tea as well... arranged not by myself but by the mother and the daughter who began firing questions at me like detectives interviewing a suspect. If only it had been a police questioning I could have kept repeating 'no comment,' like they do all the time on 'Morse' and 'Lewis' but unfortunately that wasn't an option. So within a very short space of time the two of them had extracted more information from me than I'd volunteered on my date with Lorraine. I didn't sign a confession though.

Then it was time for the family members to return to their own homes... and guess who had to do the transporting?... aye, Jim boy. Fortunately I'd stuck a couple of gallons of petrol in the tank before setting off.

Daughter Ingrid and the kids lived only about a mile away on a rough looking council estate and I dropped them off first. Doris the mother however lived a good distance away in sheltered housing. So West Denton was my next port of call and Lorraine's mother kept up a constant stream of chatter as I tried to find my way across the city. I didn't know how old she was and didn't like to ask but she was knocking on a bit so I made sure I escorted her to her front door before taking my leave.

I'd made an arrangement to return to Lorraine's flat the following evening because she assured me my mucky laundry would all be washed and dried by then. I was hoping she'd been inoculated against beriberi and typhoid. The day in all honesty had gone better than I'd expected after my initial nervous introduction. So I was feeling quite chipper as I drove away from West Denton and headed for Shankhouse. Now it was time for a few jars of nectar at my local pigeon ducket.

There was only myself and Chunk from the famous five in attendance that particular evening. Jim Pint was behind the bar as per usual and there were also two oldish blokes sitting quite close to our gang's table when I arrived shortly after eight.

"Hi Jimmy kemmycaaaal," shouted an inebriated Chunk from our table as I made my way to the bar. He sounded full of drink. Jim Pint warned me to watch out because our friend was stotting. He'd been on a bender.

I took the advice on board, looked over and gave a grin, "Hi Chunk, what's that all about... the Jimmy Chemical thing?"

Chunk must have been doing some serious arm-bending. He was slurring some of his words and his eyes were glazed, "Well I've got to call you summat. Yer not Jimmy Book nee mair... cos aah'mm Chunky-Chunky Booky and that posh bloke just gave ye a new job sellin' kelmer wotsits... chelercums. S'not improttant man... not impottran aahh just thinked up a new name for ye."

I shrugged at that, "He offered but I haven't accepted yet," I said as I carried my pint to the table."

"Are you not tekkin the graft then Jimmy boy?"

"I dunno Chunk. I've no idea about terms and conditions. Is there a basic wage or is it commission only? I haven't a clue whether I'd be expected to work up in Scotland. Anyway the guy could just have been showin' off and playing at being mister big shot."

"Cupmanny car though." Chunk was certainly well gone with the ale.

"Aye that's true. I quite fancy that. Anyway where's Albert?"

He gave a snort, "We're not joined at the hip man. Anyway wor Albert's buggered off to the hoosey-hoosey wi' the owld lady. Aall the fives aah'mm still alive... eight and seven... aahmm off ter heaven."

The two old blokes at the next table must have had their fill of Chunk. They picked up their drinks and moved away down the other end. Chunk didn't like it... he'd taken it personally and shouted at their retreating backs, "Summat aahh said was it... hey-hey dickheads... d'yer knaa who I am? Aahmm Chunky Booky muckle-smart cookie." He was mortal drunk.

I tried to carry on as if nothing was happening, "But I thought Albert's mam was dying."

"So did Albert... but she keeps hingin' on. That owld boot's not gannin ter pop hor clogs man, she's messin wi' his heed, she's a witch... hubble-bubble... tripe and onions... fee fum fo-fo. That's beside the point man. Albert gave her that joolry stuff... that brooch thingamajig and she magicked hersel' better. She thowt she'd put it on and gan oot flashin' it roond. She was flattered."

"She was flattered?"

"Aye."

"With the brooch?"

"Nah... by a steamroller." He began howling and laughing like a drain. He was well away with the fairies. Suddenly the laughing ceased, he gave a big belch and he banged his fist down hard on the table. It sent my pint flying... away from me thankfully but I still jumped up in case my trousers got a soaking. Jim Pint vacated the bar and came rushing over.

"Chunk man... howay. I think ye've had enough."

Chunk was trying to focus but his eyes were rolling all over the shop, "Ye knaa what thought did divvent ye? Haddaway hairy face afore ye get yer arse kicked." Then without another word he laid his head down on the beery table, closed his eyes and began to snore.

"Bugger... what am I gannin' ter dee wi' him?" Jim Pint looked worried. "I don't fancy my chances... kickin him oot."

"Aah'd dee nowt for the time being Jim. Let him lie. He might have pulled himself together by closing." To be honest it didn't seem likely because Chunk sounded like a pneumatic drill.

"Aye... but what if he hasn't?"

"I'll stay until closing and if he's still in a state then we'll phone for a taxi and hoy the bugger in. If he fancies takin' a swing just mek sure ye duck. We'll let his wife handle all the the flack at the other end. You've got his address haven't you?"

"Not his address. Aahh knaa it's just past Etal Road... on Laverock Hall Road, ... but aah've nee idea what number."

"So we'll just tell the taxi bloke to dump him on Laverock Hall Road. Surely he must have staggered home in a state before."

"Aye okay Jimmy, that sounds like a plan," he clapped me on the shoulder, "Howay I'll pull ye a pint and we'll have a whisky." Jim Pint seemed relieved that I'd offered to hang back with him. He wasn't relishing the prospect of having to deal with Chunk on his own.

I thought I'd better go and have a word with the two old blokes and give some sort of apology, but they were already finishing their drinks and donning coats. It appeared they'd seen enough for one evening... so I left them alone. It wasn't my pub after all.

Jim Pint didn't charge for the whiskies and I put away more than a few as we sat and talked. There was just we two... with Chunk still comatose, snoring and farting and supplying a noisy soundtrack. We ignored it for the most part and carried on chewing the fat until, after a period of relative calm and quiet, Chunk suddenly produced a huge rattling, squelchy, explosion. Jim and I looked at each other... and that moment of eye contact set us off. We couldn't do anything other than burst into silly laughter. How weird it is that grown men always turn into schoolboys when toilet humour makes an entrance. We were chortling away something rotten.

"Bet ye he's shit himself," said Jim Pint.

"He sartinly hasn't done his pants any favours. And his knickers will be formin' an escape committee," I remarked as we continued the sniggers and snorts, "Bet ye the weather forecast folk on the telly are talkin' about an earthquake in Northumberland tonight."

"Ha-ha... when he gets oot the taxi there'll be laddies followin' behind him wi' a bucket and shovel."

"Wimmen lookin' oot their front doors wi' gas-masks on."

"Only the posh ones... the other folk'll use clothes pegs."

"They'll seal Shankhouse off and send men in white coats from Porton Down to spray everybody wi' Dettol."

We carried on for ages until we ran out of funnies... then silence reigned for a while as Jim topped up our glasses. Blokes can be so infantile at times... but it's what menfolk always do, revert to childish humour when they've had a few drinks and females aren't present. Apart from that it's enjoyable... and hilarious while it lasts. Humour over we proceeded to while away another hour by sorting out the world's problems and generally talking rubbish.

It was ten-thirty precisely when Chunk finally lifted his head from the table, shouted something unintelligible... then grunted. The sudden noise surprised us and we both watched him as he stared straight ahead for a few seconds, then yawned, gave his face a couple of sharp slaps and shook his head before looking over to the bar. "Bloody hell aahh must have dozed off. Could yiz not have given me a nudge?"

Jim Pint and I shared a glance, "Ye looked like ye needed a kip man Chunk, we didn't want ter disturb ye," I told him.

"Me face is aall wet... some bugger must hev spilt some beer."

"I'll lick it off for ye if ye like Chunk," I joked.

"Bog off Jimmy... only women get their tongues near my mooth." Chunk was suddenly sober. It was weird... his powers of recuperation. He took a grubby hanky out of his pocket and began rubbing the wet from his face.

"Are ye feelin' aall right now Chunk?" I asked.

"Course aah'm aall right. What ye on aboot?" He seemed to be unaware of his drunk episode... or perhaps pretending. I wasn't sure which.

"Ohh nowt... just ye looked a bit peaky earlier on."

"Did aahh? Nah... aahh feel champion."

"D'yer want a drink afore I close up Chunk?" asked Jim Pint.

"Nah, thanks Jim, aahmm gannin yem. Wor lass'll dee her dinger cos aahh left a bag of fruit on the bus. It was for her mother... the owld battleaxe."

"D'yer want me to call a taxi?"

"No thanks Jim. I'm gannin ter walk yem. It'll tek more time up afore aahh have to face the music. Anyway Jimmy ex Book and Jim Pint I'll see ye both tomorra if the missus has calmed doon by then." With that, Chunk stood up, buttoned up his jacket and headed for the door. Then he stopped dead in his tracks. He put out a hand to steady himself against the door frame then turned around slowly with an embarrassed grin on his face.

"What's up Chunk," asked Jim Pint, "Hev ye forgot summat?"

Chunk's grin had morphed into a grimace, he shook his head again, "Nah man... aahh think aah've shit mesel'... bugger."

Jim Pint and I were in absolute stitches as Chunk turned again and left the pub without another word... with our laughter following him out into the street.

I took my leave of the Folly shortly afterwards. I'd come to a few important decisions that particular evening so tomorrow promised to be a very busy day.

"See ye tomorrow Jimmy?" asked Jim Pint.

"I'll probably pop in at some stage but I'm going to be tied up with some things I need to sort out."

I had the strangest feeling that my Folly days were coming to an end. By the tone of the question in Jim Pint's voice I had the impression that he was also thinking along similar lines. When I walked away from the pub that night I halted after a few dozen paces, I don't know why, and I turned around to look at the old building. Jim Pint was standing outside watching me, and that in itself was odd. He raised a hand and waved. I waved back, then turned and continued walking. My Shankhouse sojourn was reaching its finale.

CHAPTER 18

Off The Hook

I rang the Glasgow number the following morning. The more I'd thought about the offer the more I realised that I couldn't afford to turn it down if the terms and conditions were decent and the offer was genuine. I needed the job more than it needed me.

Ring-ring-ring... the phone was picked up almost immediately. "Good morning... McAlpin Hygiene... Caitlin speaking, how may I help you?"

"Ohh hello, my name is James Bates. I was asked to give Roger a call."

"Would that be Roger MacDonald or Roger Murray?"

I glanced quickly at the business card just to make doubly sure, "Roger Murray."

"Sorry Mr Baines but Mr Murray isn't available."

"It's Bates."

"Sorry... I didn't quite catch..."

"My name... it's Bates not Baines."

"Apologies again Mr Baines... in fact there's a note here in front of me saying that you might be in contact today. May I transfer your call through to Mr Murray's wife?"

"Yes, yes of course. I didn't realise Rebecca was employed in the business."

"Mrs Murray isn't... but she does help out occasionally when we're short-staffed or extremely busy." There were a few beeps and squawks before she came back with, "Just putting you through now Mr Baines."

The next voice I heard was that of Rebecca... it was unmistakeable. I was busy pushing ten-pence coins into the BT slot... it was eating money.

"James, so very nice to hear from you. Roger was sure you'd call... I wasn't."

"Nor was I Rebecca."

"Roger's usually spot on when he's weighing people up. He's really enthusiastic about you joining us."

"I haven't yet?"

"No... true, but I'm sure you'll like what you hear tomorrow."

"Tomorrow?"

"Yes... can you make it into the office by two o'clock? We're a stones-throw from the Ibrox stadium." She wasn't really asking, she was instructing.

"What's the traffic like? I've only driven in Glasgow once."

"Don't come by car James. Train then taxi... but keep your receipts and we'll cover the expenses. You'll be leaving in a company car. Bring your licence with you... I'm assuming it's clean. And your home address of course... telephone number, the usual."

"But I haven't accepted the job yet."

"You will... I guarantee it. As I said Roger has a good gut when it comes to business matters. You won't be disappointed with his offer."

I had the feeling that I didn't have much say in the matter, "It would be handy to have the business address. Roger's card only has his job title, the McAlpin Hygiene logo and the phone number."

"Ha-ha, yes... good thinking Batman." She gave me the address and I scribbled it down, "I've another call coming through James and I need to take it, so we'll see you in Govan tomorrow?"

"Yes... two o'clock... thank you." The phone went dead... end of conversation, charming I thought. They seemed to think it was fait-accompli. Now I needed to get my finger out and make arrangements for the following day.

I only hoped that my laundry had been done as promised otherwise I'd have no clean shirt to wear.

Walker again. My washing wasn't only clean but also ironed and in a pristine pile. I turned up at Lorraine's as arranged around seven o'clock and goodness knows why but she seemed really glad to see me. Not as glad as I was to see my fresh laundry and my white shirts on wire hangers.

"Have you had your tea yet?" were her first words as she opened the door and I entered the flat.

"No... not yet, I was going to get some fish and chips later on."

"Do you like faggots?" she asked. Ehhh... What kind of a question was that?

I shrugged, "I don't mind them... if they're polite and realise I'm not a member of their club."

That made her laugh out loud, "I take it you've never had faggots before?"

"Honestly... no. I've heard of them but I don't know what they are. The name is a bit off-putting."

"If you just think pork offal with some herbs and breadcrumbs. They're an acquired taste but with salt and pepper they're tasty enough and fill you up so I've been told. I've never had them either if that's any consolation. I've done some with potatoes, cabbage and peas and I made enough for two." She paused, "Come on through to the kitchen... the table's set." She didn't wait for a response. She turned and led the way so I did as I was told and followed her through. I was about to have my first and last confrontation with faggots.

Fortunately I'd remembered Lorraine was partial to a whisky and lemonade and I'd bought a half bottle of Bell's on my way over to Walker. She was pleased that I'd remembered and we had a glass each to kill the taste of those damned faggots. They were awful and I could tell that she wasn't too keen either. Her friend from work... a lady named Jill Sim had recommended faggots, so Lorraine had bought some. We both regretted her decision.

"That friend of yours," I remarked as we sat in the living room after the meal, "Don't punch her too hard... she might actually like feasting on things that taste like brown wallpaper paste."

Lorraine chuckled, "I think she was actually recommended faggots by our boss Mary Telfer. I don't think Jill has ever eaten them either."

"Is she fit and healthy your friend Jill?"

"Yes."

"Then I guarantee she's never eaten faggots."

We both chuckled before lapsing into a silent interlude for a minute or two. Then Lorraine asked...

"So what time did you say your train was tomorrow?"

"Eight twenty-five... to Edinburgh Waverley... then change for Glasgow Central. I'll be there around twelve-ish... so that will give me plenty of time for a mooch around before the interview or whatever it is they've cooked up."

"From what you were saying it sounds like you've already got the job."

"Yeh it certainly sounds like it."

"But...?" A one-word question from Lorraine.

I thought about the response for a few seconds. Then it all came tumbling out.

"It's not so much a but... well maybe it is actually. First of all I don't know if there's a retainer or whether it's commission only. I don't suppose that will make a great difference anyhow. After all there's a company car with the job. Secondly I haven't got a phone number as yet until I fix myself up with a different flat... because I can't continue using the Folly phone number... Jim Pint would do his nut. And thirdly I've got the taxman hanging over my head and time is running out. They're a priority... but I'll think of something."

Lorraine gave some thought to what I'd just said. Then she stood up and taking both tumblers she walked through into the kitchen without comment. When she came back into the living room she was carrying two well-filled glasses of whisky... her glass topped with lemonade. She gave a smile as she handed over one of the tumblers. Then she sat down on the settee, turned to face me and we chinked.

"Here's to success and a new job," she smiled as she spoke and we chinked again. "We'll both have plenty of time to think of solutions after I've dropped you off at the station in the morning."

"What... ehhh? Dropped me off? I can't spend the night here... I need to get back to Shankhouse."

"Why is that? Your clothes are here and clean. Do you have your driving licence with you?"

"Yes."

"Then what is the point of driving back to Shankhouse? You'll have to get up really early to catch a bus into Newcastle then walk from the Haymarket down to Central Station. Or drive of course but then where would you park your car? Then you'll probably be coming back in a company car so you'll need to pick up your own car. How will that work?"

"I... err hadn't thought it through really."

"Okay... so I'll make you a bed up on the settee. And you can give my telephone number as your home number. That sorts out one of the problems doesn't it?"

"But why are you doing this? I mean... you haven't known me for five-minutes."

Lorraine smiled, "Sometimes five minutes is all you need."

"But..."

"No buts. Give my phone number as your home number. You can make this place your new address... temporary or otherwise. As I said, that sorts out your new flat searching problem. Then we'll take it from there. I'll drop you at the station on my way into work."

"But we aren't even... you know... an item or anything."

She smiled again, "And we may never be... time will tell. But for you it solves two of your three problems. And by the way my intentions are completely honourable." She gave a little laugh.

"So what do you get out of it?" I was having trouble getting my head around this unasked-for generosity.

"I'm not looking to get anything out of it... not as such. If anything it would be company I suppose. For a few weeks at least... then after that we'll see where life takes us."

That didn't quite ring true, "I can't imagine someone like you needing some stranger for company. I'm sure you've already got plenty of friends and acquaintances."

She beamed, "Thank you for that. I do have friends and acquaintances but most, if not all, are married or have families. I don't mind my own company most of the time, but you know, sometimes it would be nice to have another person kicking around the house. Watching something funny on the telly by yourself isn't all that it's cracked up to be. Laughing alone isn't proper laughter. Ohh and by the way... you're no longer a stranger."

I was still somewhat taken aback by the entire situation but there was very little else to be said on the subject. We spent the remainder of the evening chatting, laughing and eventually sleeping.

CHAPTER 19

Driving Home For Christmas

—————————————————————■—————————————————————

Finding my way out of Glasgow in my year-old company Vauxhall Cavalier was the most difficult part of that eventful day. Finding Ibrox Business Park had been a doddle because I arrived in a taxi. However, driving your way out of Glasgow when you're a stranger is an absolute misery. By the time I left from Govan that day, around four-thirty, I had myself a new job and a decent motor but the watery sun had already retreated below the horizon. A nervous night drive was on the cards.

After a number of wrong turnings and misread road signs I found myself on the road to Carlisle. That was not the town that I'd been aiming for... that had been Berwick. But rather than turn around to brave the Glasgow nightmare again I decided to carry on. A run across from Carlisle to Newcastle on the A69 wasn't a bad second prize. I seemed to drive for an age on roads I had no idea about and tackling them in the December darkness was exhausting. I eventually stopped for a break in the little village of Crawford.

I soon found myself in the Crawford Arms Hotel and spent a quiet hour sitting alone with a few beers as I looked through the paperwork I'd been supplied with during my time with Roger in the offices of McAlpin Hygiene. The order pads they'd supplied were pristine and untouched by pen. I hoped that wouldn't be the case for much longer.

McAlpin Hygiene was in its infancy as an independent chemical company. At that particular time there were only three salesmen on the road... one of them being Roger, and I was to be number four... covering Northumberland, Tyneside and Durham. Looking through the display folder with the itemised product specs I wasn't impressed. It was going to be hard work generating decent sized orders with the limited product range on offer. However I had been impressed by the sheer enthusiasm of Roger who'd given up a directorship in a large established company in order to go it alone.

Roger was working long hours on the expansion of the product range while it was to be my brief to keep the orders clicking through and expanding the customer portfolio. The terms he'd given me were extremely generous. A two-hundred pounds per week retainer for the first six weeks while I was building up a customer base... bearing in mind that Christmas and New Year would take a bite out of those first weeks. After that a straightforward twenty-five percent commission from week seven onwards on a self-employed basis.

As I sat in the bar going over things in my mind I could see the difficulties ahead but I could also see the potential for expansion and advancement if I could square the circle. And at least I was now driving a decent car... one which had been retrieved from a previous salesman. He'd been covering the eastern borders region before being sacked. And not just because of a lack of incoming business but as Roger so succinctly put it... 'that bugger was one lazy bastard.' I was determined that I wouldn't suffer a similar fate.

Before I left the bar of the Crawford Arms Hotel that evening I made a swift phone call to Lorraine. Two rings were all it took before she picked up and answered.

"Hello."

"Hi Lorraine it's me."

"That's not possible... me is here, so that must be someone called you."

"Yes... very droll. I'm on my way back."

"In a company car I presume?"

"Yes."

"Where are you now?"

"Still in Scotland... a place called Crawford."

"What time do you think you'll make it?"

"After ten... before eleven. Have to go I'm running out of phone money."

"Okay, see you then. I'll have something hot for you."

The mind boggled. I put the phone down.

The something hot turned out to be fish finger sandwiches. I enjoyed them but they weren't what I'd been conjuring up in my head on the return journey. Nevertheless they went down a treat and were followed by cake and custard before a wee dram.

As soon as I'd walked through the front door of the flat Lorraine informed me that Roger had phoned to check that I'd made it home safely. They'd had a little chat and Roger asked her to tell me to ring him when I returned. I was on the phone as soon as I'd taken off my jacket and dumped the paperwork and display folder. Roger had given Lorraine his home number.

"Hi Roger... made it," I replied to his initial 'hello' when he'd picked up.

"Hi James, it's taken you a while."

"Yeh... I set out for Berwick, took a few wrong turns and ended up heading for Carlisle. I stopped off for a bite to eat in Crawford."

"Yes, it can be a pig getting out of here if you don't know it well. Anyway you're home safe and sound."

"Aye, ready for food."

"Yes Lorraine said she was making something for you," then he paused, "James, I had a thought just after you left. Don't know why I didn't think of it before then. Now feel free to say no if it's going to be too much trouble," he paused again and I knew that his 'too much trouble' comment meant that I would have to agree with whatever he'd thought up.

"It's Christmas on Sunday... so there's still Wednesday through Friday to crack on with," that was a strange comment because it was my intention to start cold-calling in Newcastle tomorrow morning... and he already knew that.

"Yes Roger I know that. I'll be out there tomorrow."

"Yes James, bear with me for a minute," I could hear the shuffling of papers during the pause.

Then he was back, "So, I've drawn a line across England for the furthest expansion we can accommodate over the next twelve months. We go down as far as the Humber on the east... then draw a line over to the west. That will take in

Hull, Leeds, Bradford, Blackburn and Preston... roughly."
I had an idea what was coming next."

"Yes, I get it... so?"

"So I've been thinking that..."

I jumped in, "You're thinking that maybe I could pick up some of my old customers in Hull and around East Yorkshire and give whoever the new guy down there turns out to be... a head start."

"I...err... yes, precisely if it would be worth our while." Roger seemed taken aback that I hadn't been surprised by his train of thought.

"And what kind of figure do you reckon I need to be hitting to make it worth our while Roger?" I asked.

"Hmmm, well I've worked out that if you could pull in a grand without discounting then we'd break even."

"A grand in two days?"

"Two and a half if you start off early enough. I've great faith in you and so has Rebecca for some reason. We have done our research you know. So do you think you can hit that target?"

I didn't reply to that immediately, "So how come a grand in orders would only be break even?" That had me somewhat confused.

"Additional delivery costs would take up most of the profit. And of course I'm writing a cheque for you... which will be with you before Christmas. I'm doubling your weekly retainer for your first week."

I added my own input to his statement, "And you will of course be paying for my bed and breakfast and half a dozen bottles of whisky?"

"What's that James?" My comment had thrown him somewhat.

"A bottle of spirits for a decent order Roger... that's how it works. Naughty I know, but my old customers will expect nothing less. I've a few targets in mind just immediately off the top of my head... and hopefully I'll top a grand if the right people are at work... and of course the B&B is an unforeseen expense. Petrol I'd be using anyway although not as much."

"So that's going to cost me another hundred?"

"Yes... but you'll have a foothold for your new salesman and, with a bit of luck, some of the bigger companies to boot."

"I'll write another cheque if you're up for doing it."

"I didn't think I had much say in the matter Roger."

He laughed, "I think we're going to have a happy marriage James."

"Maybe so Roger... but I don't want to be starting a family for a few years."

He laughed again, "Goodnight James, good luck... and keep me posted. I'll fast-track your cheque."

"Goodnight," I said... but the phone was already dead and I was left with a problem. Now somehow I needed to dig out a thousand pounds worth of business in less than three days. It was going to be far from easy.

I'd put the phone down and was standing staring at it... thoughts swirling around in my head when Lorraine tapped me on the shoulder.

"Supper's ready... come and tell me all about it."

When supper was over and we were sitting having a drink I talked and talked for ages but when I'd finished everything was out in the open... including my impending departure for Hull and the amount of the incoming cheque.

It was midnight by then and I was worn out.

"So you've got an early start Jim... we'd better get some shuteye." She stood up, took my hand, pulled me out of my seat and led me through into the bedroom. I protested vigorously of course (nah... only kidding).

Like A Bat Out Of Hull – I set out that Wednesday morning at five o'clock and I was in Hull by nine. I spent the first few hours sorting out digs and buying whisky and boxes of chocolates. By noon I was making my first business call and I was totally focussed on the job in hand.

Working Hull and East Yorkshire again was both bizarre and comforting at the same time. Bizarre because I was walking into places where I was greeted as if I had taken my last order there a week ago instead of a five-year hiatus. Comforting because some of my old contacts were no longer with their old employers but I was still managing to pick up orders.

The bottles of whisky and the chocolates played a big part in the order process of course... it was Christmas time after all. After a lucrative few hours I knocked off at five o'clock and returned to my digs on Springbank West. A quick change of clothes then down to the local chippy for a bite to eat. Then it was off around the local pubs which I'd sold to in the past. I didn't knock off until almost closing time but I'd managed to pick up some extra business. Not a huge amount but every little helped.

I rang Lorraine to let her know everything was working out fine and she seemed pleased to hear my news... and my voice. Then I was off to my bed. I slept like a log that night... my day had been long and tiring but a lot more productive than I'd expected. I'd managed to hit half of Roger's target already but I wasn't going to phone up and give him any news until the final evening. Tomorrow I was going to shoot at the big boys... British Aerospace, Capper Pass... and my old employers BP Chemicals. Friday I'd be concentrating on the hospitals, the city mortuary, Hull jail and the abattoir... my call list had been planned in advance.

Thursday and Friday flew by. I was motoring along... head down and backside up and trying to wring as many orders as possible from the allocated hours. I only discounted two orders during those few days and I made up for it by price-loading other orders. Christmas coming has the strangest effect on normally sensible and cost-conscious people. Bonhomie and seasonal generosity were being chucked at me in abundance and my order pad filled up rapidly. By the time I called a halt on Friday evening I'd topped two thousand pounds by quite some distance.

My phone call that evening to Roger with my running total was met first of all with disbelief: then when the news of my success finally registered and the amount of the combined orders had sunk in he was gobsmacked. I was glad that it was merely a phone call because if he'd been standing in front of me I was convinced he'd have kissed me. He was over the moon and he admitted he'd been worried that I wouldn't even hit the break-even figure.

"Wow... I have to say I'm totally impressed James. I'm glad we managed to get you on board. So are you driving home tonight or have you decided to leave it until tomorrow?"

"Tomorrow Roger... I'm knackered. I need something to eat and then get my head down. Apart from that I have an appointment tomorrow."

"Christmas Eve?"

"There's no flies on you Roger... it certainly is."

"Surely you can't have more business to pick up on a Saturday... the day before Christmas."

"I promised I'd pop in to someone's birthday bash with a wee present. I'll have to keep the promise because she's the lady who gave us the biggest of the orders... and I don't want to jeopardise that one."

"Who on earth gets themselves born on Christmas Eve?"

"Yeh, my feelings entirely. But it has to be done."

"Watch your alcohol intake James."

"Don't worry Roger I'll be in and out of the party as soon as I can manage it without causing offence. That order is worth six hundred quid but I need the official order number."

"Okay James do what you have to do and can you get those order slips into the post as soon as possible?

"Sure thing Roger I'll post them tomorrow,"

"Good man James. Give me a call after the big day is all over... ohhh, and merry Christmas to you and yours."

"Same to you Roger... have a good'un." The phone went down.

Then it was Lorraine's turn.

"Hi... James calling base."

"I've been waiting by the phone... how have you done?"

"I've more than doubled Roger's target."

"Good grief... that's fantastic but I bet you're tired out. Ohhh by the way there's a letter here for you from Alba

Hygiene... recorded delivery. The postie just managed to catch me before I set out for work this morning."

"What's it say?"

"I don't know. It's addressed to you... I haven't opened it."

"Well open it then... it will just be a cheque I think."

"Okay... hang on, I'll go and get it." There was silence for a minute.

Then she was back, "You were right Jim it's a cheque together with a copy of your contract and a little welcome letter. Should I read it out?"

"Nah, I'll see it when I get back. How much is the cheque for?"

"Wow... five hundred pounds."

"Yeh, brilliant... so Roger's as good as his word."

"Didn't you think he would be? He sounds genuine on the phone."

"I hoped he'd be genuine... but you never know until you know."

Then I heard Lorraine having a nervous clearing of her throat before she began, "Anyway Jim... I hope you don't think I'm being pushy or interfering but I've sorted out the payment for your tax bill."

There must have been a full ten seconds of silence before I could gather my thoughts to reply. "You've what?"

"I've arranged a bank loan to pay off that debt."

I was almost lost for words. If that was the case then a great weight had just been lifted from my shoulders. "But the debt isn't yours Lorraine."

"Well it is now... because the bank will want their money back plus interest within six months. I'm hoping of course that you'll take on the repayments otherwise I've made a huge misjudgement."

"No misjudgement…I don't know what to say."

"Thank you would be a good start."

"Yes… yes of course… thank you. But that means you're going to have to put up with me for six months."

She took a brief moment before responding, "I'm hoping it will be a lot longer than six months," then she waited. My answer to that would define the remainder of my life.

"Yeh… me too." And with that our fates were sealed.

"So what time can I expect you home?" Suddenly Lorraine's Kingsmere Gardens flat was now being called my home.

"I've a call to make tomorrow to pick up an official order number. That completes the biggest of the orders but I should be done by early afternoon."

"Okay… but drive careful Better late than not at all."

"Have you heard that Chris Rea single that's just been released?"

"Chris who?"

"Chris Rea… never mind, anyway it's called Driving Home for Christmas. I'll be doing that tomorrow afternoon. I'm hoping to be back around eight or nine if the traffic is okay."

"Okay… see you then," she paused, "I've missed having you around." With that the phone went down at her end before I could reply. I stared at the receiver in my hand and thought to myself… 'isn't life strange'… then I hung up.

Mistletoe and Wine – It was Christmas Eve and I did attend that birthday bash in a local pub, the Corner House.

True to her word Eunice had rustled up an official order number and she handed it over together with a kiss on the cheek. No going back on that purchase commitment then. I gave her a birthday bottle of whisky and a card I'd bought that very morning. Unfortunately she was so far gone by the time I left that I doubt whether the birthday gift would be remembered. I hung around for a few drinks... chatting and being generally pleasant with her friends but I was champing at the bit to be off. I gave it a decent amount of time then I slunk away without a goodbye.

I'd been out early that morning doing some panic buying... having realised I hadn't bought a single present. By the time I'd finished funds were running low. Not panicky low but nevertheless I'd need to manage my spending. The car had sufficient fuel for the return journey and I had enough money in my back pocket for a stop off somewhere. Of course I had a chunky cheque waiting for me when I got back and that put a smile on my face. My tax worry had evaporated... although I'd need to repay Lorraine... but all things considered life was looking rather promising.

The return journey was an awful grind. It hadn't occurred to me that maybe the entire population of the British Isles would be heading somewhere for Christmas and driving on the same roads as me... but they were. I hate driving in heavy traffic... always have and always will. It sucks the pleasure out of a motor-car journey.

After those awful hours of yuk driving I finally pulled up behind my old car in Kingsmere Gardens. It was nine o'clock on the button. It suddenly occurred to me that my old motor might fetch a couple of hundred if I could tidy it up a bit and find a mug to buy it. Locking up the Cavalier I picked up my holdall, my paperwork and my bag of last-minute purchase Christmas gifts and headed up the stairs to my newly-found sanctuary.

Lorraine must have been keeping a look out for me because the door opened as if by magic as I reached the outside landing. She was standing in front of me grinning like a Cheshire cat. Not only that but she had some sort of a bandana contraption around her head with a piece of mistletoe dangling from a wire extension which was bent over and waving about over her brow. It looked cute and the invitation was unmistakeable. It was definitely one I couldn't ignore. Cue loads of kissy-kissy stuff for the next minute or so. I had to tell Lorraine that I'd had my tonsils out because she'd begun searching for them.

Eventually we managed to make it through into the sitting room and I slumped onto the settee with my holdall at my feet. Lorraine plonked herself down and snuggled up beside me.

"Was the journey okay?" she asked.

I proceeded to tell her how lousy it had been and it had only been the fact that I'd be seeing her again very shortly which had dissuaded me from committing murder by vehicle on a number of occasions. She snuggled closer into me.

"It's Christmas tomorrow."

"Get away... honest, why did nobody tell me? I could have bought some pressies."

"I've bought a bottle of wine for you coming back. Do you prefer red or white?"

To be honest I'd rarely had wine. Nevertheless I plumped for red. Lorraine went through into the kitchen and came back minutes later with two full wine glasses. She handed me mine, sat back down beside me and said...

"Here's to the future... for both of us."

I responded, "Let's make sure it's a good future... for both of us." We chinked glasses and drank. It felt right somehow.

"I thought I'd do the Cliff Richard thing for you." She said, waiting for my response, but I was none the wiser... a Cliff Richard thing? maybe she'd booked a summer holiday.

"Cliff... ehhh? I don't get it."

"You know... the number one... Mistletoe and Wine."

"Ohhh aye... silly me. I didn't know what you were on about. Nice one. It must have taken you ages to make that mistletoe head thingy."

"I didn't make it. My friend from work did because she knew I was looking forward to you coming back." That meant of course that she'd been telling folk about me: I hoped she'd only been telling the good bits.

"Anyway Lorraine, thank you for the welcome: it was a nice surprise. I've got something for you too," I said as I sat forward and rummaged in the gift bag at my feet. I handed her three wrapped presents. She looked shocked.

"Presents... for me? I haven't bought..." she didn't finish the sentence, she was embarrassed.

"Ahh man... I didn't expect anything. These are just a few little things to let you know how much I appreciate what you've done for me,"

"But...?"

"No buts," I chuckled. "Bet you can't guess what the big one is." Of course she could. There's not many ways you can wrap a bottle without it looking exactly like a wrapped bottle. My wrapping skills of course still needed some serious work.

She quickly tore off the Christmas gift paper. "Ohh what a surprise… a bottle of Glenlivet," She gave me a great big smile and an even bigger kiss. She handed the bottle to me, "Tumblers are in the top cupboard: put plenty of lemonade in mine." The silly bugger was still doing the lemonade in malt whisky thing. I'd need to give her some serious tutoring. Nevertheless I sloped off into the kitchen to do as I'd been asked. I was back two minutes later with our drinks in hand. She'd opened the second present… a box of Milk Tray chocolates and was busy with the third which I'd had professionally wrapped with a bow and tied with ribbon. It took some opening and while she was struggling away with the ribbon I'm still standing there with the two glasses; waiting to hand one over.

When she'd dispensed with the wrapping paper and ribbon she was faced with a little box. She opened it and gave a gasp.

"Jim it's…"

"A cornucopia… it's a symbol of abundance and nourishment. The name is from the Latin and its translation means 'horn of plenty' or something." I knew this because the manager of the jeweller's shop in Hull had given me the benefit of his knowledge.

"No Jim… I mean it's really beautiful. So thoughtful. How did you know I preferred silver?"

I gave a snort, "I didn't… but I couldn't afford the gold one."

"Stop standing there like a waxwork dummy and put the drinks on the coffee table," she said as she stood up with the cornucopia and silver chain in hand. I did as I was told. She handed me the cornucopia, "Put it on for me." She turned her back to me and I proceeded to thread the chain through the eyelet. Then I put the necklace around her neck... fastening the clasp at the back.

"All done."

She turned and gave me a brief kiss before heading for the bedroom mirror. I followed and watched. She was standing there admiring her reflection with the cornucopia positioned outside her jumper.

She saw me standing at the bedroom door, "Jim it's gorgeous... I don't know what else to say. I feel really bad that I haven't got anything for you."

"Well you could share the whisky and chocolates... but I think I'll give the jewellery a miss."

She laughed, "Come on then let's go and get stuck in; I have to be up early in the morning to prepare the dinner." Then she turned and faced me with a cheeky grin, "I'd like to talk to you about a different horn of plenty," her grin grew even broader as we headed for our drinks.

Christmas day came and went so quickly and it was hectic. Lorraine's flat was only small and her family descended en masse. Family stuff was not my forte but I didn't have time to be embarrassed or feel uncomfortable. It was eat, drink, play with kids and generally enjoy the atmosphere. I'd been expecting a grilling from the older family members but they were on exemplary behaviour and it never materialised. The day just flew by and everything went off well.

It was after seven o'clock when we were finally left on our own. The dishes had all been washed and put away but there were still loads of leftovers on the kitchen table. Christmas can be such a waste of food... but I had my eye on the sausage rolls and the last slices of plate pie; those fellows wouldn't be seeing the inside of the pedal bin.

After winding down and filling our glasses we flopped together on the settee drained and exhausted. Christmas evening was spent watching Morecambe and Wise followed by the Christmas Parkinson Show. When midnight made its appearance we were already snuggled up together and snoring.

Life had taken a strange turn... and it felt perfect. Long may it continue.

CHAPTER 20

Working Nine to Five

———————————■———————————

Boxing Day was on a Monday and on the Tuesday I was out and about really early. After my exertions and successes the previous week Roger had told me to take some time out between Christmas and New Year and get myself energized for the week following. "Make the first week of January your initial week on your new patch James," Roger had insisted.

However I had different ideas because at that moment in time I didn't have a single customer in the Newcastle/ Northumberland/Durham area. I was desperate to get at least a few orders on paper and hold the order forms back so that my official first week would look more impressive. Apart from that, New Year was coming and that would mean inebriated purchasers; hopefully I would find a few of those. I always remembered one of my mother's stock sayings – 'drink in, wits out.' Those 'wits out' people were the very ones I was needing to track down. I was to surprise even myself.

Seven orders came from pubs in those first three days: one from a care-home in Blyth and one from a garage beside the Roxy bingo. None of the orders were very big but that wasn't the point; it showed a serious work ethic and successful cold calling. I was chuffed but also surprised because five of the orders had been for first-aid kits; a product I'd never sold before. To be honest I hadn't given them much attention when I'd first spied them in the demo manual.

Three days and nine orders was most satisfactory so I decided to take Friday off and retrieve the rest of my belongings from the Shankhouse digs. I still had some clothes to pick up as well as my vinyl albums, my personal book collection and some other odds and ends. I needed to say cheerio to my landlady too because my rental was up as from tomorrow and she'd been very understanding about my comings and goings. I thought a box of chocs would be a nice touch... and it was. We took leave of each other that afternoon on the very best of terms and she told me if I was ever stuck for living quarters then I knew where to call.

I had more stuff than I'd remembered and my car was chocker-block when I finished packing everything in.

Then it was off to the Folly. I didn't know for sure that it was going to be my last ever visit but I had the weirdest feeling that I was going to the pub to say my goodbyes. I didn't feel guilty about a boozy afternoon because I knew Lorraine's workplace was having some sort of an office party. She hadn't taken the car to work that day... so alcohol seemed to be on the cards... and what's sauce for the goose... as they say.

I felt a little strange as I walked into the Folly because for once I was wearing a suit: not normal attire for an afternoon session. As I made my way in I noticed there were several occupied tables to the right of the entrance. That was a big surprise... customers indeed!... Jim Pint was behind the bar as per usual and gave me a big grin as I sat myself down on one of the bar seats. Out of the corner of my eye I'd noticed a little crowd around our usual table at the bottom end; two of them being strangers. Chunk, John Milk, Bob the Knob and old Fred were sitting there as expected, but there was also a frosty faced woman in her late forties or early fifties together with a really old biddy who looked not unlike Old Mother Riley.

"Who are the two bonny lasses Jim?" I asked.

He grinned but said in little more than a whisper, "Keep your voice down Jim. The old woman is Ethel, Fred's wife... and she's canny. The other bugger... the one with a face like a welder's bench... that's Thelma, Chunk's missus, and she's well pissed."

"Drunk?"

"Aye... she was in yesterday an' all. She could barely stand man... staggering all ower the shop when her and Chunk went yem. And she's got a nasty gob on her as well... and bloody loud with-it cos she's a bit deaf."

"So what's she doing in here?"

"She thinks Chunk's been playin' away."

"Ehhh?"

Jim snorted, "Aahh knaa man.... she's roond the twist. Chunk told her some cock and bull story about the woman with the thighs... ye knaa... that hockey player woman you're workin' for. He said she'd tried to get him drunk and have her wicked way with him... can ye believe?"

"Ehhh... when was this?"

"Remember the night he went home mortal?"

"Aye."

"That was the night. He concocted some story about that wifey comin' on to him, then getting him drunk and wantin' naughties behind the pub. Told his missus that's why he'd shit hisell."

"And she believed it?"

"Aahh divvent knaa, maybe... or perhaps she's heard it all before. Anyway she reckons she's ready to murder the woman when she comes in."

"She'll have a long wait. Becky won't be back in here again."

"I know that Jimmy but as long as Thelma keeps spendin' her Christmas money then she can think what she wants. Ye'd think money was gannin oot of fashion the way she hoys it aboot." He looked over at the table then back at me, "Anyway... how's the new job going?"

"Aye it's gannin canny man. I'm doing good. It was a bit of luck Roger and Becky turnin' up here that night."

"Serendipity Jimmy."

"What?"

"Serendipity man. That's what it's called when something good happens when ye haven't been expecting it."

"Never heard that one before Jim. So this serendipity thing... it's just another name for luck?"

"Nah Jimmy... and I thought you would have known this. You can have good luck and you can also have bad luck... but you can only have good serendipity. It means a fortunate happening."

"Bloody hell Jim have you been at the Readers Digest again?"

"Aye summat like that," he replied with a smile.

"Jimmy... Jimmy, are ye ower good for us peasants now in yer bonny suit?" Chunk's shout rang out loud from his perch at the corner table.

I looked over and gave Chunk a thumbs up then picked up my pint to go and join the group. Jim half turned his back to them and said under his breath, "Watch yersell Jimmy cos she's a bitch and a half." He wasn't wrong.

Have you ever had to sit, without comment, beside a person who repulsed you and made your skin crawl? Someone who every time they opened their mouth you wanted to fill it with your fist. Yes?... then you'll know the predicament I was in when I found myself having to sit through a kind of slow torture that very afternoon. Not only myself of course but also old Fred and Ethel his wife... John Milk, and dare I say Chunk also? Because that fella looked so embarrassed and helpless as his wife proceeded to set everyone's teeth on edge. She was truly a disgusting excuse for a human.

Bob the Knob decided to do the sensible thing and he left just as I was about to park my backside. He'd obviously had enough of the present company.

"Sorry Jimmy... got to shoot off. I've a bit of business needs seeing to." He gave me a wink and a grimace as he buttoned up and brushed past me. "See yer some other time mate... good luck, you'll need it," the last bit of the sentence was said very quietly. I was about to find out why.

"It's been a while," said John Milk through barely parted lips as I took my seat... his mouth still full of wire to support his broken jaw."

"Aye John, I've been really busy."

"Is the job going all right then?" he sounded as if he was slurping rather than speaking and he kept gingerly touching the side of his face. I noticed he was still drinking his pints through a straw.

"Aye John it's going really well."

"Yeh, Chunk's been tellin me. That was a bit of luck that couple turning up out of the blue."

"Called Serendipity John."

John didn't have time to reply. Chunk's wife Thelma jumped in with big hobnail boots. "So that's the bitch's name is it?"

"Scuse me?"

"Scuse ye... aah'll bliddy scuse ye indeed. Where's that bitch now?"

"Bitch... who, what bitch?"

"Hor that tried ter get my blokes keks off... that Sharon Dimbleby yer on aboot."

"I think you misheard me pet. You've got the wrong end of the stick." I looked over to Chunk for support but his eyes were elsewhere.

"Whaatt? Come again," she cupped her hand to her ear. I had to speak much louder. Everyone in the pub could hear... and probably everyone in Shankhouse. Chunk was looking at the floor.

"I didn't say Sharon Dimbleby, I said serendipity."

"Okay...okay who cares? Selena Dipply then. Where will I find the slag? Is she with you?" she demanded. I looked to Chunk again for a little guidance but Chunk had his elbows on his knees... his hands were under his chin and supporting his head... his eyes still fixed on the floor. He seemed for whatever reason to be genuinely scared of this little loudmouthed woman. I think he was also afraid of what I was going to say next... he'd already told his wife a load of codswallop about his drunken evening... maybe he was worried the truth was about to surface.

It didn't, and I did Chunk a big favour, "Selena Dipply has gone back to America," I was almost shouting as the lie came tripping out.

"America?" she looked puzzled, "Why's she gone to America?"

"Cos that's where she lives... New York."

"Clarence never said she was American."

"Clarence... who's Clarence?" she frowned, gave me a quizzical look then pointed to Chunk who continued looking anywhere other than at me. I almost laughed... but that would have been a mistake. Chunk... or Clarence my buddy, the local hard man, had the same name as a cross-eyed lion.

I decided to embellish the lie to make it more believable, "She was just trying to pull an English bloke before she went back to the States. When Chu... errr when Clarence gave her the elbow she tried it on with me. I was tempted but I'd had a bit too much to drink and told her to bog off."

"So the dirty mare went without then?"

"Maybe."

"Ehhh?" she gave me a questioning glare. I raised my eyebrows and gave a slight nod towards the bar.

She looked over towards Jim who was busy serving two new entrants to the pub, "You mean...?"

"I'm saying nowt... mum's the word," and I gave her a wink.

"Aye, whey that's as maybe, and good luck to the owld bugger but if she'd shown her face tonight she'd have got my boot in her fanny,"

There was very little I could say to that.

I spent the next hour bored out of my tiny mind as I listened to the stupidest woman on the planet pontificating about anything and nothing... with the mistaken belief that every time she opened her mouth the word of God emerged. The emerging word of God was of course interspersed with the foulest language I'd ever heard from a woman. Come to think of it I'd rarely heard such choice language from the crudest of mining men. I was mighty glad to take my leave of the company that afternoon. I only had the one pint before making an excuse about having to do another sales call... but I think everyone apart from Chunk's missus realised why I was making my escape.

As I took my leave of Jim Pint I promised I'd pop in again just after New Year, and although I meant it at the time... I never did. I walked out of the Folly for what would turn out to be the final time, got into my car and pointed it towards Walker.

Milk & Alcohol – I was back home in Kingsmere Gardens before four o'clock. My car had been unloaded and I'd managed to find a space at the bottom of the fitted wardrobe for my books, records and other bits and pieces. I expected that Lorraine would be back soon and it was my intention to nip around to the local chippy or Chinese if she was feeling peckish. I changed out of my suit into jeans and jumper; put on slippers, then turned on the telly and settled down on the settee with a glass of the good stuff. The past week had been hectic and it was beginning to catch up with me.

The hours began ticking by and I was dozing intermittently as I watched Sumo wrestling on the telly through half-closed eyes. To be honest it wasn't very exciting. It wasn't until much later when I'd pulled myself together, had a good old stretch and poured myself another glass of malt that I realised I'd been watching a darts match.

Lorraine rolled into the flat a little after eleven o'clock... and I mean rolled. She was plastered. Conversation was brief.

"Mind you're in a bit of a state."

"Sod off."

"Okay... but I could have come and picked you up if you'd phoned."

"Excuse me I did phone."

"It's strange that the phone never rang."

"Ohh aye that'll have been me."

Lorraine proceeded to stagger her way into the kitchen: without another word she sank to her knees then lay carefully down on the floor and pressed her face into the cold tiles.

I followed her through. Her breathing didn't sound too clever, "D'yer not want to take your good dress off and get into bed?"

"Bog off."

"At least take your coat off."

That must have made sense to her. She tried to sit up and began struggling with one of the arms... she was fighting a losing battle so she gave up and lay back down with one arm half out of a sleeve... her watch strap had caught on a cuff button and pulled the sleeve inside-out. Then she began to snore and I heard the first stirrings of the retching noises. Her tummy was squeaking and growling.

That was the moment I came to appreciate how difficult it would be to dispose of a freshly murdered dead body. Not at all like it happens on the telly. This one in front of me on the kitchen floor was a live body and yet I was struggling to move it around... and without much success. I found that drunk bodies are a ton weight and assumed the same must be true of dead bodies although presumably not so noisy. If you really think about it... and just for the sake of argument... if you did indeed have a dead wife or girlfriend on your hands for whatever reason... you'd definitely need to involve other people. You'd have to have one person to lift at the feet end of the body; one at the head and shoulder end and probably a third person holding a king-sized suitcase open for you to stuff the dead body into. Presumably you'd then want to take it to a clifftop and chuck it into the raging sea below so that it would never be found. Which means of course you'd need the assistance of a massive bloke with big muscles to lift the now zipped up suitcase and carry it out of the house and into the car boot... all nonchalant like... in case any lurking curtain-twitchers had heard the screams and noticed the blood spatter on the windows. Then of course with said body now somewhere at the bottom of the North Sea you'd have to phone the police to give yourself a decent alibi in case of a court appearance...

Ring-ring-ring...

"Hello, police here... can you just hold the line for a sec while we finish beating up this suspect" thump-thump-thump, "right all done now...that was hectic, but he's singing like a canary. Now what can I do for you, important member of the public?"

"Hi there I was just ringing to report a missing woman. Her name is (*insert your woman's name here*) and she went out shopping to Kwik-Save and hasn't returned yet."

"How long has she been missing?"

"Two days."

"Aahh yes... another one. I'd give it another day or two... maybe a week sir. She's obviously not the brightest of ladies if she's shopping at Kwik-Save. Anyway they've changed all their aisles around and she's probably still in there somewhere... all confused around the milk and yoghurt section."

"Okay... another week you say? will do, thanks for your advice."

"Think nothing of it sir it's our job. And don't worry she'll turn up with two carrier bags full of cheap rubbish before you know it. Have a nice day."

Now they'd see that she had indeed been reported missing when they checked the telephone logs. Job's a good'un.

So, just to summarize... we've deduced that four people are required for the production of one murder. That my friends is way too complicated. So perhaps it just makes common sense for menfolk to accept those times when they've lost an argument with their wife or girlfriend... yet again. And instead of going down the murder route, it's eminently more sensible to surrender gracefully and nip off to the pub for the licking of wounds and a few jars of ale. Your local bar will be full of blokes mulling over the same problem. Anyway it beats having to call three pals... who you hope would be amenable to keeping their mouths shut... and asking them to give you a hand disposing of your missus.

I digress... back to reality. Because using what musculature I possessed at that time I managed to manoeuvre Lorraine's limp body into various undressing positions. Working carefully, I managed to rescue her best coat... peeling it off before the inevitable vomiting made an entrance. I hung the coat over the ladder-back of one of the kitchen chairs. Then I managed to remove her necklace, earrings and wristwatch without a great deal of difficulty. I was busy putting her jewellery somewhere safe on one of the kitchen shelves when I heard movement behind me. I turned... and just for a second Lorraine raised her head; opened one eye... saw me and said...

"Put Lena Martell on," she glared at me like Cyclops, then the one eye closed and the head went back down.

Lena Martell for goodness sake... I mean 'honestly' Lena Martell? Perhaps she was trying in her own way to induce vomiting. Listening to music like that was akin to sticking your fingers down your throat and tickling your tonsils... in my mind at least. Apologies to any Lena afficionados. However I toddled through into the sitting room; rummaged through the small vinyl collection and found a 45'... 'One Day At A Time'. I switched the player on and set it away.

"One day at a time sweet Jesus... I'm only human, I'm just a woman..." laa-laa-laa-laa... fingers in the ears time.

A voice from the kitchen floor...

"Louder, I can't fferr... snerk..." then silence.

I do as instructed and turn the sound up a notch or two, then take a minute out for myself to light up and have a puff on a fag. It gives me a little nicotine rush. When the cigarette is down to the tip I stub it out then wander back into the kitchen to make sure she's still breathing. Yep, she certainly is. I realise this is going to be one long and arduous night. I pull out one of the dining chairs... go through into the sitting room and take one of the cushions from the settee to stick under my backside. Those dining chairs aren't very comfortable. I position my chair close to the prone Lorraine but far enough away to be able to dive out of the way of the squelch if the sick becomes projectile. Then I wait... but not for long. Lena is squawking away...

"Do you remember... when you walked among men?"
... Then Lorraine joins in... "Gerrurghyarrooff" ... splat.
"Well Jesus, you know, if you're looking below,"
"Hewwyyefluggpeeair" ... sploosh.
"It's worse now than then,"
"Fluurghyblechfaguggle... pfftt...cleck... sllooshh."
James jumps to his feet and begins busying around with wet cloths and dustpans to remove the worst of the blitzkrieg. Lorraine is making rattly noises and because the record player is on repeat Lena Martell is still singing her little heart out...

"That's all I'm asking from You..."
Suddenly the words seem very apt.
"Just give me the strength to do every day,"
"Harroooghittmerk... yerk-yerk honk... Sperrloot," Lorraine still doing back-up vocals.
"What I have to do..."
And so the night progresses. As soon as the worst is over with Lorraine, and her breathing is somewhere approaching normal I find an old pillow to tuck under her head. The snores are loud and regular so I take the opportunity to nip into the bedroom and pull an album out of the wardrobe from my own vinyl stack. I silence dear old Lena and put some Fleetwood Mac on the turntable instead. I turn the volume down even though I know Black Magic Woman doesn't sound great unless the volume is up at max... but

Man of the World and Oh Well are passably okay down the quiet end.

The cleaning up is messy and stinky but after a while I've got the floor area almost back to normal; the cloths have been washed and rinsed several times and the air freshener has been doing a spot of overtime. Two scented candles are flickering away in the sitting room and there's also a plug-in Airwick or something making a nice aroma in the kitchen. I turn the heating up because it must be cold for Lorraine down on the floor then make myself a cup of black coffee. I can't get to the milk because she's sprawled in front of the fridge door. I cover her with a blanket from the wardrobe then perch on my seat with a pillow behind my back. I've purloined the pillow from the bedroom. I prepare for a fitful night with one ear cocked in case she starts again. It ain't easy dozing on a dining chair.

Seven o'clock New Year's Eve morning.

Dozing fitfully on the chair from which I've twice toppled during the preceding few hours I'm suddenly aware of movement in the kitchen. My eyes spring open and focus. It's warm because the heating has been on full belt for hours. Lorraine is now sitting on the floor, upright, with her back against the fridge... a questioning frown on her face. We stare at each other. On one side of her head the hair is neat and tidy. The other side is flat and clagged against her face. She looks almost comical but I refrain from laughing... not a good idea I reckon. Neither of us seems to want to be first to break the silence. This can't go on for ever so I make the first noises.

"Bit of a ropey night then pet?"

"My shoulder's aching. What was I doing sleeping on the floor?"

"Can't you remember?"

"If I could remember I wouldn't have asked the question would I?" She's grouchy and has a bit of a lip on. She begins tentatively exploring the flat side of her hair, "And how did I get all this porridge on my face and in my hair?" Then... just like a summer sunrise you can see understanding flooding her features. She fingers the clag on the cushion which has been under her head most of the night... she sniffs at her fingers and grimaces as realisation jumps in.

"It's not porridge is it?"

"No."

Embarrassment hits home, "How bad was I?"

"Canny bad." I reply... trying not to over dramatize.

"It stinks."

"Aahh... I've smelt worse."

"When?"

I shrug... because it had been a throwaway comment. I'd only been trying to make her feel okay about her daft night. She's staring at me waiting for an answer. Then I remember I have indeed smelt worse.

"I used to sell chemicals into the Hull mortuary. They'd pulled a body out of the Humber and it had been in the estuary for weeks. Anyway the gases inside the body had expanded the stomach and it had exploded in the mortuary and there was splodge and guts all over the shop. That smelt a canny bit worse if I'm remembering correctly."

"Well thank you mister personality for your seal of approval,"

I cottoned on pretty quickly that she wasn't impressed. She was actually looking a bit cockly. Perhaps I should have kept my mouth shut and just agreed that she smelt the worst of all time. Actually I remembered another time... when I was selling my chemicals into the abattoir. But maybe best not ehhh? better to keep the old trap shut.

"I'm going to jump in the shower," she said as she levered herself up onto her knees then cranked herself up to a standing position. Why do people always say that about the shower? has anyone ever actually walked up to the shower, opened the door and then taken a flying leap? Has anyone maybe stepped into the shower and then started to jump around? I don't think so... well apart from Dick Fosbury maybe... the American bloke who invented that flop thing that everyone copied.

"Make a cuppa Jim... and some toast please," she instructed as she headed out of the kitchen, making for the bathroom, unzipping in mid-totter.

I do as requested and put two slices in the toaster before searching for the Marmite. I personally can't stand the stuff but Lorraine loves it. The toast pops up and I put both slices on a plate. They're done to perfection... not too brown and not too white. I wrestle the top off the marmite jar and stick a knife in. I begin to spread... and the smell of the yeast extract almost makes me barff. I conclude that some people just have weird eating habits.

Then, spreading finished, I leave the toast and have a wander over to the bathroom and press my ear to the door just in case Lorraine is still wobbly and has taken a tumble. She hasn't... and indeed she's singing. At least I think it's singing. It sounds very similar to singing, but unfortunately not the kind you would pay good money to hear. I hope none of the neighbours are having a listen and beginning to search for injured cats.

I still have my ear pressed to the door when Lorraine suddenly opens it and I end up doing one of those Monty Python silly walks as I totter through into the bathroom and pretend I normally stumble about like that. Lorraine is out of the shower now and wrapped in a towel. It's only a little towel and because there's so much flesh on display I avert my gaze... 'Aye, that'll be right James.' Lorraine gives me one of those 'have you been keekin' through the keyhole,' accusing looks. I pretend innocence. I don't want to admit I've heard her singing. I reckon that would be the end of a budding relationship. I'm actually thinking I should have recorded the singing and then patented the noise as the latest car alarm.

"I was just coming to clean my teeth."

"Pffft," she snorted as she bumped past me."

I turned and watched the tiny towel sashay its way into the bedroom before the door swung shut. I put both of my eyes back in sockets then decide I'd better pretend to clean my teeth so she'd know I really hadn't been doing any pervy stuff.

By the time I finish the sham teeth cleaning Lorraine has made her way into the kitchen and is sitting in a silky dressing gown thingy. She's biting into the Marmite toast and she isn't pulling a yukky face so I reckon she must really like it. There's no accounting for taste is there?

She points to the plate, "Do you want some?"

What kind of a question is that? Of course I don't want any squelchy brown toast. Someone once told me that we'd sent a planeload of Marmite to one of those regions where they were having a famine and they've promptly sent the planeload back with a note that said, 'we might be starving but we're not that desperate,'

"No thanks pet... I'm not hungry."

"A big chap like you... have you already had something?"

'I didn't fancy Marmite so I chewed on a couple of dog turds instead.' That was what I should have said but I didn't want to appear crude. I just shrugged.

"I'll get something later. Anyway we need to go and get some shopping in. We're almost out of milk and tea bags."

"Hmmm, yes it takes some getting used to having two in the house."

"So are you thinking this has maybe been a mistake?"

She laughed, "No of course not. It felt nice coming back to a house with someone in it. At least I think it did... I can't really remember." We both chuckled at that.

We shopped on Shields Road that day. We stocked up with drink and lots of buffet things for the family coming around tomorrow. New Years Eve night however was spent quietly. Our first New Year together. We had a few drinks, watched some telly then played some Scrabble. I managed to convince Lorraine that pfregyx was a word... a breed of antelope from Iceland and the x was on triple letter score. She admitted defeat after that and we went to bed. Lorraine went straight to sleep which was disappointing because I'd been wanting to talk about the little towel... aahh well.

Time now to get used to each other and tackle our first full year together. It would have its ups and downs but fortunately the ups won... by quite some distance.

CHAPTER 21

I'm Into Something Good

———————————◼———————————

Hi folks Lorraine here (now there's a surprise).

I've been given the go-ahead to write my own chapter in this final volume of the 'North-East Diaries' trilogy. Jim's going to be unavailable for a while so I thought I'd take this opportunity to introduce myself to you readers out there. I'm the 'her indoors' person for want of a better phrase. And the 'I'm Into Something Good' title is all my own idea because we've been together thirty-five years now and I wouldn't change a single day of it. But let's be honest, Jim certainly lays it on thick doesn't he? He goes on more than a bit if I'm being truthful. But I wouldn't swap him for anything... well, maybe for one of those Ninja air-fryer things. I quite fancy one of those.

I digress. Anyway, going back to that last chapter that Jim wrote... I can vaguely remember the lying on the kitchen floor episode; not my finest hour certainly but I'm suspecting that Jim's made it sound a lot more humorous than it actually was. However I was zonked out so I can't argue about it... apart from the little towel thing. I know for a fact it was a big fluffy towel... so don't believe a word he says.

So, getting down to the nitty-gritty... can anyone tell me what's wrong with Lena Martell and Marmite? Because firstly, I happen to think that I have good musical taste. Nothing at all like Jim who plays all that noisy rubbish by people with daft names like Judas Priest, Def Leppard and Motorhead... I mean, what's all that about? If truth be told I'm not the world's best educated person... but I do know how to spell deaf... and leopard... and rhinoceros come to that, but it seems those heavy metal people don't do proper spelling. Perhaps they should forget music and stick to working in their scrapyards.

And secondly, just to put you all straight... Marmite is nice (remember you heard that from me) and much better than the things that tickle Jim's taste buds... kipper fillets and curly-wurlys. I kid you not. I mean come on, let's get real... he's a grown man. I bet you've never seen John Wayne or Victor Mature with a curly-wurly. Although... hang on a second, maybe John Wayne has had a curly-wurly, because... and correct me if I'm wrong... wasn't his proper name something like Sheila or Betty or something? Not that all Sheila's and Betty's or even Eunice's and Abagail's have to like those chocolate monstrosities. I'm in no way saying that wiggly chocolate is more suited to women... because that would make me a misogynist and I'm actually a 'sogy' myself... if that's the correct term... if it's not then I'm sure you know that I mean I'm female.

So that's that then... all those contentious things now sorted... Marmite is nice... curly-wurlys aren't... and Lena Martell is sick (Obviously she's not really sick... but if any young folk are reading this they'll realise how cool and hip

I am with the current terminology... apparently 'sick' now means awesome or outstanding... go figure that one out). Notice how I said cool and hip?

Enough of that for now... because as I write Jim is lying in Raigmore hospital waiting for another big operation. It's man stuff and very hush-hush so this bit of my writing may be edited out when he reads through it. I'm worried about him obviously but you can't tell that to Jim. He can't handle 'worried' and Jim definitely can't do 'serious' so he always has to give everything a humorous twist... which can be most annoying. I think I'll tell him how annoying he is tomorrow at visiting time... unless there's been some bad news of course. In that case I might do weeping instead. Even so Jim will make light of any bad news and still crack daft jokes... if he's still alive of course.

I'm not supposed to tell anyone that Jim is in hospital for an operation and definitely not about it being for a down-below man thing. He says he would end up with a mantlepiece full of get well soon cards covered in daft willy jokes... and that thought has kept my lips sealed... but it's not easy.

Knock-knock-knock "Hi auntie Lorraine is Jim about for a quick word?"

"Sorry Tracy he's in the bath."

"Really?... but he was in the bath when I called yesterday."

"Was he?"

"Yes."

"Ohhh that's quite a long time then. I quite forgot about that. I'd better go and get him out... he'll have gone all wrinkly. See yourself out... bye for now."

Telling lies is a lot harder than you think.

He did make me laugh though the day he came back from the doctor's with the news about his man thing problem. Our old doctor... Doctor Begg had retired and Jim hadn't realised that our new Doctor Dunbar was in fact a female. No-one had bothered to mention it to him and I certainly wasn't aware. This is how he put it...

"So pet, the receptionist calls out my name and I go limping out of the waiting room and into the doctor's office. I'm immediately confused when I enter because I'm looking at an attractive lassie maybe in her middle thirties. She's smiling at me and I'm thinking... she's definitely not one of the nurses because they don't do proper smiling. In all probability she's one of the office staff bringing my notes through. So I return the smile and wander over to take a seat beside the desk."

"Over onto the examination couch Mr Bates and take your trousers off."

I'm thinking 'aye so that you can go back into the reception and tell the other lasses you've seen my bum. Dream on sweet princess.'

"Trousers Mr Bates... I can't manage the procedure with them on. And pull your shorts down too."

"So I'm getting a bit panicky by this time. That lass has just asked me to drop'em and I'm too old for that stuff. So I'm just about to break the glass on the red fire alarm thingy when I suddenly notice the nametag on her shirt. It says Dr K. Dunbar... a woman doctor indeed. Mind you she could have nicked it... but somehow I doubt it. So, with great reluctance I do as requested and lower the trousers and shorts. After a few seconds staring at her computer screen she turns around to face me. Suddenly her jaw drops, her eyes open really wide... and she points down below, puts her hand over her mouth and begins to snort and giggle. I'm embarrassed and not best pleased by this time, so I shout for help. The door bursts open and a big policeman comes running in with his truncheon in his hand... and he takes one look at me with no pants on and laughs even harder..."

"Nah, only joking pet... that Dr Dunbar was really good. She was just a doctor doing her job and she put me at ease. I forgot all about her being a female. She got me up on the couch thing... did the doctor stuff then took her latex gloves off and gave me the verdict on the prostate and the hernia... all matter of fact. To be fair I can't speak highly enough of her... in fact I'll make sure I book my appointments with her in future.

"So anyway Lorraine, cutting a long story short, I've got to go and have an op as soon as poss. Ohh aye, and if things should happen to go pear shaped can you invite Dr Dunbar to the wake."

That was Jim being as serious as he could be. I realised at that point, after all these years together that he was in fact covering up his nervousness. The thought of the op had scared him and he glossed over it with humour. He'd never in a million years admit to being nervous or scared of course, but that moment seemed to reinforce the fact that we were indeed a solid partnership, because I knew he was worried... and he knew that I knew... and we both felt comfortable in the knowing.

Enough said about Jim though... he'll be back soon enough. I'm going to tell you about myself and our life together. Our chalk and cheese life together.

I made my entrance into this world on the 24th of April 1945. Somebody must have gone and told the Germans... and they must have been terrified, because just a fortnight later they surrendered. I often wonder how much of that silly kerfuffle could have been avoided if I'd been born a year or two earlier.

I was brought up alongside two siblings, Terry and Jacqueline. Both were older than myself and sadly both are now gone. My mother brought us up alone because my dad died when I was three years old. Tuberculosis they said it was... although it was commonly referred to as consumption. It was ironic that had my dad managed to hold on for a year or two he could possibly have recovered when streptomycin made its entrance.

Everyone of a similar age who is reading this will agree that life in the forties and fifties could be something of a grind. We didn't think of it as such then, when we were going through it... but with the benefit of hindsight we realise how much of a struggle life could be, especially if you were an offspring in a single-parent family. Rationing continued into the fifties and money was always tight. That was life then and we just got on with it.

Fast forward to 1988 after marriage, divorce, two children and then grandkids making an appearance. I'm sitting alone in my flat after a hard day's work at Sanderson hospital. The 'alone' bit is becoming irritating. Nobody deserves to live their life alone... do they? I'm reading through the Evening Chronicle and I happen upon the personal ads section. Some of the ads seem okay whilst others feel more like a cry for help. It makes me wonder what kind of a personal ad I would write if I was feeling desperate. Then a daft one catches my eye. I honestly can't recall if Jim's version in an earlier chapter is correct but I do remember having a chuckle at the sheer cheek of it. I do remember it said something about WLTM lady with GSOH and she must have her own teeth and no moustache. I don't know why it tickled me so much... but it did.

So we met up... and the rest as they say is history. Now however I'm sitting in my living room up the top-end of Scotland. I did tell you that we now lived in Sutherland didn't I? Probably not... but we do. We've lived in Scotland for almost twenty years now. If we'd gone much further north we'd have been Norwegian. But I'm rambling... I tend to do that nowadays, and of course I'm tired and worried, and hoping the phone doesn't ring, because at this time of night it could only be bad news. My wee Westie's head is on my lap and that's some comfort... but he realises, like myself, that one of the pack is missing. Time to stop writing. I'll write some more tomorrow after visiting... if it's gone all right of course. But for now I need to get some sleep. I bet I can't. Speak to you all later... night-night.

A Hard Day's Night

I didn't manage to get much sleep as I predicted but I did make it to Raigmore hospital for visiting. Jim hadn't long been out of the operating theatre and was very groggy... so I thought it was best if I ate his grapes for him. There was a sign on the board behind him saying 'Nil by Mouth' which confused me a little because where else could you stick grapes? I had a little chuckle to myself when I followed that train of thought. Of course I shouldn't even have driven the fifty or so miles to Raigmore. Keep it quiet but the DVLA have taken my licence away... the rotten buggers. All because I have early Alzheimer's on top of the leukaemia. But I was having a good day so I thought 'aahh what the hell.' I know that's really naughty but I'm cracking on for eighty so it's allowed. I have told you all about the Alzheimer's haven't I?... No? Sorry about that I must have forgotten.

A nice lady called Frances from the Alzheimer's trust thing comes to visit me every few weeks to see how my condition is progressing. And she says it's progressing really well... so that must be a good thing... mustn't it? Frances has Mackay for a surname because it seems to be the law that everyone up here is called Mackay or Ross or Murray or Sutherland with the odd Mackenzie thrown in for good measure. If you don't have one of those surnames you must be a Glasgow incomer... or even worse... English. Jim said we should begin to call ourselves McBates and then begin saying things like 'hoots mon' and 'lang may yer lum reek.' Honestly I was okay with that but then he said he might start wearing a tartan skirt. Aye... I don't think so. He'll be hunting through my knicker drawer next.

So, now that I've come clean about my health problems you'll be a little more understanding if I waffle on a bit. Jim says I'm really good at waffling. Ohh aye and I had a stroke as well... way back in 2007. A proper stroke... not one of those you do with your dog. They took my licence away for a whole year then too. I blame Winston Churchill. I had to jump through hoops to get my licence back but fortunately

I did hoop-jumping at school. As luck would have it my stroke was on the good side of my brain and I made a full recovery... well almost full. Can you remember that Gloria Gaynor record 'I Will Survive'? Well survive I did... and 'I'm Still Standing' (thought I'd stick that record in to show you I still have marbles to play with) ... glassy ones, not those steel things that were just little ball-bearings.

So, going back to 1989 and Jim and I were having out first disagreement. I'll call it disagreement instead of argument because men never win those.

"I've loaded the dishwasher pet."

"You don't usually do that Jim."

"Just thought I'd help."

"That's nice... did you rinse them first?"

"Ehhh?"

"Did you rinse the dishes before you put them in the dishwasher?"

"Lorraine, what on earth are you on about? The clue is in the name... dishwasher. You put them in the machine and it makes a whooshy noise and washes your dishes."

"Ohh my goodness Jim, you're a typical man. You have to give the dishes a pre-rinse before you put them in."

"Why?"

"So that they're clean."

"So what's the point of the dishwasher?"

"It's labour saving... and it only uses a third of the water that you would normally use."

"You're talkin' bollox Lorraine. It doesn't save you any labour. Not if you have to rinse them before you put them in. You're working harder."

"I wish you wouldn't use bad language Jim. Anyway the man told me how much it saves."

"Lorraine man, never believe a salesman. Think about it, you're washing the dishes before you put them in... so how are you saving labour? You're using water to rinse the dishes which you would have been doing anyway before you bought that contraption. And then the machine uses even more water to make your clean dishes even cleaner so where's the water saving? Then you have to do all that bending to get the dishes out... give them a swift wipe with a tea towel and then put them away. You've made more work for yourself... not less. And the electric meter has been laughing its head off while clicking merrily away in the meantime."

He did make a good point. I'd never thought about it like that. So there wasn't much I could say other than...

"Bugger off... and keep out of the kitchen in future."

"Lorraine I do wish you wouldn't use bad language." He was using sarcasm again. I think he put his jacket on after that and went to the pub. Not the Jubilee Club though because he'd been barred... and not the Scrogg because it was a crime pub and the clientele reckoned that Jim was a police spy because he wore a collar and tie. We'd only been there one time and it wasn't very nice... it was full of 'bampots' (notice how I'm using the Scottish word for 'nutter').

Then a really big day came... our first joint purchase. It felt weird but important. Our first purchase together was a continental tent. It was a big step for us... buying something together which was fairly expensive. Because who would get custody of the tent if we split up? We laughed about it of course and I remember saying that I should have custody but Jim could visit and take it out at weekends.

That piece of equipment saw a lot of use during the first five years. We didn't have a lot of money because of Jim's tax thing, my car payments, the mortgage and many other outgoings. For several unfathomable reasons we wouldn't have access to Jim's lingerie money for another five years. I can't remember the ins and outs of it but it must have made sense at the time. So holiday fortnight would see us load up one of the cars with all our equipment and head for a campsite. Sometimes we'd have my grandson Christopher with us and we'd head up to Melrose or Hawick. I'd sit out in the sun and Jim would play football with my grandson. I wasn't too happy about that because I thought Jim should have used a ball... (that was me trying out some humour).

Usually though we would camp at Crawford. It's a little village between Carlisle and Glasgow where Jim had discovered a pub that never closed... the Crawford Arms Hotel. That place was where I learned to play pool (more of that later). Sometimes though we travelled even further. On one occasion we camped at a place called Resipole if I'm remembering right. It was in an area called Ardnamurchan anyway and I know I have that name correct. From some other place around there we booked a day trip and visited Mull and Iona. Iona was a tiny little island and the setting for another of our disagreements. I wasn't happy about taking half a day to go and stand on a little island and then half a day to come back again. But I kept quiet for Jim's sake.

Click-click-click.

"Jim... what on earth do you think you're doing?"

"Ehhh? I'm taking photos."

"It's a graveyard."

"I know... that's why I'm taking photos."

"That's not nice. They're dead people."

"This is where the old kings of Scotland are buried Lorraine."

"So"

"So it's history man. Kenneth Mac-Alpin is supposed to be buried here."

"And what do you think his wife will say about you taking photos?"

"Lorraine, are you for real?... I said Kenneth Mac-Alpin."

"Okay, okay, got it. He's the bloke you used to work for."

"No man he's one of the old kings from twelve hundred years ago. There's loads of history all around this place. John Smith was buried here just a few months ago."

"Is he the fellow who invented beer?"

"The leader of the Labour party for heaven's sake."

"I didn't know Tony Blair invented beer?"

"I give up."

"Good... put that camera away and let's head back to the boat."

"It's a ferry."

"It floats so it's a boat... just like a bloomer is still bread." Jim didn't reply. Camera went back into the case and we headed for the 'boat'.

I won that one. For some reason Jim loves his history but what's the point of that. History is things that have already happened and they can't be changed. It's those things that are happening today and what's going to happen in the future that I'm concerned about. We can do something about that… can't we? Jim of course says that we need to study history and learn from it so that we don't continue making the same mistakes over and over. He's got a point I suppose… but there again so has a needle.

The only other time we argued on a regular basis was when we disagreed about multi-tasking. Jim has the irritating knack of being able to annoy me when he begins to press all the right buttons. I'm sure there must be lots of women reading this whose husbands have managed to press their buttons. 'I know… I know! that's Jim's double-entendres rubbing off on me'. Not that I let him rub off on me very often.

"Jim can you come and give me a hand to shift this settee so I can hoover underneath it?"

"I'm busy pet… trying to figure out the instructions for putting that occasional table together. Can't make head nor tail of it. It's all Chinese to me."

"But can't you help me with this as well?"

"Not really, I'm busy with an Allen key and I need to concentrate."

"Ohh for God's sake… I just need a hand. Why is it that men can't multi-task like women?"

(cue button pressing) … "Because men like to do one job at a time and do it properly. Women have lots of little jobs going on and end up making a right pig's ear of them all." (cue vitriol and bile).

"You conceited prat."

"Not a prat Lorraine. A prat is someone who behaves stupidly or has little ability. Entirely the opposite of the word you're searching for. Don't you mean genius or intellectual?"

Grrr... that man could be so annoying. He'll regret it later when he discovers I've put 'Fiery Jack' in his underpants.

Anyway... I've got to go now. Jim is coming home. And before you ask... no, I'm not driving; Ingrid, my daughter is picking him up from Raigmore. So I can't continue with my story... just when I was beginning to enjoy the writing. Once Jim's back he'll want to take over and check my spelling. Then of course he'll be doing all the future writing because it's his tale to tell. I do hope that he leaves my little contribution in the book though. So, bye for now folks it's been nice meeting you. (Not that I've actually met you, it was just a figure of speech). See? There I go rambling on again. TTFN.

CHAPTER 22

Hello It's Me

———————————————————■———————————————————

(It's her indoors again... cue disappointed sighs)

I picked the title of this chapter too, because I like Adele and she always tells you how old she is on her albums. I'm hoping to still be around when she does '35'. I'm not joined at the hip with Lena Martell you know.

Anyway, Lorraine here folks. I know you were expecting Jim for this chapter, and all the other ones too... but he's not able to sit at the computer for the next week or so. He's home now but he's a little uncomfortable... you know? down below. He has to sit on this squishy donut thing and have soft pillows underneath. What a pain that is for him. He's having to sleep in the spare room too in case either the dog or myself jump on him. I certainly wasn't going to... I'm past all that malarkey. Mind you our Westie Jack most certainly would have leapt on him.

Our dog is a bit put out to be honest because Jim isn't allowed to play tug with him or to take him out for walks. Not for another week or two at least and definitely not until all his stitches have dissolved. If he played tug with our dog

Jack then his stitches might burst and all his insides would come tumbling out and splodge all over the carpet... and I'd have to clean it up. Can you imagine having to pick up all those things that look like sausages?... Ughhh...

Apart from that he's having to shower twice every day and rub some sort of magic cream around the affected area. He showed me the operation scarring and it looked really sore and painful. I didn't make eye contact with his old fella though... just in case it thought malarkey might indeed be in the offing.

It's nice having my husband back home again but it's disrupted our normal routine. He's been having to sit in front of the television, watching daytime programmes and he hates them all. You should have heard the language half an hour ago when he was watching Lingo. 'And here's your second four letter Lingo beginning with an F'. Honestly I had to put my hands over the dog's ears. I turned the telly off because I was dreading some even worse letters popping up. The letter 'c' is a corker. Do you know how many rude words of four or five letters there are? Loads and loads... I googled them but couldn't find a decent one for the letter 'e'. If you can find one then let Jim know on Facebook.

Anyhow, while I'm writing this Jim is in the sitting room, reading quietly. Something about the Plantagenets. I do hope he's not thinking of ordering new flowers for the garden without showing me what they look like first. Did I tell you he's colour-blind? Probably not... but he is. He doesn't tell people about it because when they find out they invariably say something like 'so what colour do you think my jumper is then?' In answer to which Jim usually replies with a four-letter Lingo.

When I left off the previous chapter I'd briefly covered our first five years together. I'll bash on now with the next chunk of our lives up until 2005 when we moved to Scotland (if that's all right with you folks of course) ... Yes? Then let's crack on. He'll probably edit it out anyway.

Life during those years was more or less mundane to be honest. There weren't any really notable happenings in our immediate lives. My mother died and shortly afterwards Jim's dad followed suit. They were both sad occasions but Jim will probably elaborate further on his dad's funeral... when an obnoxious cretin ruined what should have been a solemn occasion.

Life moved on as it always does and we worked and paid our bills. Jim's spinal problem became an even bigger problem and he left the chemical company after four or five lucrative years because of those issues. He began to teach himself computing and touch typing. People used to give me funny looks when they asked about Jim and I would tell them he was probably locked in the bedroom with Mavis Beacon.

Mavis Beacon of course was a computer programme which taught you how to touch-type. Jim took it seriously and pretty soon he was really fast and efficient. Initially he worked for several charities until he felt comfortable with his computing and typing skills. Then he applied to join BT. He was successful.

We also formed a football team. We called it Walkergate Rangers... because the home pitch was on the Fossway in Walkergate. The Rangers bit was just added to make the team seem formidable... but obviously it didn't work. Jim was the chairman and I washed the strips and made the sandwiches.

Jim was also initially the manager of the men's team and before he proudly handed over the reins to someone else he achieved a ninety percent record... one win and nine defeats... 'ha-ha-ha'... certainly not in the same league as that Manchester bloke Pop Garlicodour.

Shieldfield Club became our regular haunt. It was where most of the men's football team congregated so we followed suit... and that's where Jim and I became pals with an incorrigible soul called Flossy.

What can I tell you about Flossy? Well... everything and nothing actually. He was a small, completely bald, wiry bloke in his fifties. He was a professional thief who'd never worked a day in his life. He was a liar... a cheat and a thrice married nutcase but he liked me for some reason. Maybe that was because I'd beaten him more than once on the pool table where he rather fancied himself as something of a hustler. He hadn't realised I played for the county and had once beaten the British number two. Okay, okay, I hear you, enough of the boasting. To continue... Flossy was also very-very funny and possessed an innate streetwise intelligence which made him stand out from the other career criminals who frequented the club. I liked him.

There were various explanations as to the origin of the nickname Flossy. Some said it was because he'd once dressed in women's clothes and had donned a blonde wig to avoid arrest over a series of burglaries. He'd then strolled nonchalantly through a police cordon wearing a mini skirt and high-heels. Unfortunately for him one of his strategically placed balloons had popped at a crucial moment... leading to his apprehension... after a huge fight of course in which he laid low three burly coppers. I'm sure that tale was just an urban myth but it added to his reputation nevertheless. Amongst other explanations for the genesis of the name was the one I came to accept... although I never mentioned it in front of Flossy. In this version a gang boss had supposedly arrived from London to set up a Newcastle syndicate. The gangster was reputedly a leading member of one of the London crime outfits during the war, and years before the Krays and Richardsons became famous nationwide. During his brief stay in Newcastle he'd indulged himself with a night or two of pleasure with Flossy's mother, a hostess... for want of a more descriptive word. She became pregnant and nine-months later a male child entered this world. The surname of the Cockney gangster was Candy... and that apparently was how our erstwhile pal received his Flossy nickname... Candy Floss! We never did discover his proper Christian name, because it wouldn't have been polite to ask.

Did I tell you that Flossy was also a magician? If not then I apologise, that's my memory on the blink again. The thing is, Flossy could do things which had no logical explanation. I mean weird and wonderful things which even now I still talk about and wonder how on earth they happened... unless of course he was truly magic. 'Nah' I hear you say, 'there's no such thing,' but honestly folks, I believe different.

"Hi Flossy."

"Hi Lorraine... fancy a game?"

"You'll be letting me get my coat off first?"

"Plenty time pet, there's somebody on the pool table just now. You'll need to put your money down and go and knock them off."

"What's the matter with you putting your money down?"

"Skint."

"You always say you're skint."

"I know pet but this time I really am. That's why I'm nursing this pint that Davy Davison bought me."

He seemed genuine on this occasion although you never could tell because he always had a twinkle in the eyes which hinted at a fib being presented. Nonetheless, with that I pulled a five-pound note out of my jeans pocket and proffered it to Flossy, "Here you old rogue... get yourself a couple of pints... you can owe me."

I remember him looking so surprised at what had been for me a simple friendly gesture. "You're not a bad lass Lorraine... for a woman. You must have some male hormones in you."

"Give over Flossy, you'll be wanting Christmas cards next."

He laughed at that comment then said... "Do you want me to double your donation?"

"What?"

"Double your five-pound donation."

"And how do you intend to do that if you're skint?" He wasn't making much sense, "Unless of course you're going to tear it in two. By the way it's a loan... not a donation."

"Nah man, I'm not going to tear it. If I can double the value of that fiver then you have to promise never to tell anyone about what you're going to see."

The mind boggled, I really couldn't imagine what he was up to, "Okay Flossy it's a deal." I was expecting to see him go and nick someone's handbag or something similar.

"And you mustn't ask me how I made it happen or the moment will be spoiled." He was being serious.

"Okay."

"Promise?"

"Yes promise." I was good at keeping promises.

He handed me the five-pound note. "I'm going to stand back from your table so that I'm nowhere near the money."

I stood with the money in hand, "Okay... now what?"

"Now you have to confirm that what you have in your hand is a five-pound note?"

"Of course it is... I just gave it to you." I thought that bit about confirmation was quite needless but nevertheless I inspected the fiver and made a big show of inspecting both sides just to indulge Flossy. He seemed satisfied.

"Now put it down on the table and put a bar towel over it." I laid the note on the table but there was no towel handy so I had to wait a few minutes while he wandered over to the bar and returned with one over his arm. He handed it to me. By this time Jim was watching what was going on from the far end of the room beside the snooker table.

"Check the bar towel first to make sure it's just an ordinary cloth and that I haven't tampered with it."

I did so. It was just a run of the mill bar towel. I inspected both sides then gave Flossy a grin, "Now what?"

"Now place the towel over the five-pound note." As I did so... Flossy stepped back so that he was at least six feet away from the table.

"And...?"

"Peek underneath to make sure the fiver is still there."

I peeked, and it was, "Okay, it's still a fiver."

"Now put your glass of pop on top of the towel."

"It's whisky not pop."

He sighed, "Okay then... put your glass of whisky on top."

I did so.

"Good girl... now spin around three times and say, Hubble-bubble money double."

I gave out a giggle, "You're kidding... right?"

"You'll spoil it if you don't do it." He was still six-feet away.

I thought 'what the hell'... it was all a harmless wind-up anyway. I did as told and turned around three times quickly and Flossy still hadn't moved an inch. "Hubble-bubble money double," I felt such a fool coming out with that especially with Jim and some of the other folk watching.

I gave Flossy a huge embarrassed grin, "What now?"

"Sit down, knock your drink back, lift the beer towel up and then hand me the tenner."

"Hand the tenner to you?"

"Aye of course. It was my fiver you put on the table."

I had to think about that. It had been my fiver originally but I had given it to Flossy... so logically it was his.

"And you're telling me that when I look under the towel the five pounds will magically have become ten pounds."

"Aye."

"Is this going to make me look silly?"

"No."

There were about a dozen interested spectators by this time... Jim being one of them. He'd moseyed over from his game on the snooker table and was standing there, next to Jackie Walker, cue in hand, chalk on his shirtsleeve, and with a puzzled look on his face. I didn't want to make a complete idiot of myself, but I had no option at that point other than to continue with the charade. So I sat myself down, drank the whisky and lemonade... then very carefully lifted the black and yellow bar towel. I was surprised. Well actually, stunned would be a better word. Sitting on the table in front of me was a crisp new ten-pound note. It wasn't possible... surely? I must have sat for a good few seconds just staring at it. I lifted my head to look at Flossy who was still standing in the same position... at least six-feet away. He raised his eyebrows as I glanced over. He smiled and I began...

"How...?"

He grinned broadly and held his finger to his lips... "Shhh..."

I remembered what he'd said about not asking and telling. I just sat there open mouthed. How on earth had the five-pounds turned into ten pounds? I was certain that Flossy hadn't moved a muscle during my turning around routine and there wasn't anyone else near to my table. It was to all intents and purposes impossible.

"Flossy... what the heck...?"

He grinned from ear to ear as he stepped up to the table, picked up the ten-pound note and said, "Paul Daniels asked me how that was done."

I was still gobsmacked... "And what did you tell him?"

"I told him to bugger off, it wasn't a trick... it was proper magic." he laughed, and with that final comment Flossy pocketed the tenner and turning on his heels headed for the bar.

As he left Jim came and joined me. "How did he do that?"

"No idea."

"You must have seen something."

"I didn't see anything. What he just did was impossible."

"Check your purse."

"I didn't bring my purse. I only had the fiver in my pocket for emergencies."

"Are you definitely sure it was a fiver you gave him?"

I didn't dignify that question with a response... I just glared.

"He must have had the tenner stuck on one side of the towel and you missed it," Jim offered.

"Right, smarty-pants... I didn't miss it. I checked it, both sides... you saw me. And anyway, where did the fiver go?"

Jim just shrugged, dropped his eyes and began checking his wallet even though Flossy hadn't been anywhere near him. We both ended up being utterly bemused by what we'd witnessed. The other folk who'd been watching seemed to be equally baffled. Not a single one of them came up with a plausible explanation and although he was approached several times that evening by various regulars who'd witnessed the magic or trickery or whatever it had been... Flossy would not be moved and remained tight-lipped.

Eyes down. The next occasion with that old reprobate was equally as mysterious. It must have been a full month later before we saw Flossy. We were in Shieldfield club yet again but on this occasion we were in the upstairs function room. It was dancing night and Jim had a face on him like a smacked backside. I loved to go dancing... Jim didn't. You know how people describe rubbish dancers by saying they have two left feet?... well Jim had three. You see some folk glide across the floor like romantic poetry in motion. My husband was more like a poor Limerick... who stumbled, stuttered and laughed every time he stood on my foot. He did a lot of laughing... and I grimaced a lot, but at least I'd managed to get him there. I'd told him it was to be big bingo night, held during the dancing interval and the jackpot hadn't been won for weeks. It now stood at fifty-five pounds. That pleased him... although the jackpot could only be won if you shouted before the fifty-fifth number.

So instead of our usual game of pool we were enjoying a different kind of evening, but guess who was trying to pull himself an unattached lady? Yes, it was Flossy and he looked moderately respectable for once. He'd even attempted to fasten a tie to his almost clean shirt... but a Windsor it was knot (notice the play on words?). He was up and down like a yo-yo asking women up for dances and having very little success. Most ladies in the room were well aware of Flossy and his reputation.

After a while we thought he must have sickened of his unsuccessful evening when he came over to join us. He parked his pint glass on the table.

"Hi Jim... Hi Lorraine, fancy a dance?"

"You not having much luck then Flossy? I grinned as I asked.

"Aahh you know how it is... I've slept with most of them and they're terrified of so much ecstasy in one small bundle."

"Small bundle is it?" I began fencing with him.

He grinned at that, "It won't be small later on when I escort Maggie home."

"Maggie?"

"Over there beside the stage," he pointed with his head.

I looked over. There was a good-looking woman of roughly my age sitting alone and she gave a smile and a brief wave when she noticed Flossy looking. How on earth?

Flossy answered before I could ask the question, "It's her first time here. Only been divorced a few months. I think she's glad of the attention."

"Flossy... you old dog."

"Maybe, but my bite's better than my bark," he grinned, "Now about that dance?"

"It's a quickstep."

"I know... I learned to dance in prison."

"Really?"

"Course not. I did gardening and kitchens usually. I learned to dance when I was a bit of a lady-killer... years ago."

"Come on then... but no standing on my feet... that's Jim's job."

Jim just grimaced and got stuck into his pint.

Flossy took my hand and led me onto the floor. I didn't know what I was letting myself in for but surprisingly he was really good. I mean exceptionally good but that only made me feel sorry for him. He had a big smile on his face as we quickstepped across the floor and he was foot perfect. That's where the feeling sorry bit came in. What a waste of a life.

We stayed up for the next dance too... a cha-cha if I remember correctly and this guy had all the moves. It made me see him in a different light. We returned to the table after that dance... both out of breath.

Jim chirped up as we sat down, "You need to practice that spin turn of yours Lorraine. It was a bit clumpy."

"Shut up."

"Okay."

"Your wife is a pretty good dancer actually," Flossy remarked.

"Well that's because she's had me as a teacher," Jim grinned.

Flossy laughed out loud, "I was watching you on the floor earlier Jim. Have you ever thought about putting your shoes on the right feet."

That put Jim back in his box. Just then the Maggie lady came over to the table. She smiled at us before bending down and whispering in Flossy's ear. He grinned in response to the whisper. She handed him a bingo ticket and then made off towards the ladies cloakroom.

Flossy stared hard at the bingo ticket and then handed it to me. "Got to go folks... something's just come up," he chuckled, then handed the ticket to me. "That's an extra ticket for you Lorraine. Maggie's ready for the off. So consider that to be your fiver back bonny lass, and you can buy me a few drinks with the rest of your winnings next time you see me."

"Aye Flossy, that'll be right. I never have any luck with the bingo."

He placed his hand on my shoulder and squeezed, "Tonight your luck will change. Two little ducks, all the fours, clickety-click and two fat ladies all on the same card," He squeezed again, "I guarantee... one hundred percent that you'll walk away with the jackpot tonight. Believe the magic Lorraine... believe. And don't forget who supplied the magic."

With that he gave us both a thumbs up and hurried off in the direction of his missing lady friend. Good luck Flossy... or should that have been good luck Maggie?... yes, probably Maggie.

Without taking you all on the rollercoaster of emotions during a jackpot bingo game... suffice to say that my husband ended up with bruised arms. "Got that one," nudge, "got that one as well," heavier nudge... then two fat ladies, "Jim, got that one too," ... super nudge.

"Will you stop banging my arm... I'm trying to mark two tickets and on one of them I'm only waiting for three."

"Number three?"

"No man... three numbers."

"But Jim I'm only waiting... 'two little ducks... twenty-two.'

"House ye bugger... here-here," I was up on my feet and screaming like a banshee, "Over here, over here." I'm waving my arm around with the winning ticket in hand and being ultra loud... just in case the committee man is hard of hearing and begins to shout the next number.

Jim has a sickly grin on his face because everyone is looking at me and I think he's maybe a wee bit embarrassed. Someone comes over to rescue the ticket and take it for checking. I have so many bits of me crossed... eyes, fingers, arms, legs... hoping that I haven't by some chance marked off a wrong number.

I hadn't. I'd bagged the big one... which would revert to a starting amount of thirty pounds next time out. So we were paid out the fifty-five pounds with all eyes upon us but it felt really strange. Some of the people in the room who only minutes before had given friendly smiles were now glaring malevolently at me. Jealousy and envy were rearing their heads. But I didn't care... I was rich and it was only natural that all the poor people in the room should resent my newly-won wealth. I reckoned I had won enough for a frivolous holiday in some exotic location... Cullercoats maybe or even abroad to Seaburn. I was one extremely happy lady that evening.

Unfortunately I didn't get to buy those few drinks for Flossy. The next I heard he was back in prison having broken his parole or something. Rumour had it that he'd seen the Maggie lady home and sometime during the night had vacated her bed and made off with her purse and various saleable silver items. It didn't look like Flossy would be able to quickstep his way out of that one.

The question that had no plausible answer though, was how in heaven's name had Flossy guaranteed us a winning ticket? He'd been so definite about the outcome, but it hadn't even been his ticket. It was a mystery with no logical conclusion. Jim of course had his own opinion about the outcome. Bent committee men and backhanders. But that made no sense to me when you actually thought about it. I wasn't about to give out any backhanders. Anyway, that couldn't be true because who on earth had ever heard of bent committee men? That would be just as bad as believing in bent policemen. No way man... impossible. Pffft... as if!

So excitement over for the time being, we got on with normal life. We packed in our stewardship of Walkergate Rangers not long after Jim had begun working for BT. The club had ballooned to a point where there were now three age group teams for kids as well as the men's team and an embryo girls team. It was all too much to manage and hold down a full-time job as well, so James withdrew gracefully from his sporting hobby.

It only took Jim about six months to be given a full BT contract and shortly after that he moved onto a permanent nightshift which had been formed for the forthcoming rollout of nationwide broadband.

Ohh aye, and we got married after ten years of living together. We just set off one day to Morpeth Registry office with two witnesses. One of Jim's BT work colleagues, Julie Fairhurst was the main witness and his nephew David Long was the other. We'd kept it very hush-hush because the last thing we wanted was loads of presents and fuss. We were both middle-aged and experienced at marriage failures so we didn't advertise our wedding. It was all straightforward, uncomplicated and over in a flash. We'd arranged to meet up with various family members on the evening at an Italian place just off Benton Park Road. That surprised them all because they thought they were coming to celebrate Jim's work promotion. We fooled them all.

Don't Leave Me This Way – That's what I'm imagining you'll all be saying when I tell you that Jim will be back writing tomorrow... and I'll be going back to being 'her indoors' again. 'No-no please we want to hear more from you because you're so sensible' I hear you cry. Sorry folks... my lord and master has ordained that he will in fact vacate his squishy donut and once more take over the reins of literary excellence... Pffft – I should coco. Nevertheless I'm being cast asunder tomorrow so I'll need to cram lots of life into my last paragraphs.

We sold the flat in Kingsmere Gardens and utilizing the profit from the sale as well as finally drawing on the mysterious lingerie money we paid cash for a house in Gillies Street, still in Walker, just off Welbeck Road, but almost Byker. We were now mortgage free but we needed to spend a lot of money on making the house and garden into something desirable. It was work-work-work with very little respite. Jim would do his ten-hour nightshift and arrive home in time to hand the car over to me. Then I'd go and do my shift at Sanderson. I'd return home after five o'clock, then make the tea before waking Jim. We'd have maybe two hours together before it was time for Jim to shoot off for his next shift. We were making good money but life was a grind.

We spent loads on the house and also had some truly super holidays. Corfu, Crete, Malta x 3, Majorca x 4 and generally they were all enjoyable apart from the fact that James hated flying and would turn into a real wimp as soon as we approached the airport. Talk about a big girl's blouse.

Then Jim had a little heart attack. He recovered within a month but the very next year he had a biggie. This next bit is true... I mean everything I've written is true but this next bit sounds far-fetched.

Sanderson hospital podiatry office – Ring-ring-ring.

"Good morning, podiatry, how may I help you?" chunter-chunter-chunter.

"Hang on, I'll just get her for you Jim... Lorraine it's Jim for you."

I take the phone, "Hi, what you up to? You should be in bed."

"I've just phoned an ambulance pet. Just to let you know I'm having a heart-attack."

"You're kidding." Shock, horror.

"Got to go, I'm on the floor and they're at the door."

"Jim man... what the...?"

"RVI... they're taking me to RVI," phone gets hung up.

Half-an-hour later I'm at the RVI in one of the crash wards watching Jim in obvious distress and looking very ill indeed.

I don't know what to do. I feel so useless, "Are you Mrs Bates?" asks a white coated fellow with a clip board in hand.

"Err... yes," the change of name still spooks me sometimes.

"I need you to authorize the next procedure we want to give to your husband."

"Okay... and what's that?" I point to the clipboard.

"It's a disclaimer form. Your husband has had a rather severe heart attack and we really need to give him a special kind of large injection which can only be administered once. It will probably save his life but there's a chance it could also go the other way... and we need your permission to proceed."

"You mean he could die?"

"Well, we expect not, but yes it's a possibility... or he could have a stroke. I'm afraid that is the case but the chances of it happening are much less than if we do nothing and he doesn't have the injection at all. We really need you to decide quickly so we can get to work on him."

I had a matter of seconds to decide. It was an awful choice to have to make. If I signed the form and they went ahead with the injection and he died... how on earth would I have lived with that knowledge for the rest of my life. But it was a Catch 22 situation. He might die with the injection and he would probably do so without it. Jim would sometimes say... 'Life often gives you difficult choices.' This was one such occasion. I signed the form and crossed my fingers.

I was still in there when they put a team around him and gave the injection. It was a big bugger straight into the stomach. Some machine was making beeps and we stood waiting. I admit to having a few tears... mainly for Jim but a few others for myself, and the thought of having to live with the consequences of the form signing.

Jim went quiet for a while. He'd stopped the moaning and after a little while he began rambling instead. His language was choice... trust him. Eventually he managed to focus on me and eked out a smile, "Hi pet, you made it," his voice was slurred and different, "Watch out for that big ******g giraffe behind you." I glanced over my shoulder. Obviously there was no actual giraffe.

The clipboard doctor touched my arm and whispered, "He's hallucinating... which is good. It means the injection has worked and he's stabilising. You'll need to leave us to do our job now. I'll get one of the nurses to let you know when we've got him settled and hooked up." With that a nurse took me by the arm and led me out into a corridor. She pointed me towards a waiting room and coffee machine. I felt very much alone and scared. I did manage to find a payphone to let my work colleagues know I wouldn't make it back that day.

Two hours later I was sitting at Jim's bedside. He had tubes going in to various places and there were machines flickering and flashing with one making the expected beeps. But he now had some colour back and he wasn't cursing and hallucinating.

"Where's me grapes?" he asked... but in a subdued voice.

"I haven't had time to...."

"I know... just joking."

"Not funny."

"I know. They're transferring me to Freeman tomorrow."

"They never said."

"They will. They just told me ten minutes ago."

"Why Freeman?"

"Cos that's where they do the big heart operations."

"How big?"

"Dunno really, but as big as it takes."

"Are you scared?"

"No... I'm still here so scared is pointless. Unless they're going to fly me over to Freeman of course."

We both had a little chuckle at that. As it turned out it was two days before the Freeman transfer and he had his big op on day four. It's pointless telling you how it turned out because he's still here and writing books... so hazard a wild guess. It would be ten days before he made it home and a few months of recuperation. But I have to say that BT were absolutely brilliant during that period and took many weeks to slowly ease him back to work.

I was due to retire from the NHS the following April and Jim had taken the hint that a medical retirement may be on the cards for him. So we began planning for life after work. And we began looking northwards to Scotland for our retirement move.

That's all from me... for now anyway. Bugger-lugs is back tomorrow and he'll be picking holes in my writing. If anyone fancies starting a Twitter cyclone thing to get me back for another chapter feel free. I've got the writing bug and I think I'll start my own book... but you know the crack with Alzheimer's? I'll probably have forgotten by tomorrow. Take care readers... and keep your hand on your halfpenny.

CHAPTER 23

Hoots Mon, There's a Moose

—————————◆—————————

Loose Aboot This Hoose

Oh dear, letting my wife loose with two chapters wasn't such a good idea. I thought it would be fun and that she'd have a harmless mess around with some memories. Also I thought it would keep her out of the sitting room so I could swear at the telly in peace. I didn't expect she'd put so much personal stuff in there and now I think I'd feel like a real Scrooge if I dumped any of it.

I'll leave it as it is for now... otherwise she'll give me earache and sit me back down on my donut. I can't take any more of that. However, I may have a minor tinker with her spelling later... especially her rinoceras.

But first things first. We're into April 2024 and I'm being pushed to finish this third volume of the North-East Diaries trilogy. So let's crack on.

Easter has just been and gone and the village of Rogart has returned to some kind of normalcy since Covid decided to fade away. Personally I'm still worried that it's just hiding somewhere and waiting for us to forget about those traumatic years and let down our collective guard. Then it will nip back with a vengeance and our hospitals will be back to bursting point. To be fair, after almost fifteen years of this government the hospitals are already creaking at the seams and it wouldn't take a lot to totally overwhelm them.

Now just before I finish the tale by getting stuck into our last twenty (almost) years up here in the Highlands I need to have a good old rant about daytime telly. Why? You ask. Well I'll tell you… it's because I've had to sit in front of the box for the last two weeks (almost) with my willpower slowly ebbing away (almost) with the sheer pointlessness of the daytime bodge-job telly-filler programmes for the brain-dead. I'll get onto the programmes in a minute, but first the adverts. Some of them have had me at screaming point… shouting abuse and throwing buns at the screen. Fortunately I'm not a good shot… but honestly?…. an example… you'll have seen this one or something very similar.

A lady enters someone's house through French doors… a big smile on her face… "Eeeh George, my canny old next-door neighbour with the salt and pepper hair and the friendly smile… you'll never guess what I've just done after watching daytime adverts?"

"Ohh hello Nellie, this is a surprise, my excitable, slightly younger next-door neighbour. I thought you'd be out at your Zumba class. Whatever you've done must be extremely important for you to come barging into my kitchen while I'm dicing vegetables for my beetroot, kale and feta salad. So come on spill the beans… what's the big announcement?"

"Have a guess."

"Hmmm, I don't know. You've joined the Postcode Lottery?"

"Wrong."

"You've sent aid money to Gaza/Somalia/Afghanistan/Scunthorpe?"

"Wrong."

"You've signed up to Amazon Prime?"

"I did that a while ago... by mistake and it took me ages to de-register. But no that's not it."

"New glasses from Specsavers?"

"No."

"Hearing aid from Boots?"

"No."

"Sent money to the Battersea dog place?"

"No."

"A new phone from E.E?"

"No."

"Okay, I give up."

Big triumphant smile, "I took your advice and joined Golden-Oldies Insurance for old folk and not very well folk over fifty-five."

"Did you now?"

"Yes, and I didn't even have to do a health check."

"Wow."

"And do you know they'll even pay out when I'm dead?"

"Wow."

"Unless I pop in the first two years of course."

"You're not going to do that... are you?"

"Of course not silly, I take that biofungulata stuff every morning and it's full of probiotics and wiggly bacteria things that make your gut all healthy and your poo's nice and squishy."

"Wow... I didn't know about that. I could do with squishier poo's."

"Yes, they were talking about it on Loose Women. Janet Street Porter was showing photographs of her squishy....."

"Grrr... get out of my house you total moron."

I could go on about the adverts for ages but you get the gist don't you? As for the programmes, well honestly... is this what we've come to? All sitting around waiting for a phone-call from Holly Willoughby and when it rings having to shout out 'Albert Tatlock' or 'Wee Willie Winkie' or something equally stupid so we can make an arse of ourselves trying to win a few hundred pounds on that big wheel thing. I mean... can you imagine phoning your old mother who's living alone... and when she picks up the receiver she begins shouting out 'Wee Willie Winkie'. You'd be straight on to Social Services wouldn't you? Anyway, that though aside, this is how it usually goes on dumb-down tv.

"Congratulations... you've picked up, who is it calling?"

"Lilian."

"Well done Lilian, you're the first caller to remember to shout out Albert Tatlock."

"Yes... little chubby old bloke with a flat cap. Ken Barlow's uncle."

"Yes of course, well done you. And where are you calling from Lilian?"

"My sitting room."

"Ha-ha, yes of course, and what do you do for a living?"

"I breathe in and out."

"Ha-ha, yes of course." Wheel goes around. Click-click... clliikkk.

"Ohh, well done Lilian... you've won a thousand pounds... what will you do with it?"

"None of your business."

"Ha-ha... yes of course... but remember if you can answer the next question you'll also win a hessian bag full of jigsaws, t-shirts and a mug printed with a photo of Phillip Schofield when he was still employed."

"Don't bother, just send the cash." Phone goes down... Holly still has permanent fixed grin. Then, because silly playtime is over off we go for an in-depth discussion with a self-professed expert on Brazilian bum lifts gone wrong. Cue concerned faces. Blown up photograph of one of the Kardashian backsides on the back wall. The world has gone mad.

So, I'm sitting watching Hello Britain, Good Morning, Scotland Today or Lorraine or something else... I can't remember because they're all the bleeding same. The female half of a presenting duo has just finished the regular bit featuring older, dumpier women parading up and down a catwalk in new 'make you look younger' togs. The telly folk are hoping that we'll ignore the prices and we'll all immediately jump onto our mobility scooters and shoot off to Primark or wherever. They must be on a massive commission.

"And that was Gladys, looking absolutely stunning in the kimono style wrap from JCB... the cardy from Silversurfers and the duffel coat and chunky shoes from Massey Ferguson. Thank you Gladys... you gorgeous older lady with bingo wings. And that wraps up today's fashion parade folks. (cue canned applause) ... And after a very short break we'll give you that special something you've all been waiting for."

With that winding up moment the adverts come on. They continue until we've all had our fill of Chang Bimbo the new electric car with a driving range in excess of fifty miles and a charging time of under forty-eight hours. Followed of course by the eponymous Crypto only, less malarky, more smarty, and a puzzled consumer standing with a potato in his hand. Ads over we eventually flash back to the studio where we now have two presenters cosied up on a sofa, always one male, one female, with a table in front of them. On the table is a plethora of food filled plates and pots and the two presenters are picking away and pretending all the morsels are delicious... the best ever. Female looks up, pretending to be surprised that the cameras are now back on them. She puts a hand over her mouth and does a make-believe swallow... to make you think she's actually eaten some of the food.

"Sorry about that... you've caught us out," she giggles, "But boy have we got a treat for you today folks (smug smile). Because believe it or not we have Pierre Lafarge cooking for us. Welcome Pierre," female presenter extends her arm and throws a huge false smile. Camera pans to the guest chef, a snake tattoo crawling out of his jumper and writhing up his neck. He's unshaven, two dangly earrings and some metal in his bottom lip. This is diversity in action. He's standing behind the kitchen range so we can't see if he's wearing hot-pants and high-heels. To be fair he's wearing a white jacket and a tall white hat.

"It's Peter Fargo pet, but thank you for the intro."

271

Male presenter looks at his notes, "Yes... well, minor hiccup. But first of all can you tell the viewers about your awards Pierre... the Michelins and the other achievements."

"It's Peter."

Grimace from male presenter, "Okay Peter, it shows humility going incognito. But tell them about the Michelins and your awards while working at La Belle Foofoo in Marseille."

"Where's Marsay?"

"France... your birthplace."

"I'm from Gateshead man. Born and bred."

Presenter looks uncomfortable and shuffles papers. "But your awards?"

"Aye... right enough bonny lad, I've got four Michelins on my car. One in each corner... so five if you count the spare. I also have a couple of ASBO's and I managed a GCSE in home economics. If that's what you're on about."

Fluster-fluster-fluster, time to ignore the ongoing train-crash, "So what are you cooking for us today Peter?"

"Gypsy toast... you know? bread dipped in milky egg and fried."

Male presenter's face has a sickly grin and he's avoiding the camera, "Don't you mean grilled aubergine with almond and parsley pesto?"

"I don't shop at Presto, it's gone now man. Anyway what's an aubergine?"

The presenters are whispering, "It's a right cock-up this. Who the f.."

"Don't swear Algie, we're on live. Just pretend this is normal and they'll edit it later on and pretend it's a wind-up for Red-Nose Day."

"But who the f.. sorry, who the heck is that over there."

"Peter Fargo apparently."

"But what's he doing here?"

"Just ask him... it can't get any worse."

"You've never watched Pointless then?"

"Yes."

"How does Alexander Armstrong do that show with a straight face?"

She shrugs and face goes blank.

"You know the... and what will you do with the money if you win today's jackpot?"

"Ohhh, I don't know... I might put a fiver towards it and splash out on a MacDonalds."

"All I'm saying is... it can indeed get worse."

Screen suddenly goes blank to save the day. Ater a moment or two a message flashes up... 'Our apologies for the break in transmission. We think it's hackers... probably from Leeds United or Millwall. We hope to have transmission back in half a jiffy.

Hopefully the screen will stay blank for the remainder of the day... at least until The Chase comes on. Mind you, just as an aside, that Bradley Walsh is getting up his own backside a bit isn't he. Trying to join in with the questions and pretend he's a real smarty-pants like the proper chasers. Not that I've taken much notice of it of course.

Okay... rant over. It was just something I needed to get down on paper, because now my rant will be around forever. Shouting at the telly or even telling someone about your pet hates is all well and good. But where do your words go once they're spoken? Have you ever thought about it?

Is there a word graveyard somewhere so that folk can lay flowers and say things like 'I remember those very words... they were so kind and somehow apt, I used to pop around to their house to hear them every day. I'll miss those words for as long as I live'. Pfft... rubbish and baloney, they've gone forever and they'll be forgotten. Your verbal rant will never be remembered. So write it down folks and when you've gone to meet the big fellow in the sky make sure you leave your writings to someone who can read.

Here endeth the lesson. Rant now definitely done.

Sorry for that time-out folks. Bee in bonnet. Now let's crack on with the info about our new country and new home.

Mull of Kintyre. Don't ask why I chose that as an introduction. We ended up a few hundred diagonal miles north-east from McCartney's place but I couldn't find anything with Easter-Ross in the title so it will have to do.

September 1st, 2005. We're standing in the kitchen part of our newly bought cottage, a few miles outside the thriving town of Tain in Easter-Ross. We've driven up here from Newcastle, starting early to beat the arrival of the removal van and we've just entered our new abode. There's very little in the way of furniture following us up here. We'd sold or given away most of ours because we'd bought the cottage contents along with the building... all the piney, country cottage furniture you'd expect to see. But the inside is completely bare... not a stick in sight. We look at each other.

"Bugger," I exclaim.

"Double bugger," Lorraine replies.

We're both at a loss. Our furnished cottage has turned out to be unfurnished. I don't know what to do so it's no good Lorraine looking to me for answers.

Lorraine points at the floor and screws up her face, "Have you seen...?"

"The mouse droppings," I reply. "They're all over the shop. Not just the floor but all over the kitchen units too."

"What are we going to do?"

I shrug in reply, "I haven't got a clue." I really need a good swearing session but Lorraine doesn't like bad language... unless it's hers of course.

"Go and ask a neighbour Jim."

"That's a laugh, we haven't got any. Remember that's why we bought this place? No more nutty neighbours."

"Yes, I know but I could do with a cuppa and there's no electric."

"Yeh, I'm parched myself. So don't panic... we'll drive into Tain and find a café or something. I noticed a Co-op so we can stock up with grub for tonight and buy some candles until I can contact the electric folk."

"But what about the furniture van?"

"It's paid for, so I'll just leave a note on the door in case they come while we're out. They can just dump the stuff in the living room. There's just the bed and the three piece and that Ottoman thing... and the cases of clothes of course." I don't know what else to say.

We looked at each other and that look spoke volumes. At that precise moment in time we were both thinking... 'Oh God, what on earth have we done'. Lorraine must have been thinking about all the work that was needing to be done in the cottage. I was more concerned about the mouse droppings. I was going to have to be a rodent killer and I'd never killed a mouse in my life. How do you go about it and where to buy a gun?

We were just about to set off for food and sustenance when a voice rang out from behind the closed kitchen door.

"Hello, anybody there?" It made us both jump. We looked at each other, surprised, and then I moved across the kitchen and opened the door. Standing in front of me was a thickset fellow with a profusion of grey hair topping his over-large head. Below it a smiley wizened face. Late sixties I immediately thought to myself.

"Hi there... what can I do for you?" I asked, while returning the smile.

He held out a meaty hand, "Pleased to meet you, I'm Eddie from the house down the track and just past the big gate." I shook the outstretched hand. The grip was firm.

"Hello Eddie, I'm Jim Bates," I turned to indicate my wife, "And this is Lorraine my better half," Lorraine snorted, "So we're your new neighbours I suppose."

"Aye, we've been expecting you." He paused and bent down to stroke a Jack Russell which had been hiding behind his legs, I hadn't noticed it until that moment, "And this is Kipper, our best friend and resident mouser. You may be needing his services by the looks of things," he grinned as he looked past me into the kitchen, perusing the floor covered in droppings.

"Aye Eddie, that could well be. I'd offer you a cuppa but we don't seem to have any electric."

"Aye, about that... the electric people are booked for Friday... tomorrow. I arranged it but I couldn't get them to come any sooner," he gave a resigned shrug.

"I don't suppose you would know what has happened with the furniture that we've bought and paid for?"

"Aye, about that as well. The solicitor asked me to put it into £10 a week storage. Because the sale took so long they thought it would be better to keep it safe... and mouse free."

"So, where is it?"

"It's all under tarpaulins in the stables," he turned and gestured towards a three bay stable building opposite the cottage.

I was a little confused by that, "So I take it that mice and other rodents are barred from the stables?"

Eddie laughed, "Aye, I thought it was daft as well but that's what they asked me to do... so I did it. You've seen the residential caravan site down the track as you drove in. An empty cottage with goodies inside might have been a temptation for some folk, and at least the stable is padlocked."

"So how much do we owe for the storage?"

"Sixty quid by my reckoning... but fifty should be acceptable."

"And who do I pay?"

"Me of course," Eddie grinned.

Somehow I wasn't surprised. I immediately earmarked Eddie as a chancer... but a friendly chancer. "I'll pay you when I've been to the nearest cash machine Eddie but for now Lorraine and I really need to go into Tain and have something to eat and drink."

"Fair enough," he replied, "When you return your furniture will be back in the cottage. Nice to meet you both." And with that he turned and strode off towards his own humble abode followed by his canine companion.

"We need a dog Jim," Lorraine said as she watched Eddie disappear down the track with his Jack Russell, "It's time to add to the family."

There was no arguing with that. Lorraine had been looking forward to life in the country. Now she could have the Westie she'd always wanted because she was retired. That was all well and good but my immediate thoughts were more down to earth. The cottage needed a huge makeover if we were to enjoy this phase of our lives and that was going to take some serious planning backed up with serious money... and I still needed to earn. No full retirement for me for a good while yet.

That first foray into Tain was interesting to say the least. We drew out a bundle of cash from an actual bank. Remember, this was 2005 and banks still had branches... with real people serving customers. The high street still had shops; proper ones that weren't of the charity or pound variety. But best of all there were pubs and eating establishments... with real people serving and with real customers eating and drinking. We didn't realise at that moment in time that we were experiencing the swan-song of normal life. In those halcyon days the term 'on-line' was usually nothing more than an exciting train ride; Amazon was just a long river in South America; Sky was something up above you, occasionally blue but generally full of clouds and Pappa Johns was soiled male underwear. If you're over the age of forty you may remember those days with a sense of desperate longing... we certainly do.

After stocking up with groceries and candles we decided it was time for food and we hunted out a decent looking place. The eating establishment we found ourselves in was The Royal Hotel. It was all very nice and posh. We seated ourselves without fuss and were pleasantly surprised to be quickly attended to by an attentive waiter who smiled as he supplied us with menus. We gave him our drinks order and he departed. Lorraine and I perused the fare on offer. We ran our gaze over the long and confusing list and then looked questioningly at each other.

"It's a bit expensive," Lorraine offered.

"Sod the expense," I replied, "But I was just wanting pie and chips or something to fill a hole. I don't know what most of this stuff is. Garlic mushroom and goat's cheese frittata... what the hell is that?"

Lorraine nodded agreement, "And this one, steak with creamy soy and wasabi sauce. I know what steak is... obviously, but what's creamy soy and what's wasabi sauce?"

I shrugged, "It could be a dish from the American west. That Indian bloke Tonto used to call the Lone Ranger something like Kemo-Wasabi. Buggered if I know what the creamy soy is though. I think I'll just go with number eighteen, the 'coq au vin' for now."

"What's that?"

"Chicken done in wine I think."

Lorraine ran her finger down the menu, and stopped, "Hmm, so I'm assuming vin means wine and coq means chicken."

I tried not to sigh. Lorraine hadn't taken French at school so a sigh would have been patronizing. "Yep pet, got it in one... well done. But vin is pronounced like 'van' and not vin as in tin... and coq isn't pronounced like coke, it's pronounced cock... like in shock."

"Why?"

"Just because that's how the French say it."

"Are they stupid or something?"

"Aye, I suppose so," there was nothing else I could say without going in too deep, "Anyway, are you up for the coq au vin?"

Lorraine pulled a face, "Hmm, I'm not sure about that. You know what I'm like about chicken. It's not my favourite so I wouldn't want a lot of it. It's not a whole chicken is it? you know, like one of those tiny bantams. Because that would be too much for me... and what kind of wine is it?"

"I don't know Lorraine. I've never had coq au vin before. I've heard the name on the cookery programmes and that's about all, but if we're in a posh restaurant we might as well order posh food."

A young girl brought our drinks to the table. A pint of lager for me and a glass of pinot noir for Lorraine. The drinks were welcomed like old friends and I took a mouthful. Lorraine was still unsure about the food order though.

"Will you have some of my chicken if there's too much for me? It'll be such a waste if they give us a whole chicken each." She was sipping at the wine and obviously enjoying it.

"Yes, yes okay, I'll have some of yours if there's too much. I'm sure it will be portions and not a whole chicken but you could ask the waiter." Lorraine was totally old-school and detested waste in any shape or form. She was glancing around the room looking for the waiter's return and half-whispering the French menu order 'coq-au-vin' and pronouncing the 'vin' correctly.

A few minutes later the waiter arrived at our table, all smiles. He stood with note pad in hand and pencil poised. "Are you ready to order... sir... madam?"

I ran my gaze down the menu, "Number eighteen for both of us... thank you." Looking back to that moment I should really have taken over completely to forestall Lorraine but I was too slow. As soon as she opened her mouth I sort of knew what was coming.

"Can I ask you to just give me a little coq... I'm not really that keen and I don't want too much of it." She gave him an apologetic smile. Lorraine in all honesty was completely oblivious to the impact of her words.

The waiter half-turned so that his back was to Lorraine. He was pretend writing on his notepad. I couldn't hear any laughter but I could see it in the shaking of his shoulders. It was a few seconds before he turned back to face us. Lorraine was still completely blank.

"Is there anything else sir... madam, more wine perhaps?" His mouth expression was completely passive but his eyes were laughing their socks off. It was all I could do to keep a straight face. Lorraine gave me a little victory grin. She'd just asked a question containing a real French word and was looking self-satisfied.

My voice was cracking somewhat... with the effort of holding the chortles back, but I managed. "We'll both have a Merlot, thank you."

"Madam is currently having pinot-noir sir. Would you prefer the same wine again madam?" He addressed Lorraine directly.

She was well up for this now, "Yes, I think so, this 'van' is very acceptable. So same 'van' again please." Lorraine was entering into the spirit of the occasion. Anyone passing our table would probably have decided she was a French lady on vacation... 'aye, that'll be right James'...

"Will sir and madam be having a sweet?" the waiter asked.

"Sticky toffee pudding and custard twice," I replied hastily. The waiter nodded, wrote it down and left without another word.

Lorraine didn't object but she asked, "How do you say sticky toffee pudding in French?"

"They don't have it in France Lorraine... it's only served here in the UK." That was a complete lie of course but I didn't want Lorraine going all Joan of Arc on me and trying out her foreign pudding pronunciation. Apart from that I hadn't the foggiest idea how to ask for sticky toffee in French... 'steekee-terrfee avec crème anglaise s'il vous plait'... nah, best to leave it.

After all that silliness we actually enjoyed the meal, the wine and the exemplary service. When we'd finished we headed back to our cottage with renewed enthusiasm. A new life was awaiting us.

Lorraine has had a brief word in my ear and what she said made sense. Our North-East Diaries days were over on that very day we moved to Scotland. Any further writing we're about to begin should be a completely new endeavour and the opening salvo of our Highland Diaries. Hopefully they will prove to be equally as entertaining if we do eventually write them. So this isn't an ending... it's just a different beginning and hopefully a continuation for all the readers who've followed the trials and tribulations of our main characters throughout the pages of the North-East trilogy and perhaps the 'Doggie Book' too. Thank you... each and every one of you.

CHAPTER 24

Where Do You Go To (My Lovely)

———————————————— ■ ————————————————

(Featuring Lorraine Again... cos Women Always Have The Last Word)

'So by hook or by crook I'll be last in this book'. Those words were written on the back page of my friend's autograph book which she'd persuaded all of her pals to sign when she retired from the NHS. I don't know why that particular snippet should have been buzzing around in my head but nevertheless it was a memory snatched from my working years. Believe me folks memories are precious and we should cherish them before they fade away forever. You'll be aware that mine are fading somewhat, and sometimes it feels like I'm trying to grasp fog but I have my Jim and he helps me with the memories. Whenever I become frustrated and struggle to remember something he'll say to me... "Don't worry about those memories... we'll make some new ones... some better ones, and we'll remember them together." He's canny really.

Jim said something to me yesterday which didn't make sense at the time. Thinking about his words now though...

well, they make perfect sense. I'd said to him something like...

"You know Jim, I keep forgetting some of my memories."

Then he said, "No you don't Lorraine... because it's impossible to forget a memory."

"What are you talking about Jim?... you know fine well that I'm forgetting things, and you have to remind me."

"Okay, I'm not trying to be clever or anything, but a memory only exists when you remember it. If you don't remember something then for you it doesn't exist... it isn't a memory until it's being remembered."

"God, Jim you do talk some rubbish," and he does sometimes, but the more I thought about his words the more sense they made. I'm in the Jim camp now. You can't forget a memory... but you can make new ones... and they'll stay with you as long as they pop into your head and you remember them.

Anyway, that memory thing aside, I had a good day yesterday. I had Jack my wee Westie out on the meadow and he had a whale of a time playing with Jen and John's new rescue dog called Ansa. So now he has two pals because he likes playing with Mike and Lesley's dog called Torin. They're both much bigger than him, but Westies just can't accept that they're little. Inside my Jack's head is the thought that he's just as big as any other dog... and he runs around and gives those big fellas what for. He's not doing too badly is he? That's my big worry... about my little Jack. He'll be five years old in August, but what will happen if I'm no longer able to take care of him? Yes I know Jim will look after him... but what if something happens to Jim? Anyway that's my big worry, and I think about it all the time.

I stayed up quite late yesterday too. I watched the snooker... and tomorrow is the final of the World Championship so I'll be watching Kyren Wilson play Jack Jones. I'm looking forward to that. Ohh aye, and a parcel was delivered yesterday and Jim snuck it away into the spare room... so I know it's something for my birthday... a belated pressie that didn't arrive on time. Good heaven's I'm seventy-nine now... I think. How on earth did I get to be that old?

Anyway, Jim was going to carry on and write about our lives up in Scotland and he was struggling with that. But I had a brainwave and told him to stop... because the North-East part of all those character's lives was over. The day we moved to Scotland was the day to make an ending of 'The North-East Diaries' I said to him... and he was relieved. He's already planning 'The Highland Diaries' or something. He hasn't decided on the title.

Funnily enough, although some memories come and go, I can remember the time when Jim's pal Sid (or Hawky) came and stayed with us for a while. I felt so sorry for him because he had no-one to turn too other than Jim and myself. His sister lived in Australia and he'd lost touch with his elder brother who, when last heard of was living in Hong Kong. That poor man's funeral only had four people there. Jim and myself and two neighbours from Kirkcaldy. How sad was that?

There's lots of other tales Jim could have written about in his books. I didn't know Tug and Charlie Chuck... and I only met Frances once. His friends from Hull and from the 'Folly' in Shankhouse were just as much a surprise to me as I'm sure they were to you folks. I can only relate to the last thirty-five years since we met and he's left a few tales out of that lot. He never told you about spoiling a holiday to Malta because he was arrested at Gatwick did he? That was an embarrassment if ever there was one. The thing is, Jim always turned into a lump of jelly when he entered an airport. Flying used to terrify him. So I'll tell the story... and this is a brief precis of that day.

So, we were going through the check in and we were in a rush. I'd lost track of time in the duty-free shop and we were having to hurry because they'd given the final call for passengers. We were going through that security gate thing when the baggage man said to Jim...

"Has anyone put anything in your baggage without your knowledge?"

I know it was a really daft question. Yes or no would both have been incorrect and the only sensible response would have been 'I don't know.' If he'd asked it of me I would just have replied with a simple 'no'... but Jim of course was already agitated and freaked-out at the thought of boarding an aeroplane.

"How the **** would I know if anyone had put something in my bag without my knowledge? Are you right in the ******* head?" I'll let you fill in the blanks concerning Jim's language.

"So you don't know if someone has tampered with your baggage?"

"I'll tamper with your nose-end you moron."

"Calm down sir, we have to ask... it's standard procedure after all the latest scares."

Remember this was shortly after the shoe-bomber incident and they were only doing their job. But Jim, already up a-height... lost the plot.

"No... there's ****-all in my baggage but I've got half a kilo of Semtex in my Chelsea boot." With those words the world went crazy. Klaxons started sounding and big beefy fellows with those machine gun things appeared from nowhere and came rushing over. Within seconds they had Jim down on the floor and they were speaking into their walkie-talkies. The immediate area was cleared like magic and they led me away too into a bare room.

The upshot was that we missed our flight. Jim was grilled for ages and they went through all our luggage and our clothing with a fine-tooth comb. My husband was given a stern lecture and a caution, then given a warning as to his future conduct. We missed our flight and had to book into a local hotel until they could find us a spare couple of plane seats. It was two days later when we landed in Malta and arrived at our hotel in Bugibba. Our room had been re-allocated so we ended up in alternative accommodation which was not the best. We did the usual tourist things... Popeye Village and Mdina - the Silent City, then on to Mosta Church, but our airport hassle had changed things for us. The holiday was still okay but we didn't enjoy it as much as usual and that was our final time in Malta. From that time onwards Jim was like a little lamb whenever we flew. He still hated the experience but he learned to keep his lips zipped.

When we returned from that Malta holiday we were heading through the nothing to declare green lane at

Gatwick. However they pulled Jim and his trolley over for a random search (but I'm sure they must have had his photo on their computer). Then they went through the suitcases. They put 400 cigarettes and a box of hand-rolling baccy on the table in front of Jim.

"You've exceeded your limit sir."

"No I haven't," says Jim, "I'm entitled to 400 cigarettes and a 10 pack of baccy."

"No sir... you're allowed 400 cigarettes 'or' the tobacco. It states in your leaflet sir... it's 'or' not 'and'."

I was expecting Jim to argue the point but he didn't. "My apologies, I misread the instruction." The apology thankfully did the trick, and he didn't mention the Semtex in his shoes.

The man put the cigarettes and baccy back into the suitcase and gave Jim a smile, "Go on, bugger off, it was a genuine mistake," and with that he turned and left the desk. Jim learned something that day.

He says he can't remember those times at Gatwick but I know he can. He can't look me in the eye when he says it... so I know he's being less than honest. He doesn't like to remember the sheer embarrassment. More Fiery Jack called for... I think.

Jim comes out with me on most days now to walk wee Jack. We have a favourite walk just behind the vet surgery and Jack squeaks like one of his toys when he realises where we're going. It's a bit of a steep climb for our old bones but Jack loves it and he goes rooting around and sniffing out trails. At the top of the steep climb is a park-bench type of seat and we sit there for ages up on the hilltop, looking out over Strath Fleet, the river and farms, and all the forestry commission land. It's sometimes hard to believe that this beautiful area is our home now... and long may it continue.

So it's bye-bye from me now. I've been really pleased that Jim gave me the go-ahead to do a little writing. I hope my minor contribution hasn't messed up the flow of Jim's story. I've really enjoyed it tremendously and I hope I haven't bored you good people too much. Five minutes ago Jim brought me a bacon sandwich but I told him I'd lost my appetite. He asked me if I'd looked under the couch... typical!

P.S. I found this poem of Jim's. It was the first one he had published. I thought it was funny anyway. He'll probably edit it out.

BUYING CONDOMS (JRB)
I was desperate to buy me some condoms
On that Wednesday morning in June
My girlfriend said 'You're on a promise'
And we were meeting up that afternoon

For she'd noticed that in my frustration
My flat.... which I kept fairly neat
Now had fingernail marks on the ceiling
And teeth marks on the lavatory seat

So she promised an hour of pleasure
As pleasurable as it could be
She wanted the first fifty minutes
With the other ten minutes for me

Where Do You Go To (My Lovely)

Now you folks are probably thinking
Splitting an hour like that was a crime
But if you'd known my previous track record
Ten minutes seemed like a long time

So I stood in a queue in the chemist's
Hoping to be quite discrete
As an old lady in front bought and paid for
Corn plasters to stick on her feet

And when my turn came I was gutted
I thought 'this must be a joke'
For a gorgeous young girl came to serve me
When I was needing a grizzly old bloke

Embarrassed I picked up some aspirin
But her smile put me quickly at ease
And she winked as she took the pills from me
'Were you wanting some condoms with these?'

'We have them in black, red or tartan
And ribbed ones to last a long time'
'Do you have a favourite flavour?
We have peppermint, strawberry or lime'

'Flavours?'........ I nervously stuttered
'Strawberry?.......'Is that what you said?'
'These things are to go on my winkie'
'Not between two slices of bread'

She chuckled away as she wrapped them
She'd decided on tartan and lime
And smiled as she gave me the packet
Then wished me a really good time

I dashed around home in a frenzy
The minutes were ticking away
My girlfriend was coming here shortly
For our sixty minutes of play

My clothes hit the floor in a heartbeat
I put on my condom with glee
And the first that she saw, as she opened the door
Was my tartan condom... and me.

She screamed as the door closed behind her
Her face like a deathly white mask
Then pointed and silently shuddered
'What're you going to do with that flask?'

I chuckled 'It isn't a flask it's a condom
Tartan and flavoured with lime'
With disgust she turned and departed
Walking out for the very last time

So my day of passion was stifled
I didn't make it as far as the bed
And as for my lime flavour condoms
I had them with my Corn Flakes instead

The End (Honest) - her indoors has gone to bed.

Acknowledgements

―――――――――■―――――――――

Firstly, I would like to thank each and every one of you who have read the complete trilogy. Your support and comments have been a huge source of inspiration to continue writing. Customer reviews, especially on Amazon supply the bread and butter of feedback and your reviews whether good, bad or indifferent are welcomed for their honest appraisals from your personal points of view. If you have a UK address then DM me on Facebook if you've left reviews for all three volumes and I'll send you a free copy of the forthcoming dog book 'A Westie's Song' directly from Amazon as a thank you for your support.

Thanks to my project manager Benjamin and consultant Domizia, whose joint enthusiasm, understanding of continuity and attention to detail has made this volume better than it would otherwise have been. Thanks also to my daughter Sharon whose insight and comments on the initial prologue and opening chapters gave me an increased endeavour to pay greater attention to nuance and detail.

A big-big thank you to Alan Dickson whose cover artwork has given the North-East Diaries trilogy its authentic feel. The simplicity of the covers immediately take you back to a time when life seemed somehow less complicated and infinitely more pleasurable. There have been many comments from readers of the volumes, stating how the artwork immediately signalled the bygone era content of the books. Muchos Grassyarse Alan.

Thanks of course to my wife Lorraine ('her indoors') who has spent many a lonesome evening watching telly with only 'Jack' our Westie for company, whilst I wheedled away my hours pounding manically on the keyboard. Just as an aside – Lorraine did indeed contribute to this volume. Some of it was embarrassing to myself, especially the airport fracas but she was adamant that it should be included because of her night on the kitchen floor episode. Aahh well, I suppose she had a point.

And finally a nod to all the folk who feature in any of the three volumes. They are predominantly North-east people but there are some now living far from home much like myself, and some now scattered across the globe. And as a parting comment... let us not forget those who are no longer with us. Our numbers have thinned somewhat during the past year or so. Arthur, Wilf, Toss, Barney et al. My thoughts are with their families.

I hope to tempt you with further writings in the near future. The dog book is up next... but after that 'The Highland Diaries'... maybe!

Printed in Great Britain
by Amazon

42538003R00172